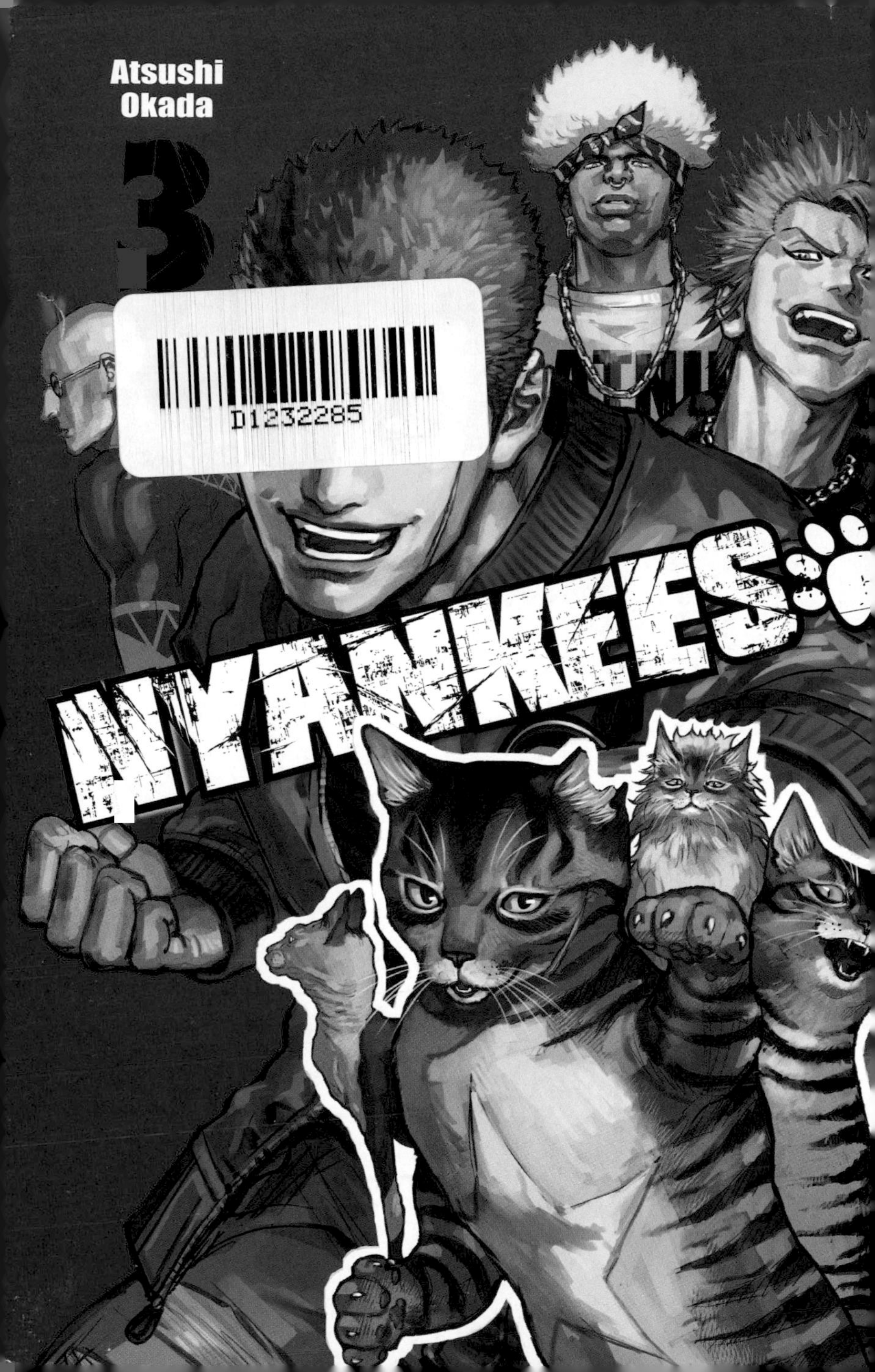
Atsushi
Okada
3
NYANKEES

C O N T E N T S

Chapter 12 ❧ **READY!!** —————— 001

Chapter 13 ❧ **Hairball Reversal** —— 043

Chapter 14 ❧ **Reunion** —————— 077

Chapter 15 ❧ **Cat Brothers** ——— 111

Chapter 16 ❧ **Intruding Felines** —— 133

CHAPTER 12 READY!!

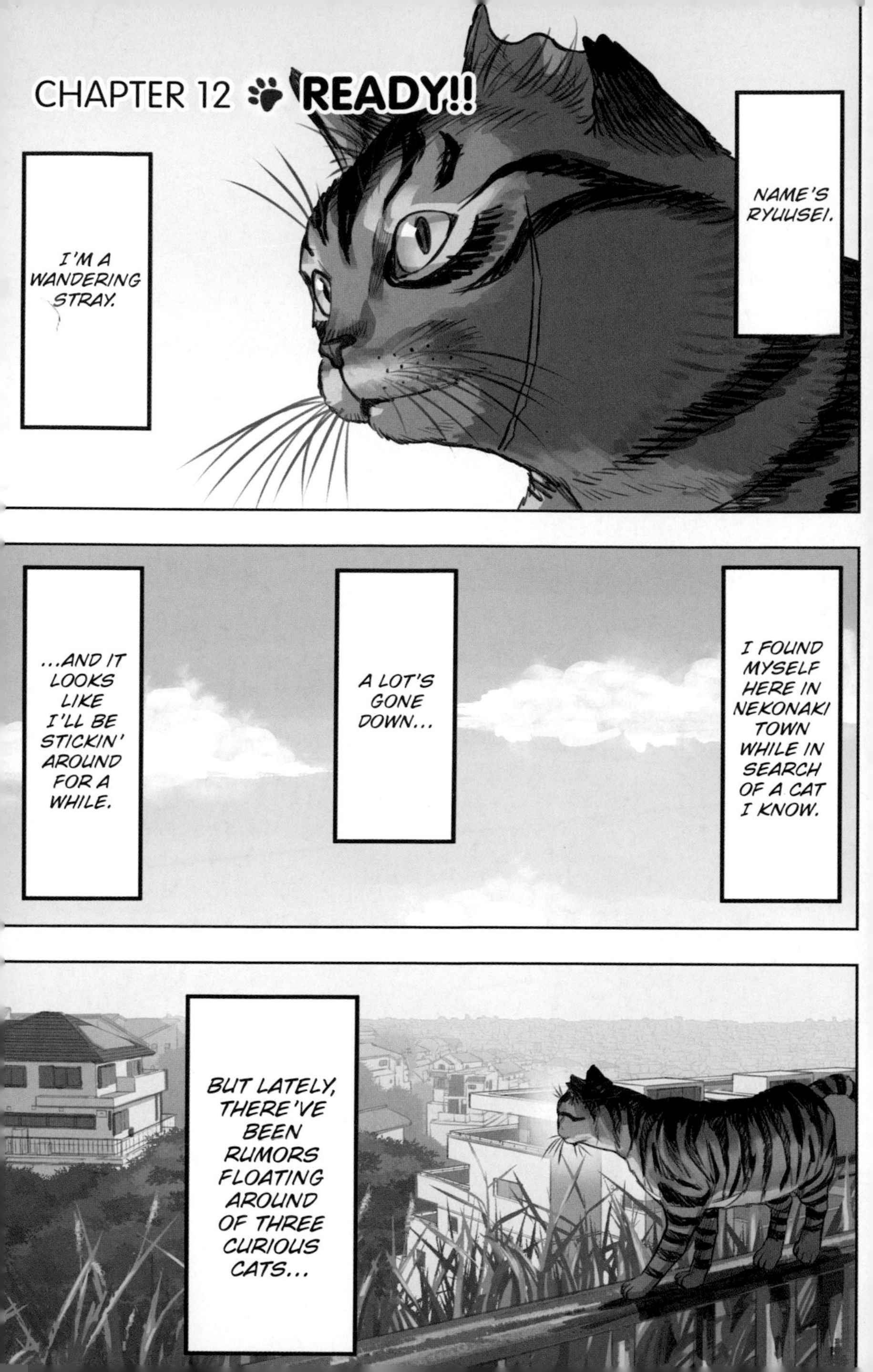
NAME'S RYUUSEI.
I'M A WANDERING STRAY.
I FOUND MYSELF HERE IN NEKONAKI TOWN WHILE IN SEARCH OF A CAT I KNOW.
A LOT'S GONE DOWN...
...AND IT LOOKS LIKE I'LL BE STICKIN' AROUND FOR A WHILE.
BUT LATELY, THERE'VE BEEN RUMORS FLOATING AROUND OF THREE CURIOUS CATS...

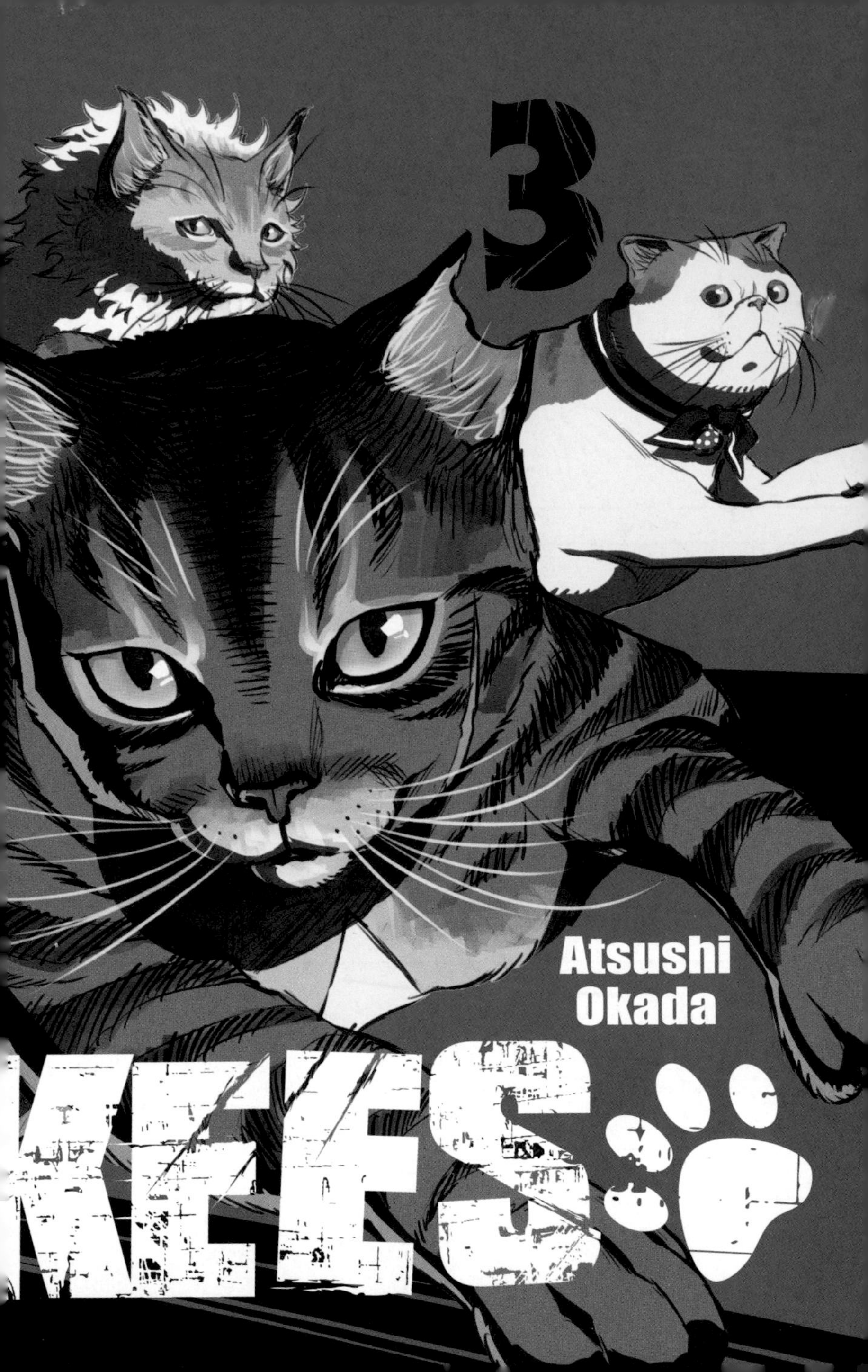
3
Atsushi
Okada
KEES

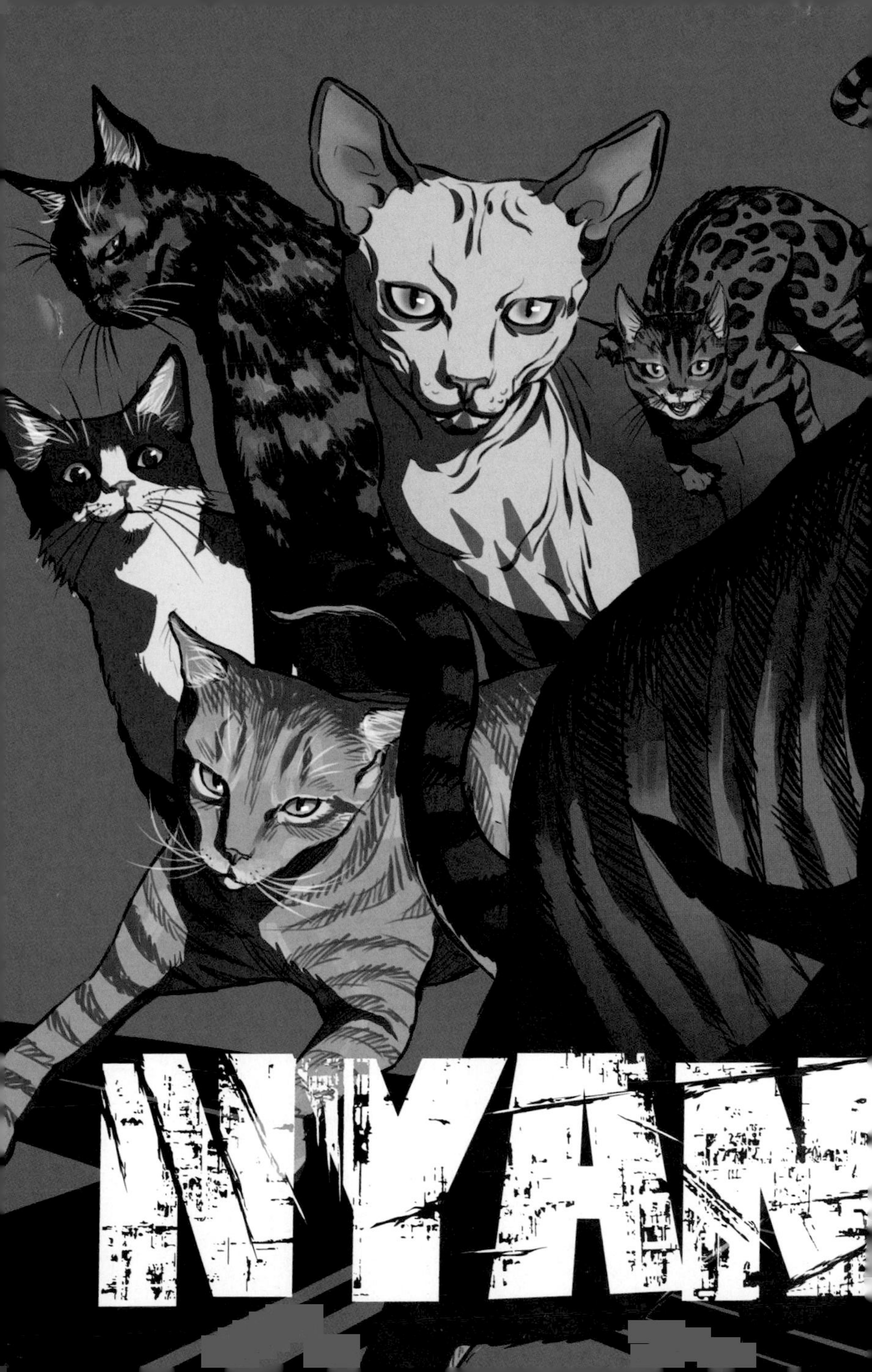
NYAN

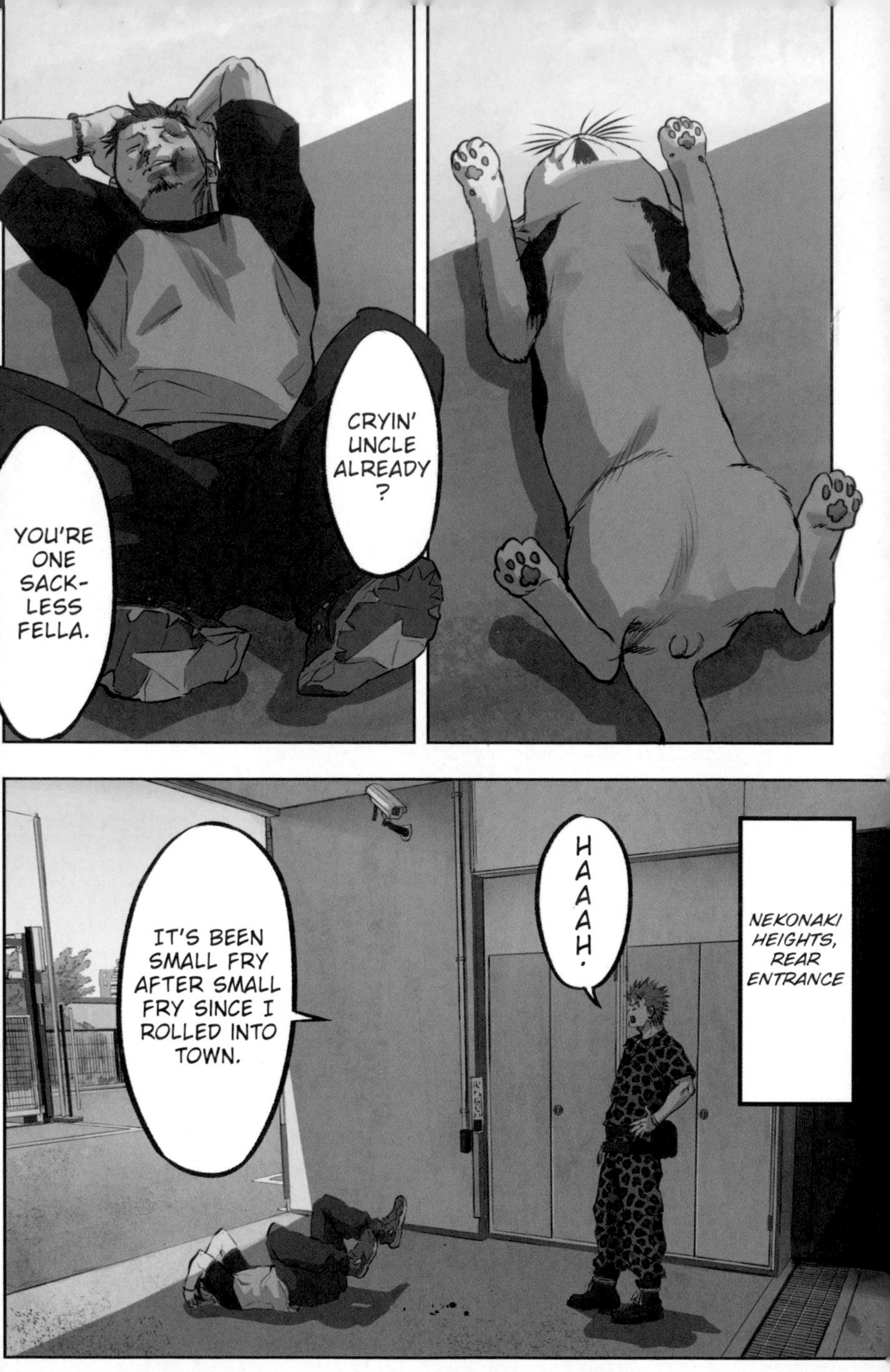
CRYIN' UNCLE ALREADY?
YOU'RE ONE SACKLESS FELLA.
NEKONAKI HEIGHTS, REAR ENTRANCE
HAAAH.
IT'S BEEN SMALL FRY AFTER SMALL FRY SINCE I ROLLED INTO TOWN.

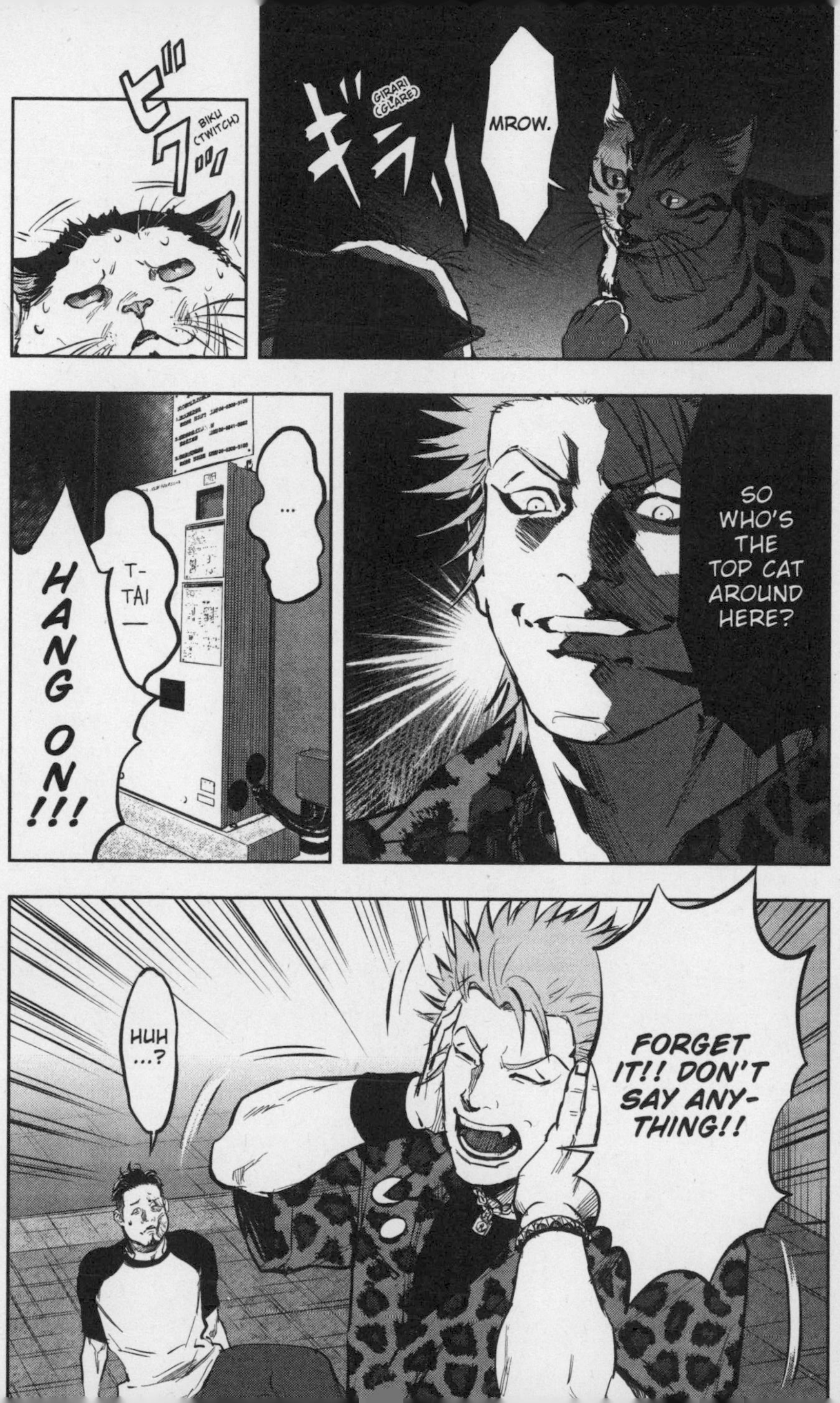
GIRARI (GLARE)
MROW.
BIKU (TWITCH)
SO WHO'S THE TOP CAT AROUND HERE?
...
T-TAI—
HANG ON!!!
FORGET IT!! DON'T SAY ANY-THING!!
HUH ...?

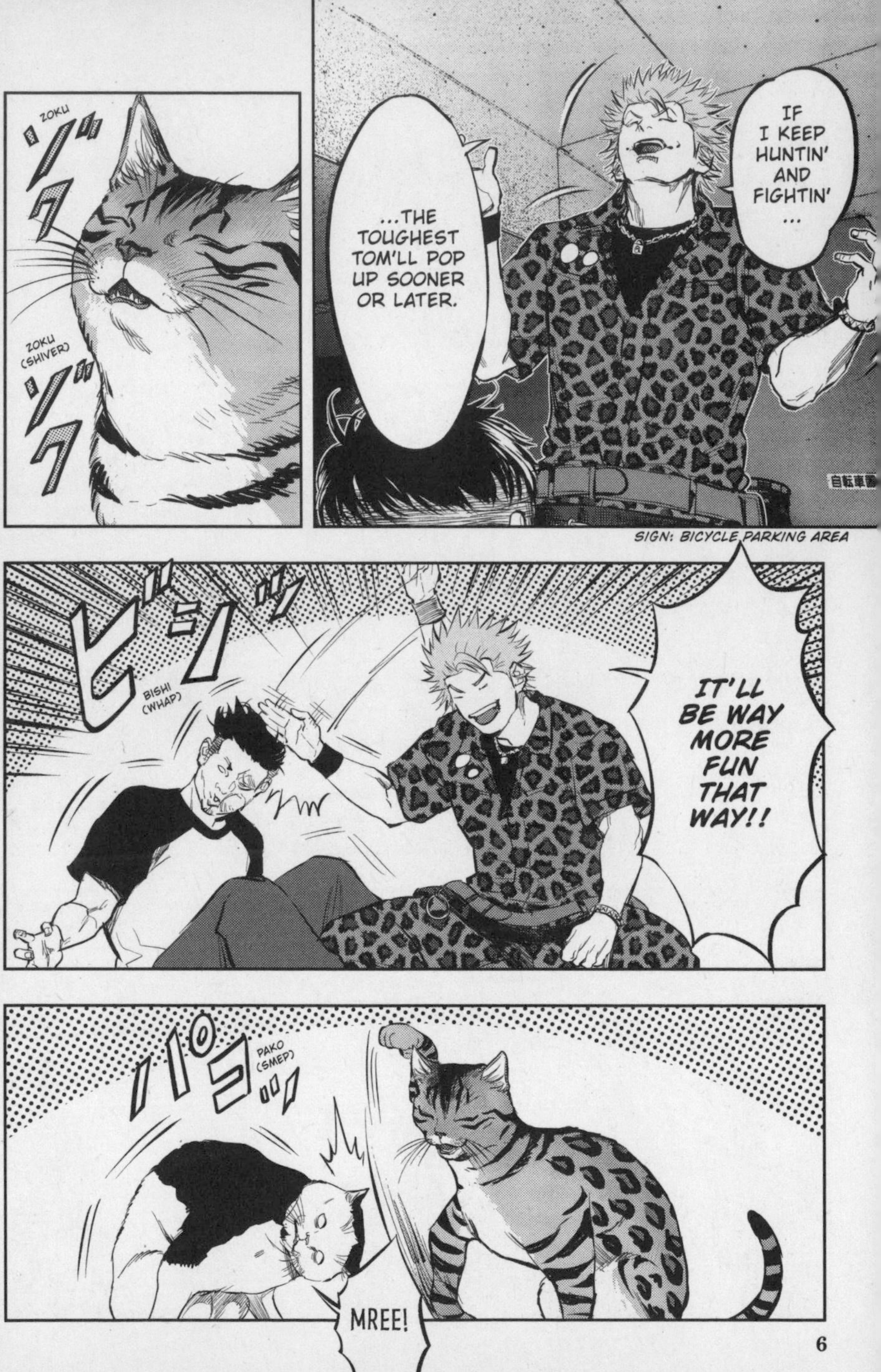
IF I KEEP HUNTIN' AND FIGHTIN'...
...THE TOUGHEST TOM'LL POP UP SOONER OR LATER.
SIGN: BICYCLE PARKING AREA
ZOKU
ZOKU (SHIVER)
IT'LL BE WAY MORE FUN THAT WAY!!
BISHI (WHAP)
PAKO (SMEP)
MREE!

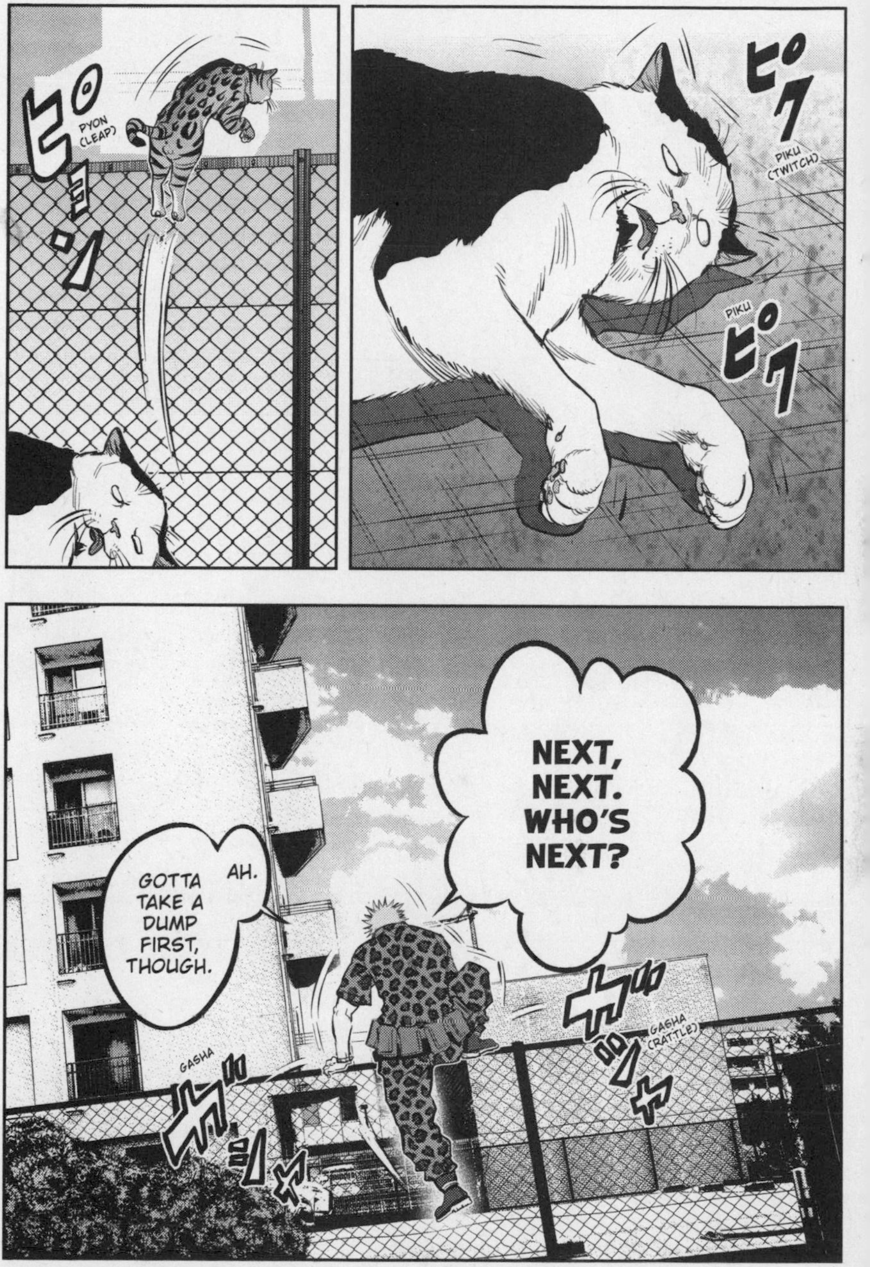
PIKU (TWITCH)
PIKU
PYON (LEAP)
NEXT, NEXT. WHO'S NEXT?
AH.
GOTTA TAKE A DUMP FIRST, THOUGH.
GASHA (RATTLE)
GASHA

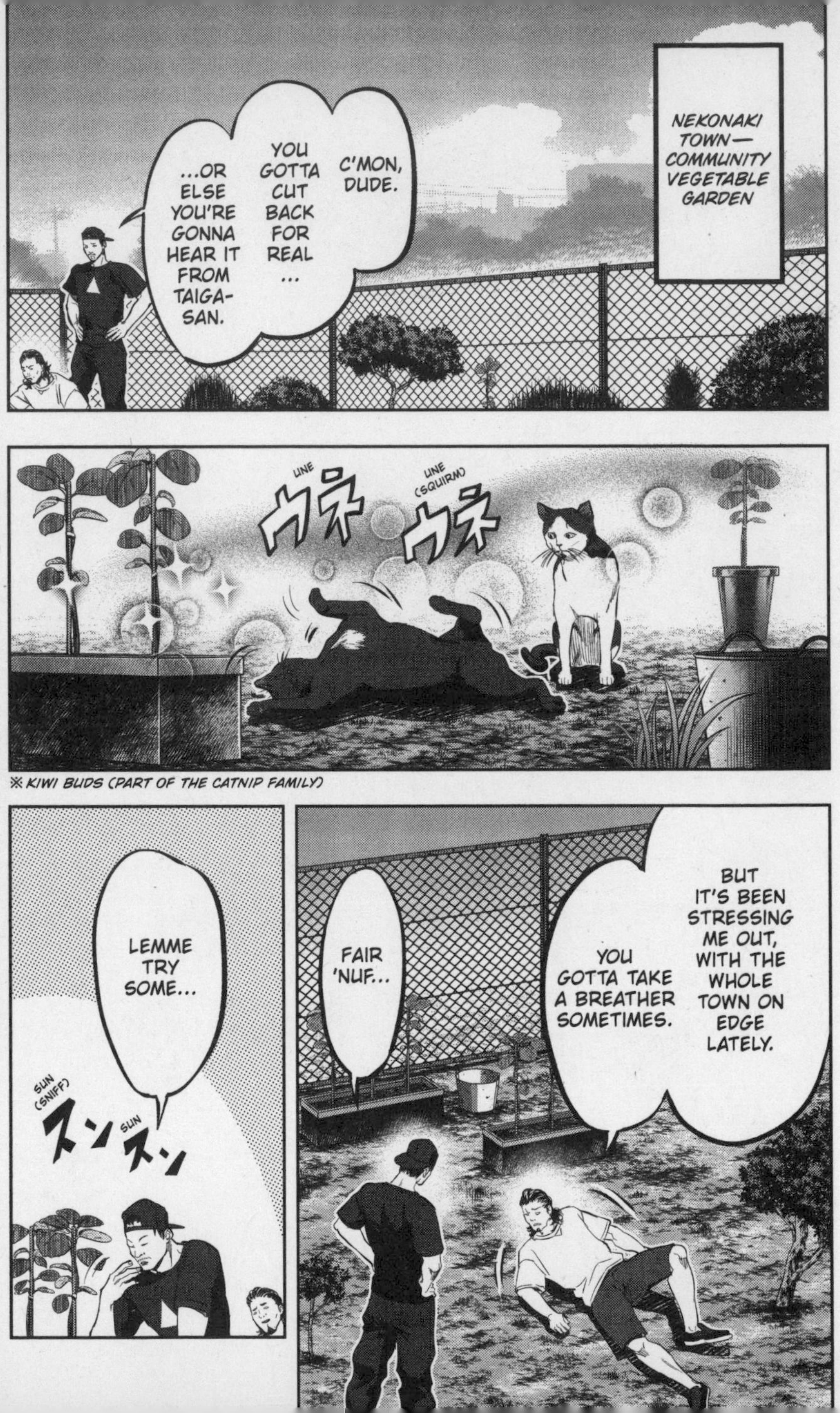
NEKONAKI TOWN—COMMUNITY VEGETABLE GARDEN
C'MON, DUDE.
YOU GOTTA CUT BACK FOR REAL...
...OR ELSE YOU'RE GONNA HEAR IT FROM TAIGA-SAN.
UNE (SQUIRM)
ウネ
UNE
ウネ
BUT IT'S BEEN STRESSING ME OUT, WITH THE WHOLE TOWN ON EDGE LATELY.
YOU GOTTA TAKE A BREATHER SOMETIMES.
FAIR 'NUF...
LEMME TRY SOME...
SUN (SNIFF)
スン
SUN
スン

※ KIWI BUDS (PART OF THE CATNIP FAMILY)

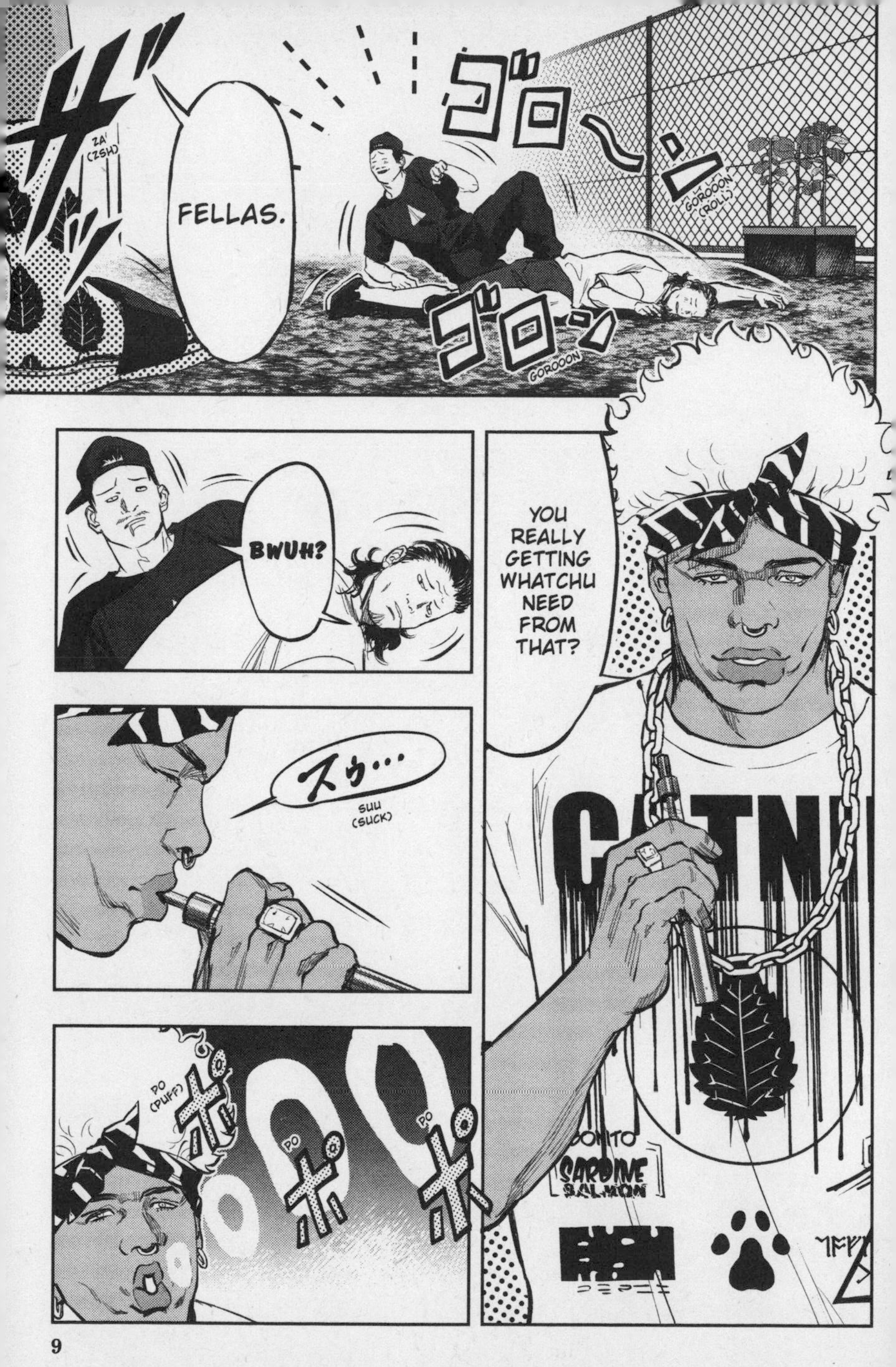
GOROOON (ROLL)
GOROOON
FELLAS.
ZA (ZSH)
YOU REALLY GETTING WHATCHU NEED FROM THAT?
BWUH?
スゥ…
SUU (SUCK)
PO
PO
PO (PUFF)

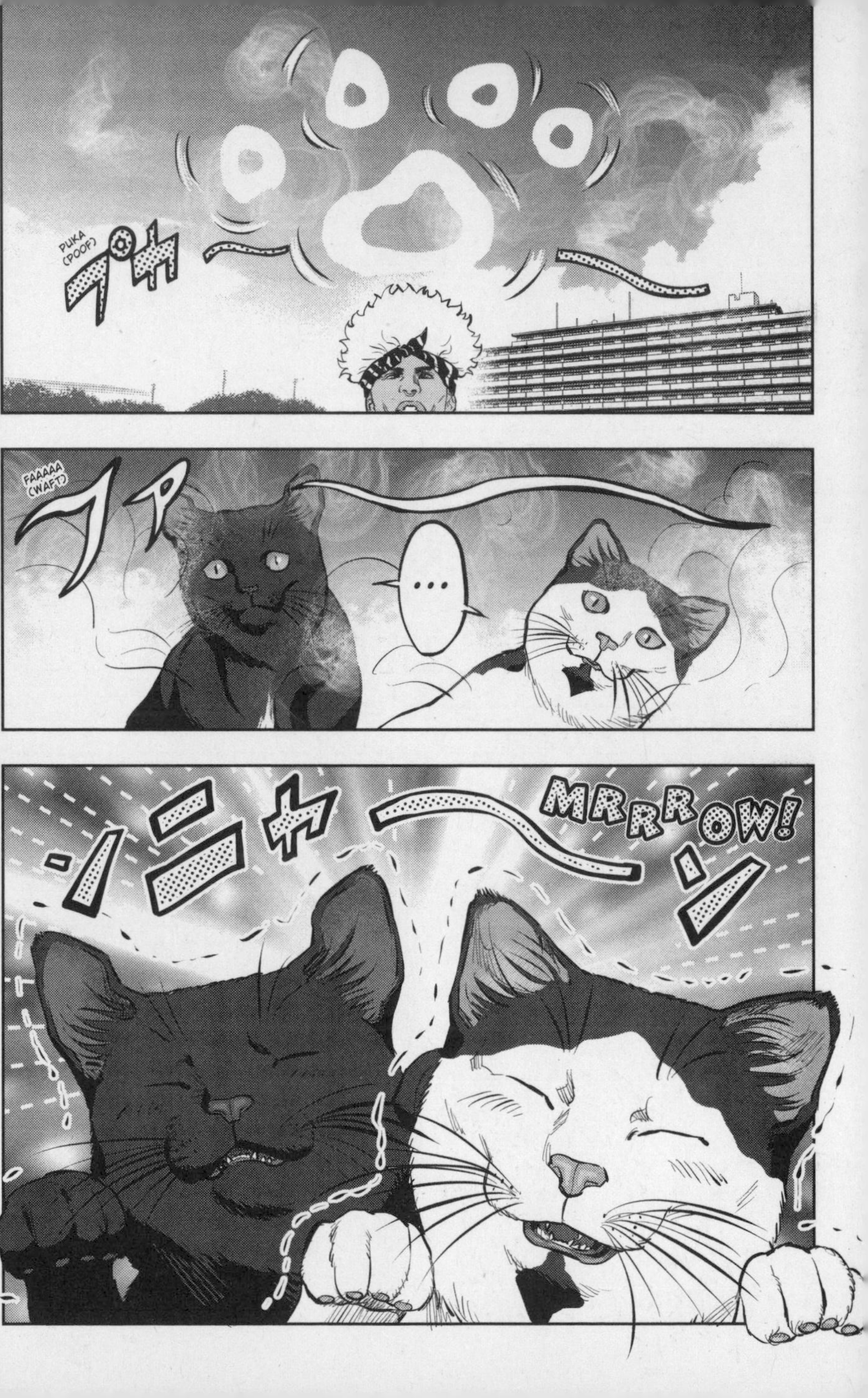

PUKA (POOF)
プカ〜〜
FAAAAA (WAFT)
ファ〜
...
MRRROW!

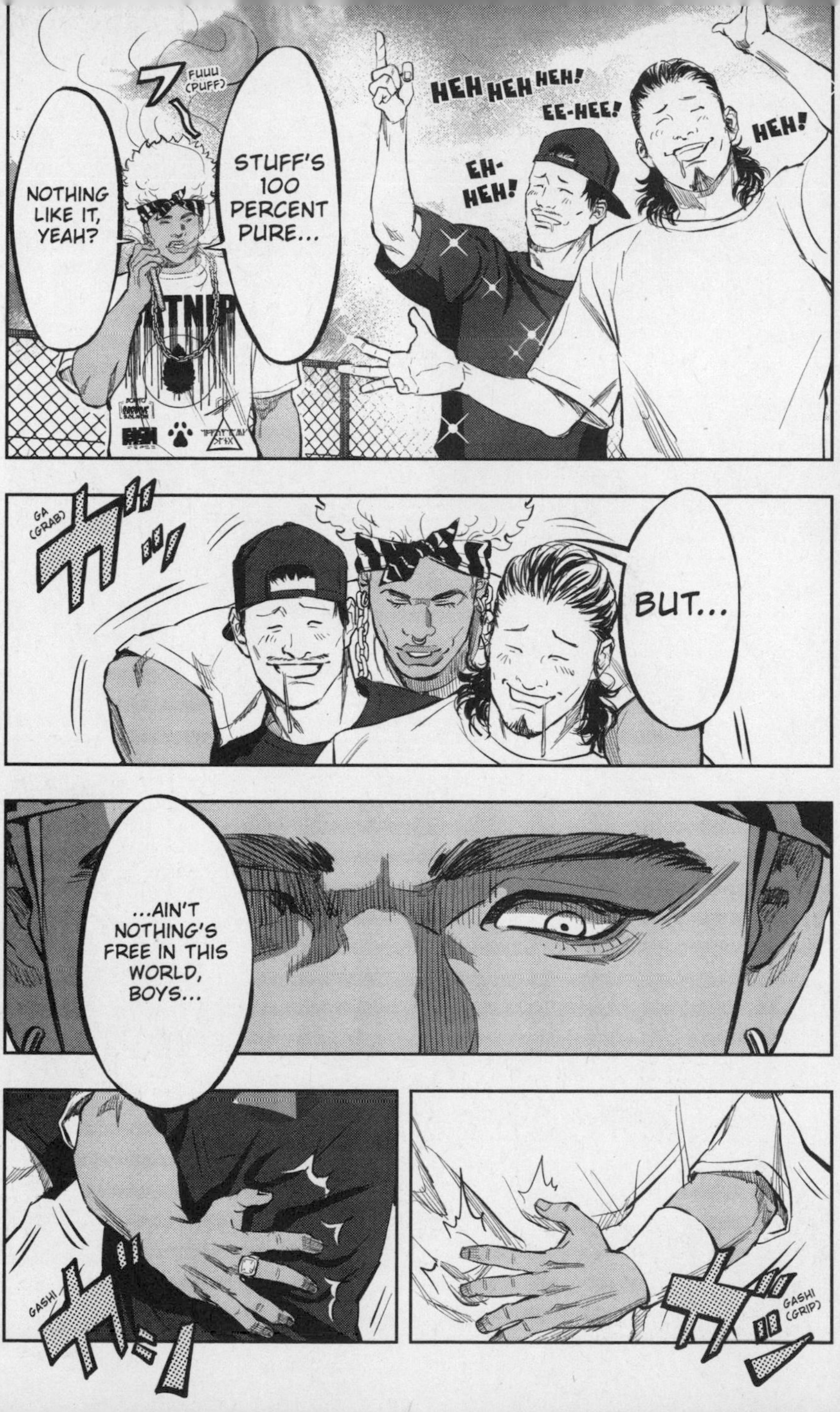
HEH!
EE-HEE!
HEH HEH HEH!
EH-HEH!
STUFF'S 100 PERCENT PURE...
FUUU (PUFF)
NOTHING LIKE IT, YEAH?
BUT...
GA (GRAB)
...AIN'T NOTHING'S FREE IN THIS WORLD, BOYS...
GASHI (GRIP)
GASHI

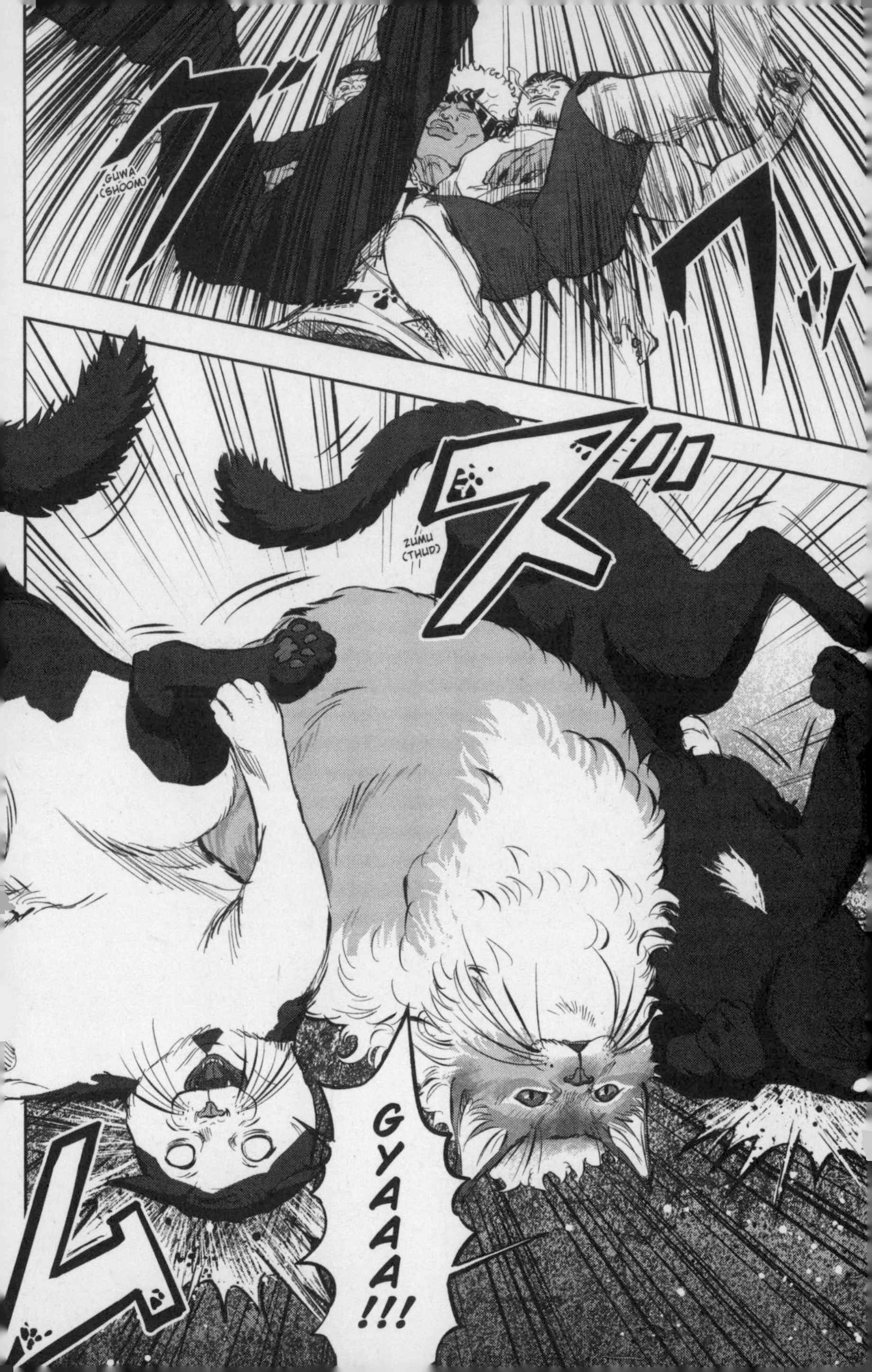
GUWA (SHOOM)
ZUMU (THUD)
GYAAAA!!!

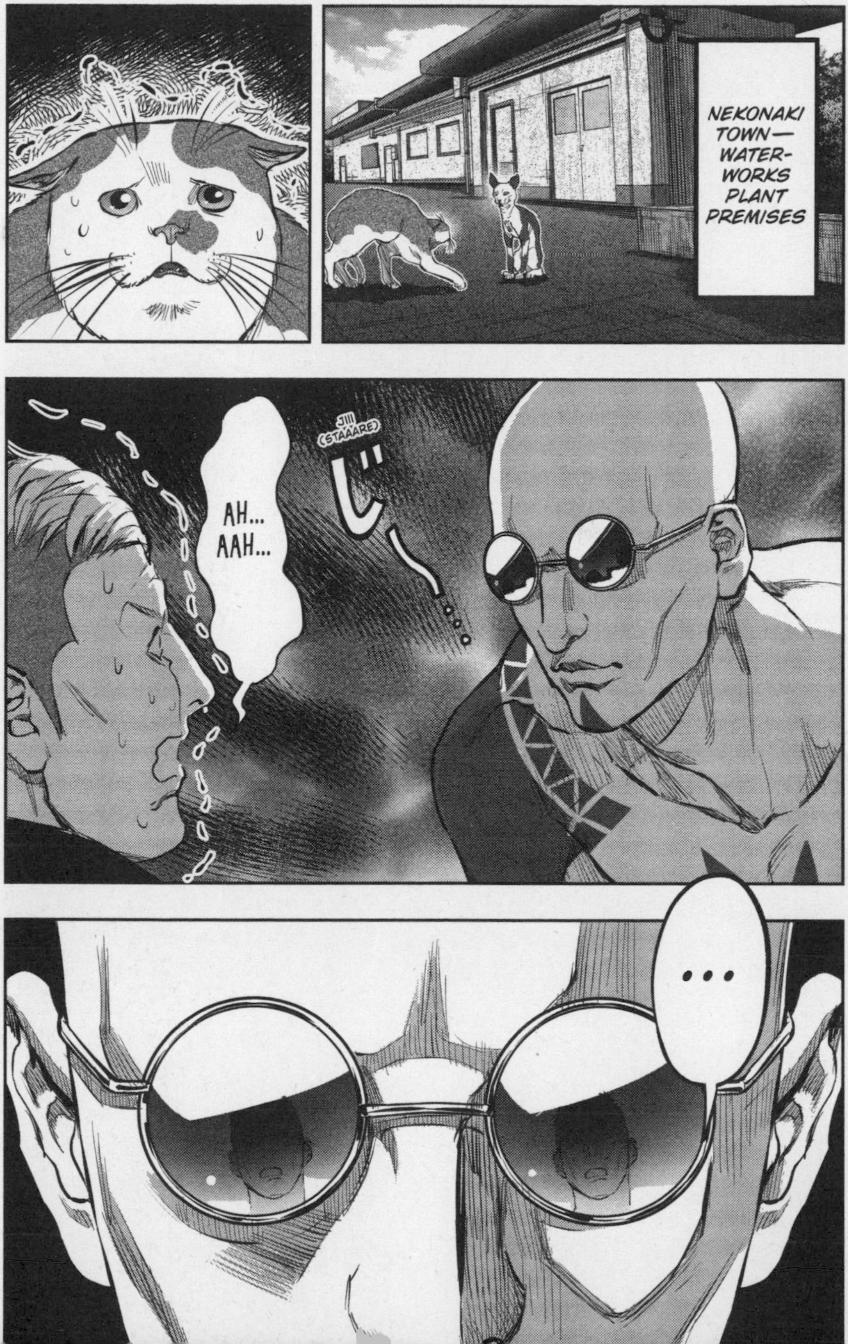
NEKONAKI TOWN—WATER-WORKS PLANT PREMISES
JIII (STAARE)
AH... AAH...
...

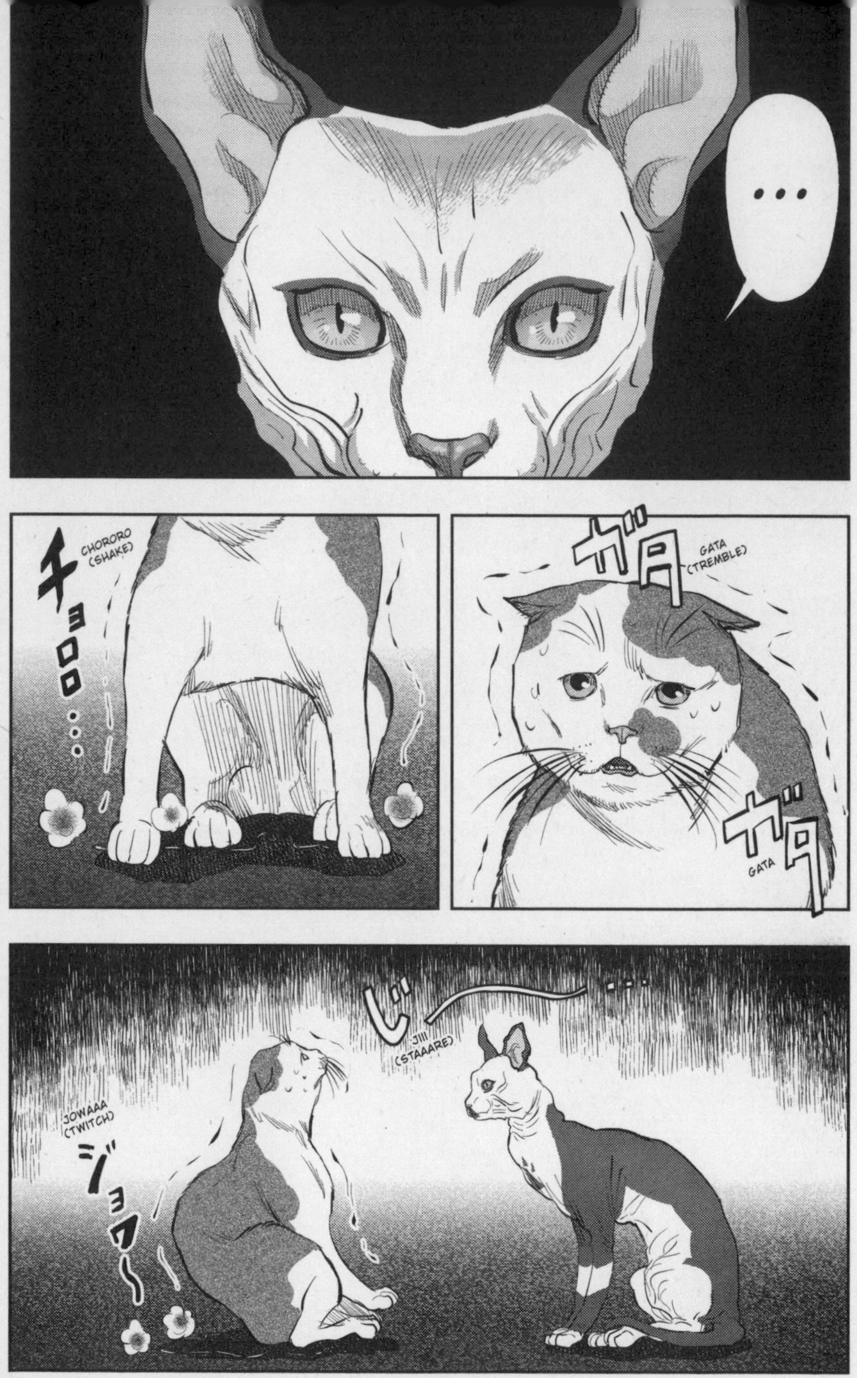
...
ガタ
GATA (TREMBLE)
ガタ
GATA
チョロロ...
CHORORO (SHAKE)
...
じー
JIII (STAAARE)
ジョワ~
JOWAAA (TWITCH)

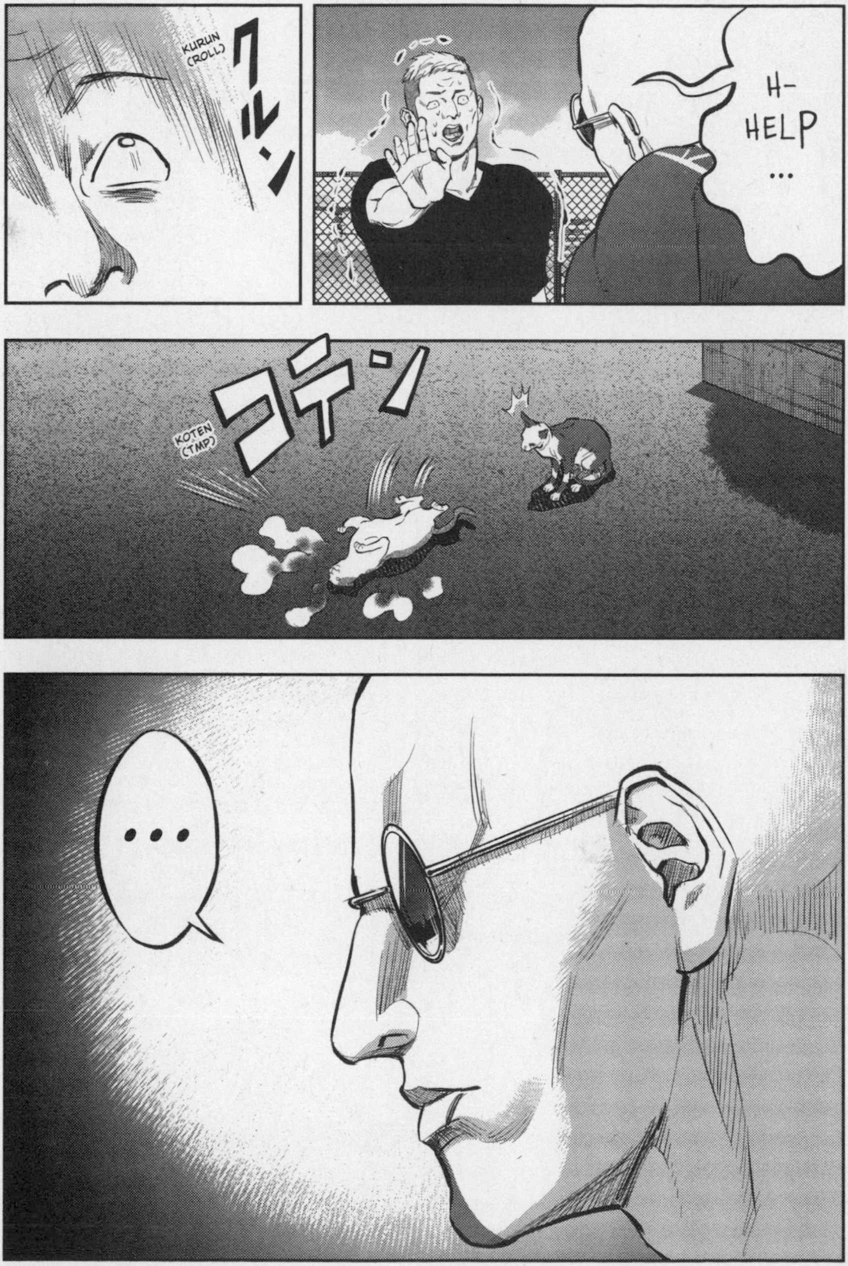
H-HELP...
KURUN (ROLL)
クルン
KOTEN (TMP)
コテン
...

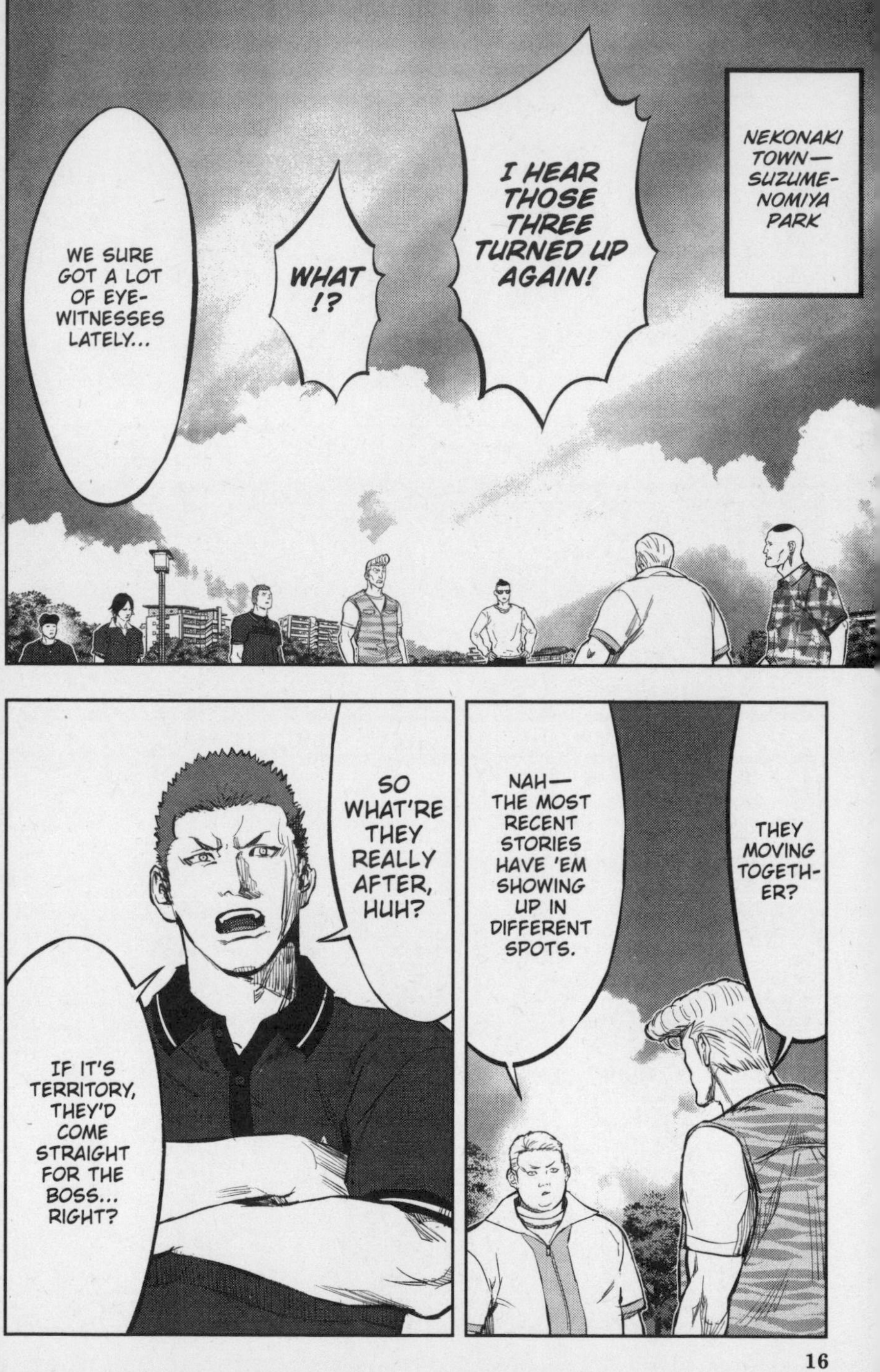
NEKONAKI TOWN—SUZUME-NOMIYA PARK
I HEAR THOSE THREE TURNED UP AGAIN!
WHAT!?
WE SURE GOT A LOT OF EYE-WITNESSES LATELY...
THEY MOVING TOGETH-ER?
NAH— THE MOST RECENT STORIES HAVE 'EM SHOWING UP IN DIFFERENT SPOTS.
SO WHAT'RE THEY REALLY AFTER, HUH?
IF IT'S TERRITORY, THEY'D COME STRAIGHT FOR THE BOSS... RIGHT?

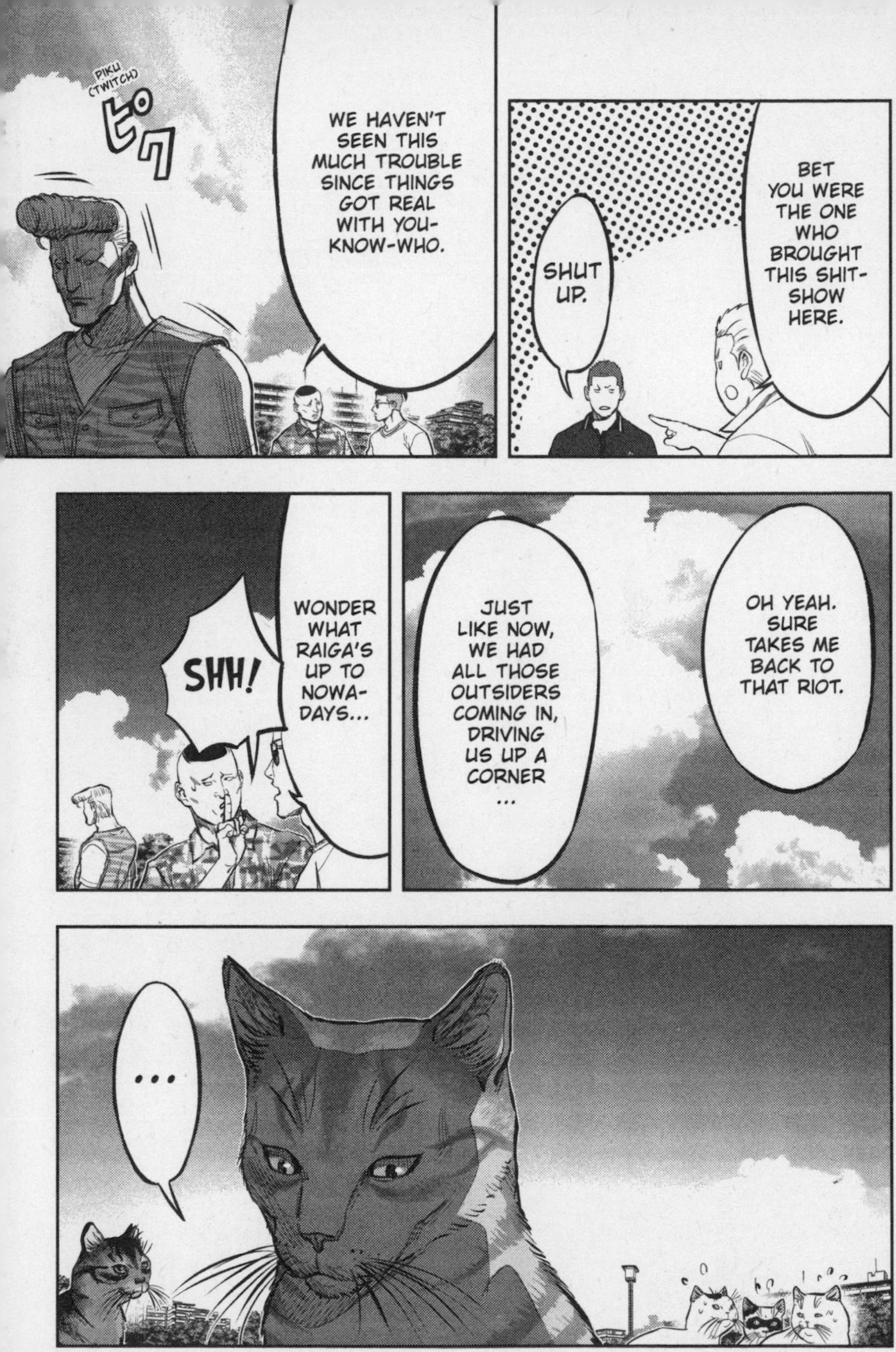
BET YOU WERE THE ONE WHO BROUGHT THIS SHIT-SHOW HERE.
SHUT UP.
WE HAVEN'T SEEN THIS MUCH TROUBLE SINCE THINGS GOT REAL WITH YOU-KNOW-WHO.
PIKU (TWITCH)
ピク
OH YEAH. SURE TAKES ME BACK TO THAT RIOT.
JUST LIKE NOW, WE HAD ALL THOSE OUTSIDERS COMING IN, DRIVING US UP A CORNER...
WONDER WHAT RAIGA'S UP TO NOWA-DAYS...
SHH!
...

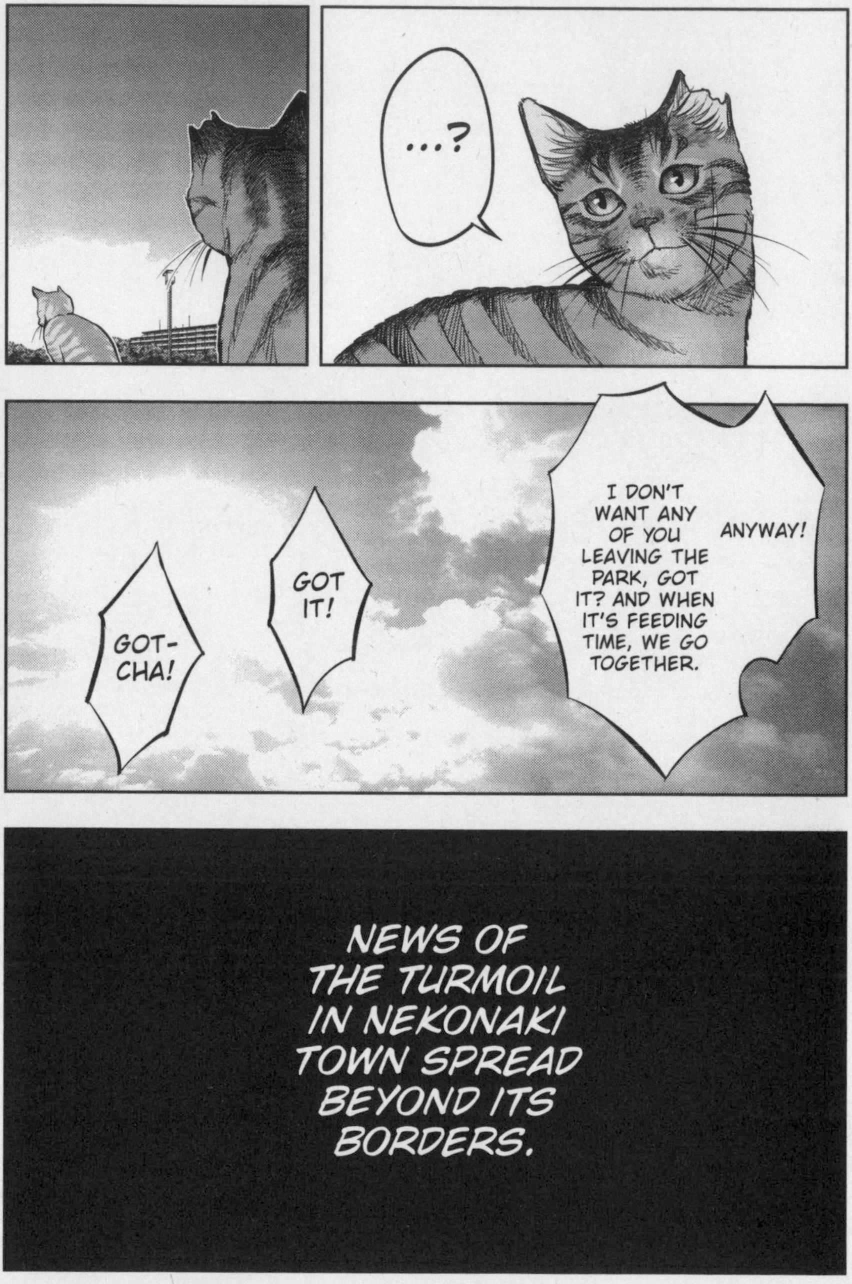
...?
ANYWAY!
I DON'T WANT ANY OF YOU LEAVING THE PARK, GOT IT? AND WHEN IT'S FEEDING TIME, WE GO TOGETHER.
GOT IT!
GOT-CHA!
NEWS OF THE TURMOIL IN NEKONAKI TOWN SPREAD BEYOND ITS BORDERS.

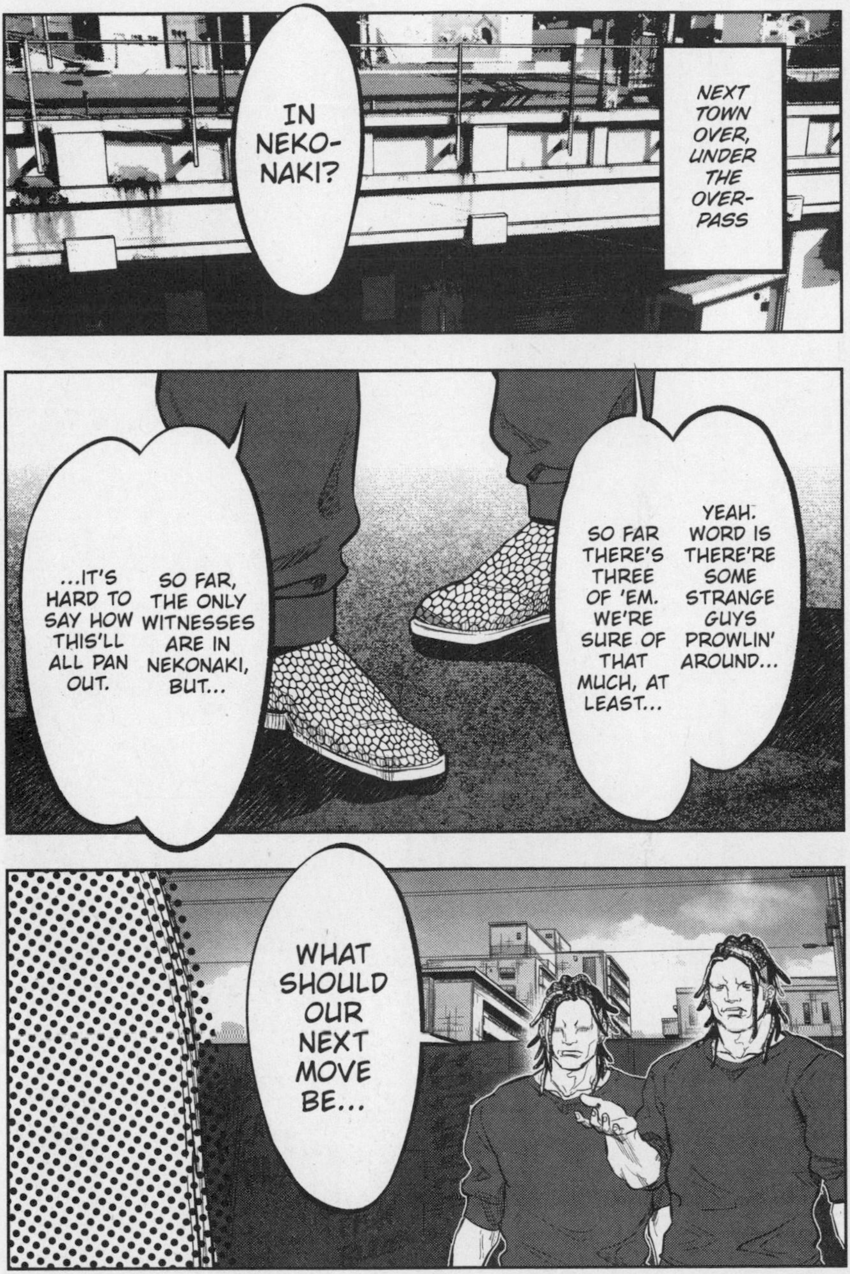
NEXT TOWN OVER, UNDER THE OVER-PASS
IN NEKO-NAKI?
YEAH. WORD IS THERE'RE SOME STRANGE GUYS PROWLIN' AROUND...
SO FAR THERE'S THREE OF 'EM. WE'RE SURE OF THAT MUCH, AT LEAST...
SO FAR, THE ONLY WITNESSES ARE IN NEKONAKI, BUT...
...IT'S HARD TO SAY HOW THIS'LL ALL PAN OUT.
WHAT SHOULD OUR NEXT MOVE BE...

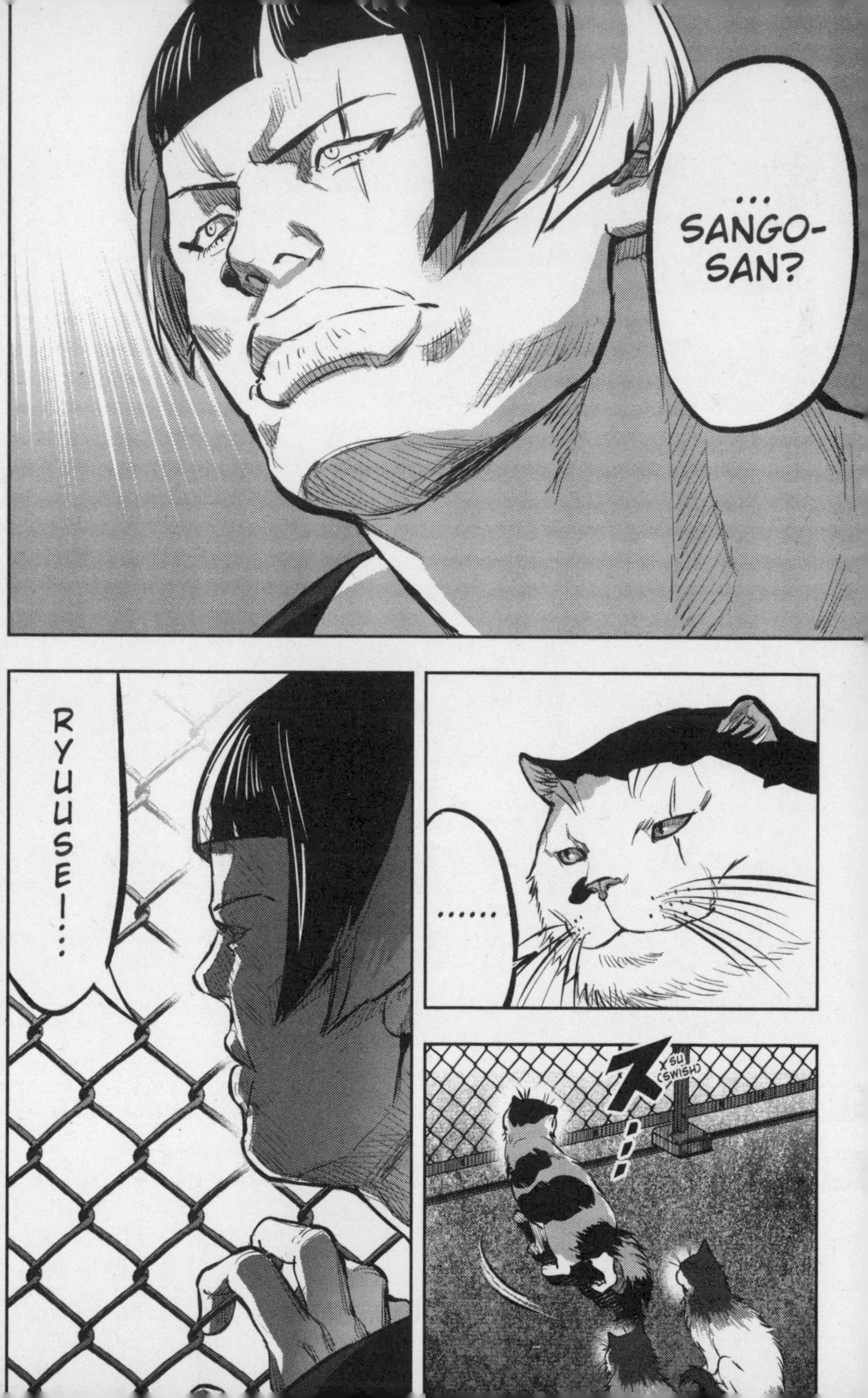
...SANGO-SAN?
......
SU (SWISH)
RYUUSEI!...

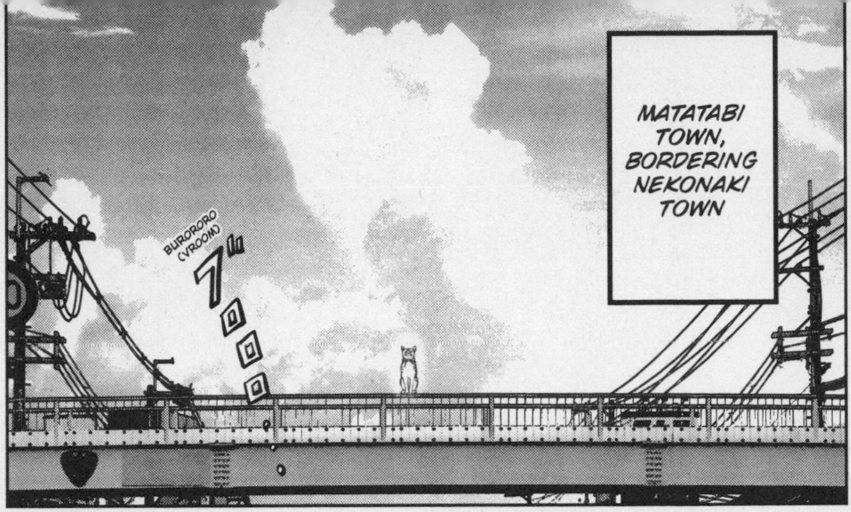
MATATABI TOWN, BORDERING NEKONAKI TOWN
BURORORO (VROOM)
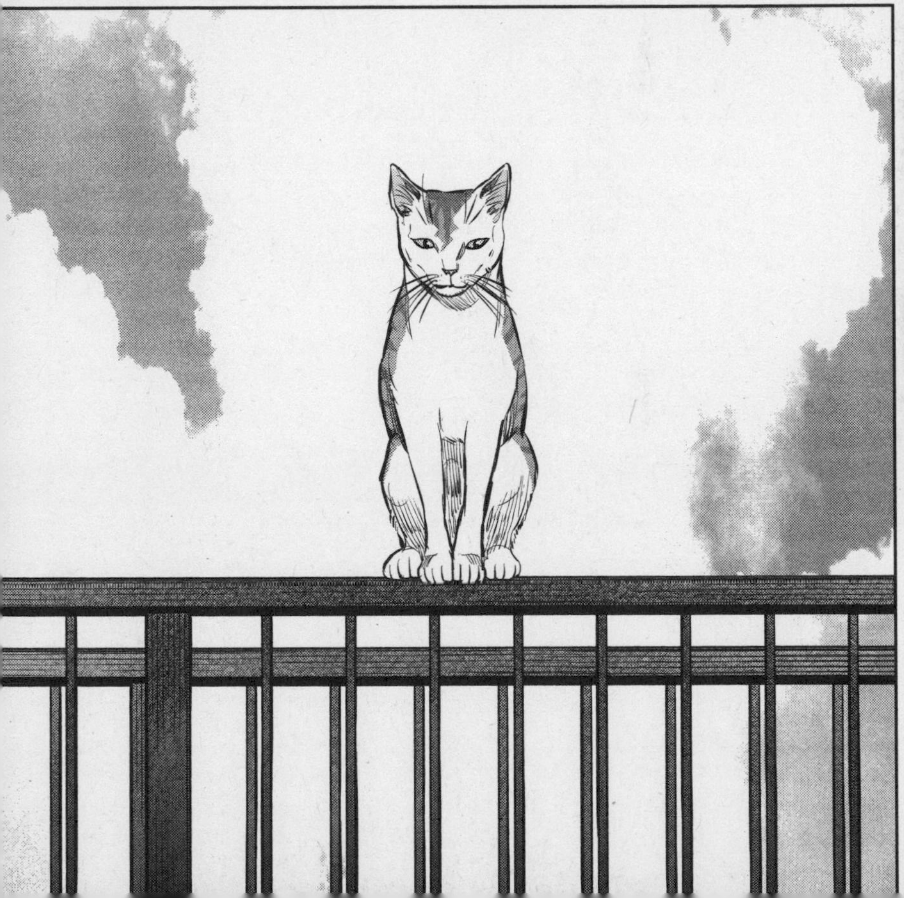

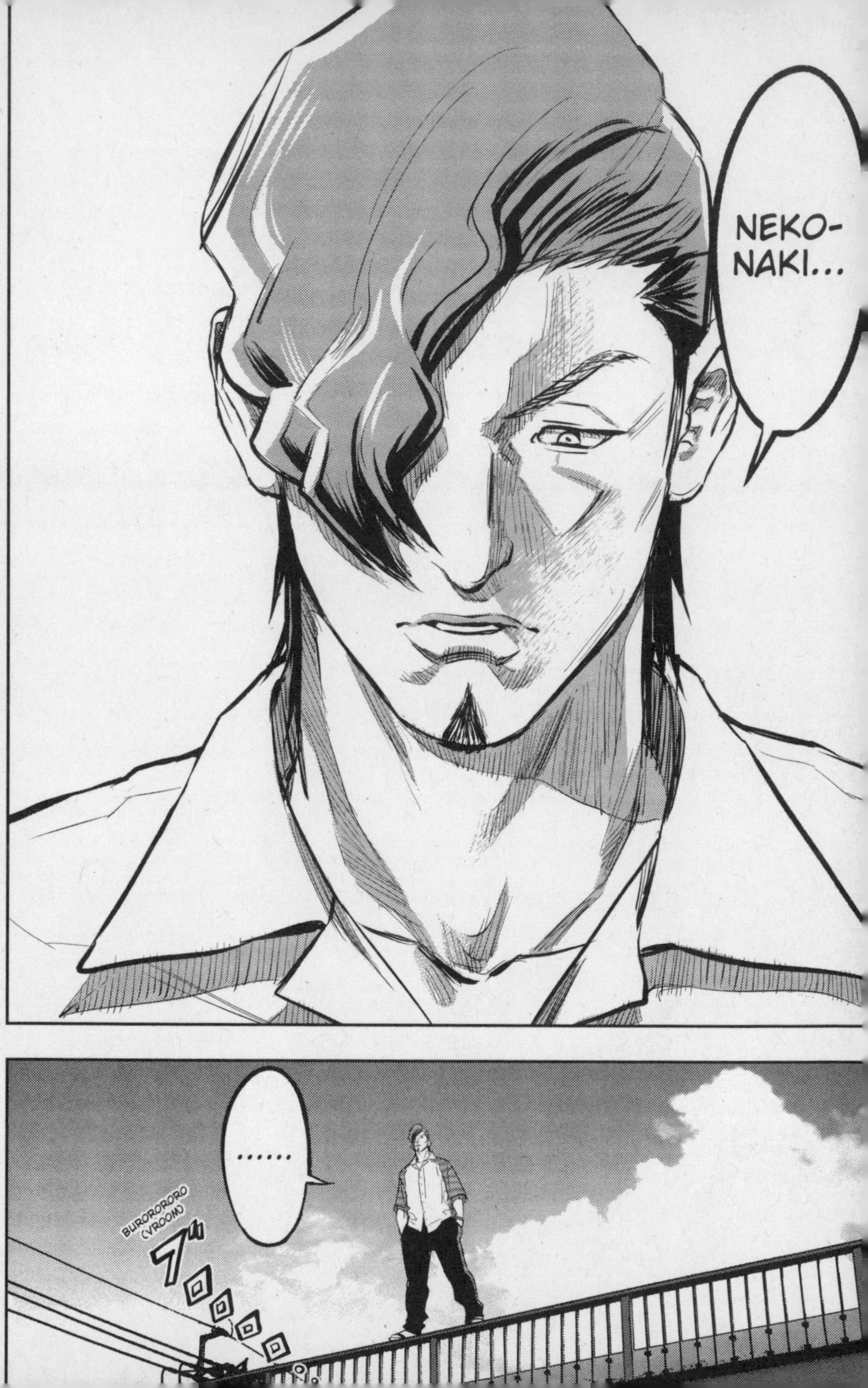
NEKO-NAKI...
......
BURORORORO (VROOM)

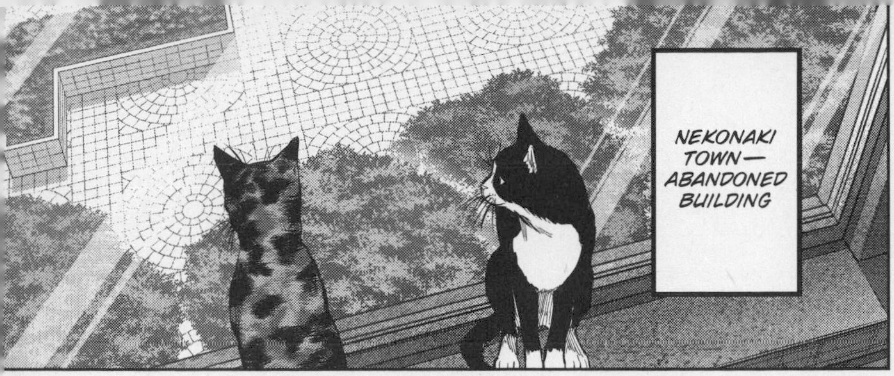
NEKONAKI TOWN—ABANDONED BUILDING
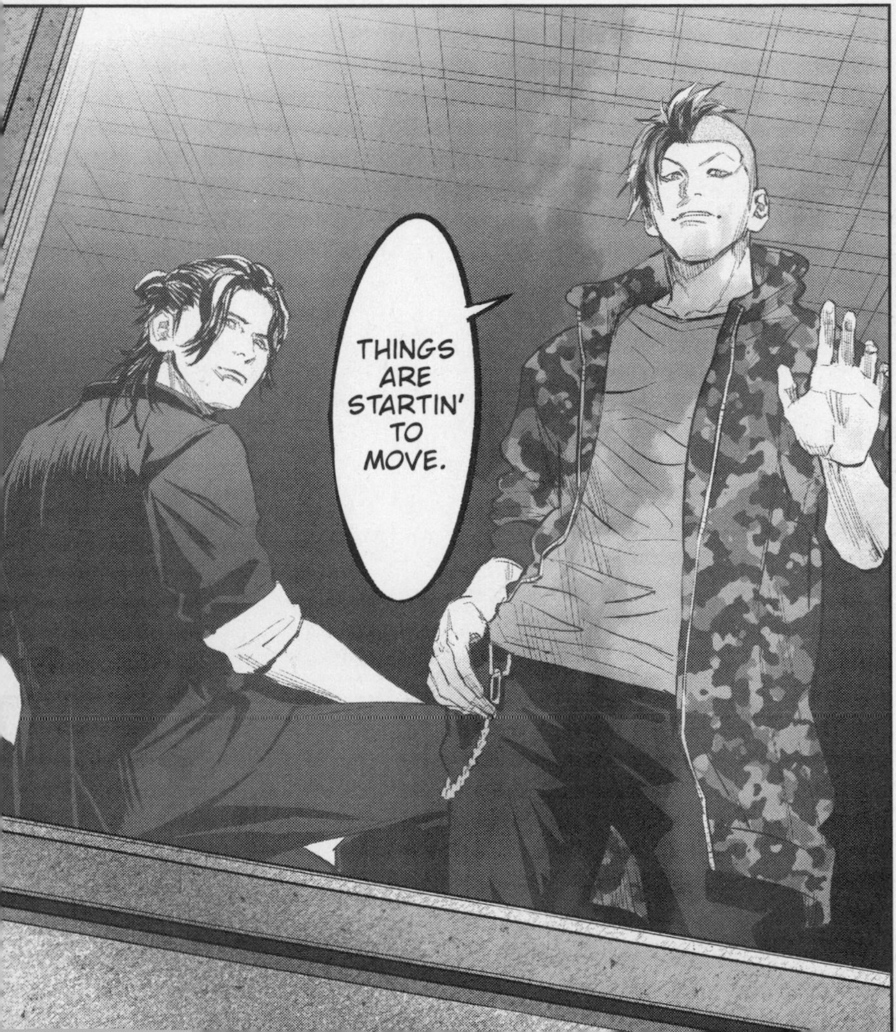
THINGS ARE STARTIN' TO MOVE.

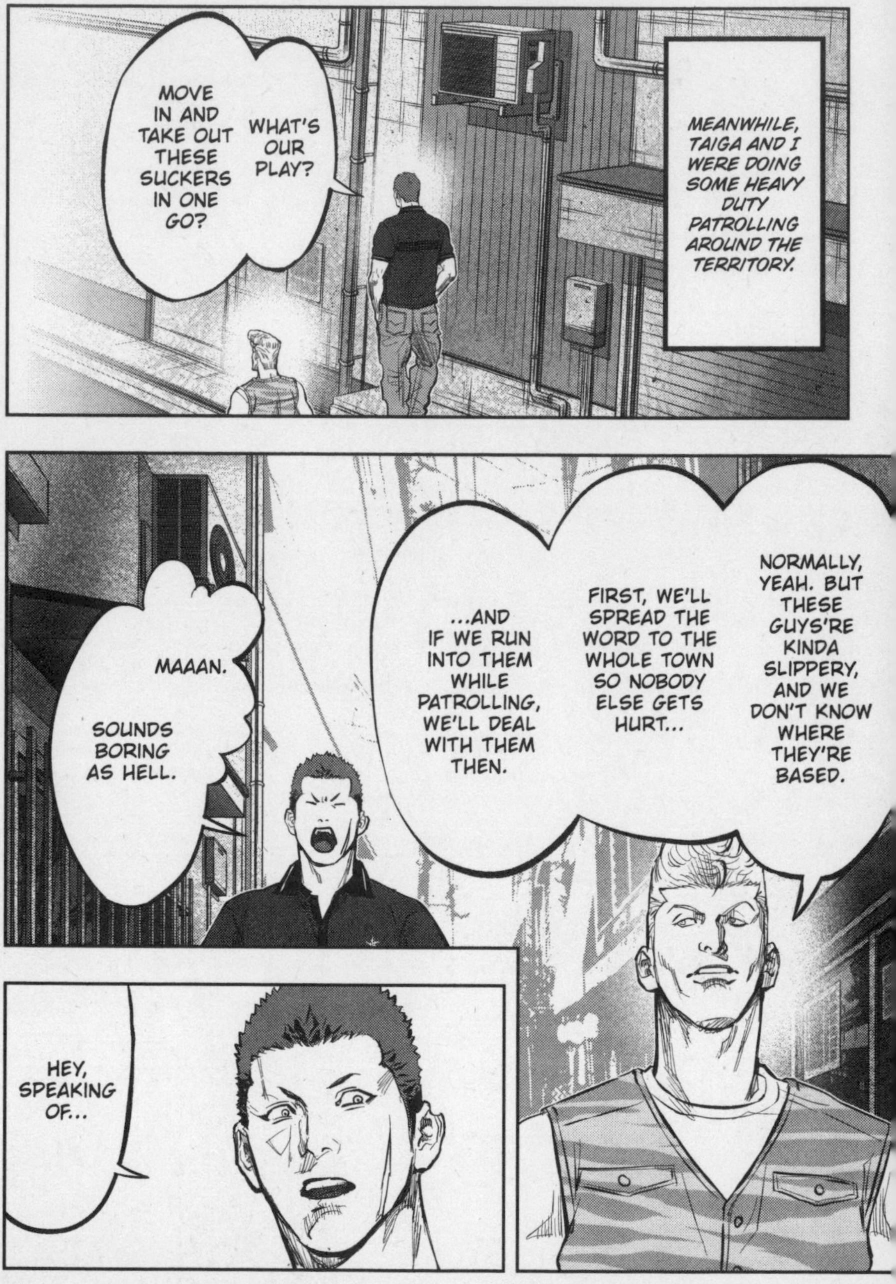
MEANWHILE, TAIGA AND I WERE DOING SOME HEAVY DUTY PATROLLING AROUND THE TERRITORY.
WHAT'S OUR PLAY?
MOVE IN AND TAKE OUT THESE SUCKERS IN ONE GO?
NORMALLY, YEAH. BUT THESE GUYS'RE KINDA SLIPPERY, AND WE DON'T KNOW WHERE THEY'RE BASED.
FIRST, WE'LL SPREAD THE WORD TO THE WHOLE TOWN SO NOBODY ELSE GETS HURT...
...AND IF WE RUN INTO THEM WHILE PATROLLING, WE'LL DEAL WITH THEM THEN.
MAAAN.
SOUNDS BORING AS HELL.
HEY, SPEAKING OF...

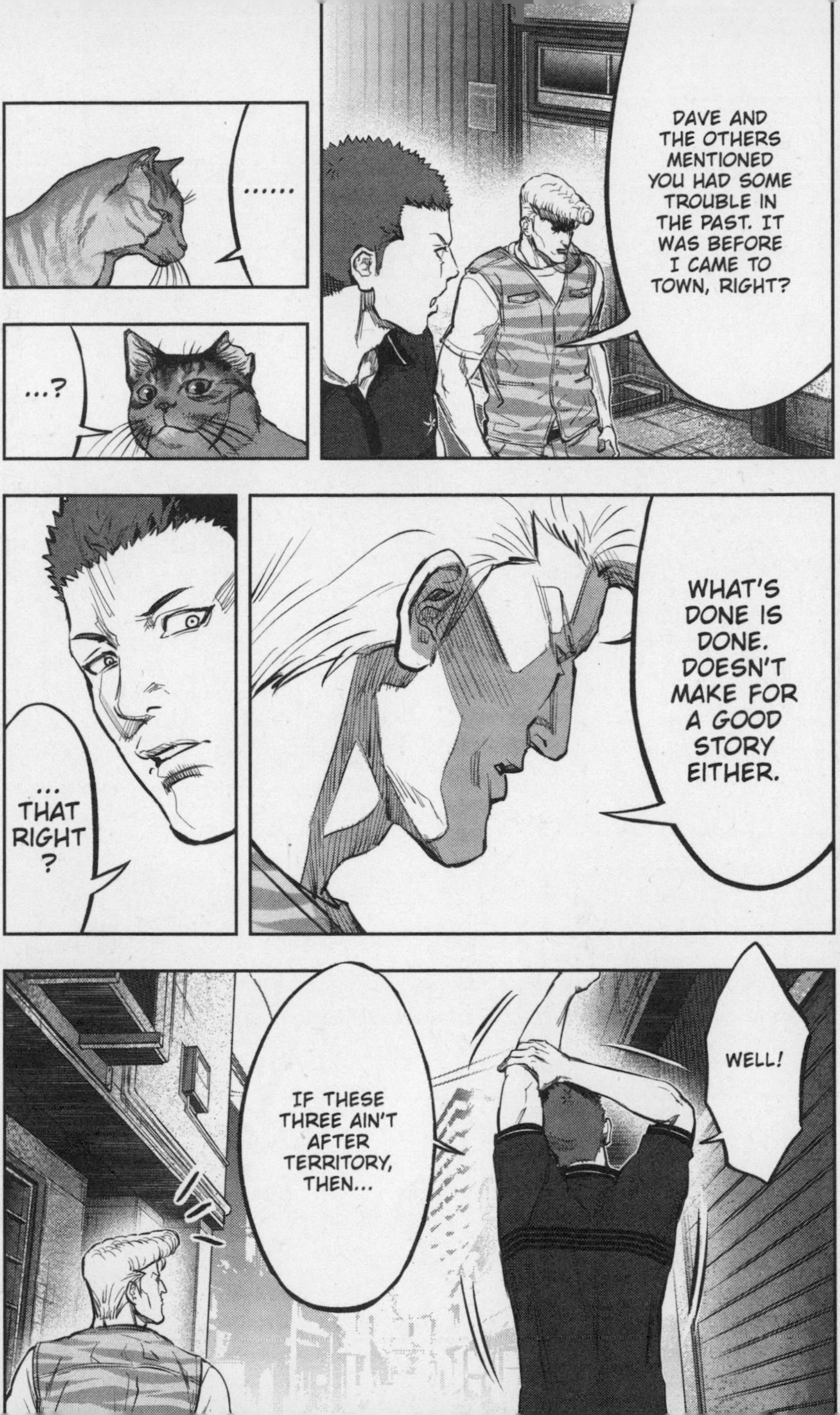
DAVE AND THE OTHERS MENTIONED YOU HAD SOME TROUBLE IN THE PAST. IT WAS BEFORE I CAME TO TOWN, RIGHT?
....
...?
WHAT'S DONE IS DONE. DOESN'T MAKE FOR A GOOD STORY EITHER.
... THAT RIGHT ?
WELL!
IF THESE THREE AIN'T AFTER TERRITORY, THEN...

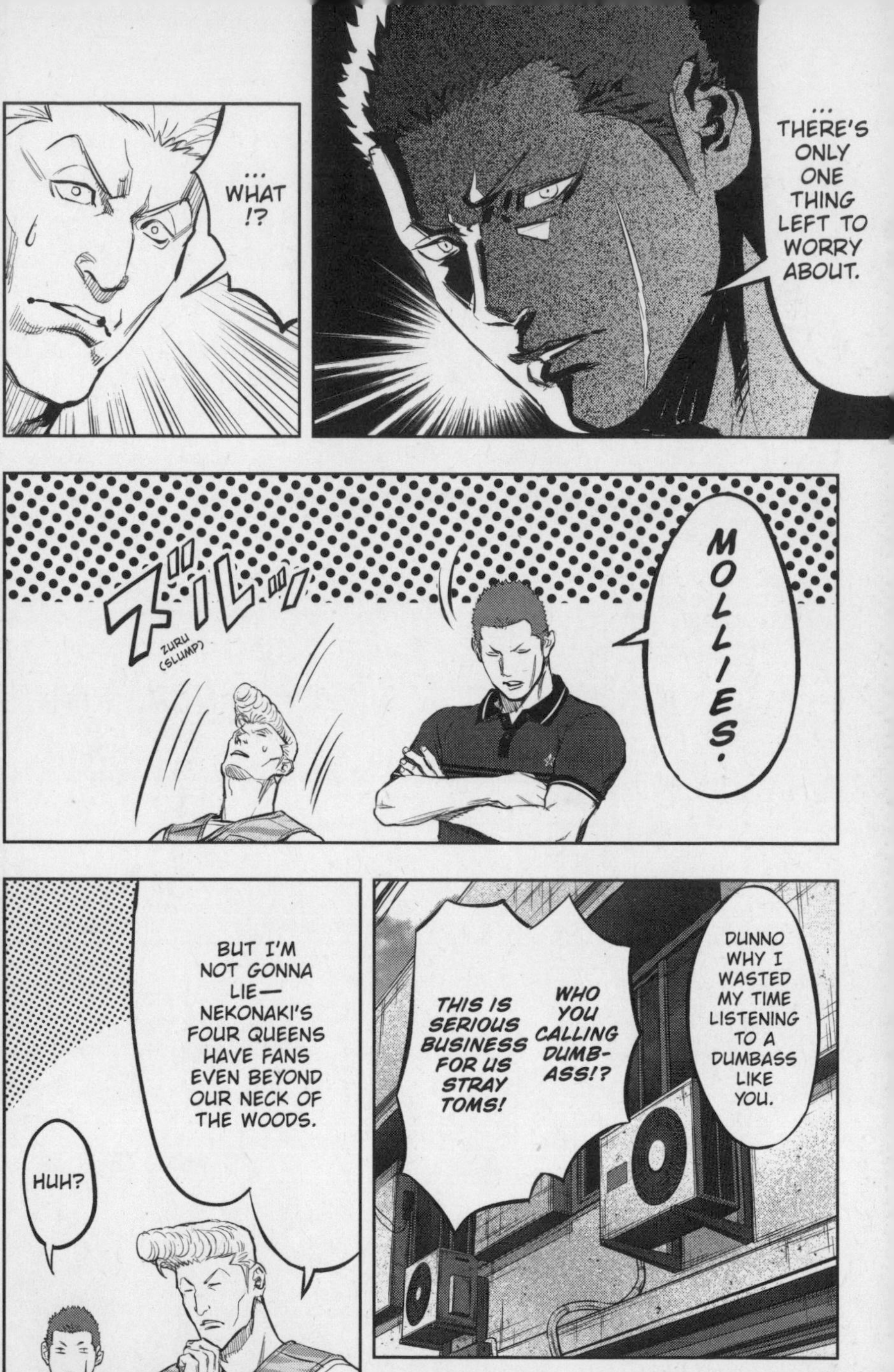
... THERE'S ONLY ONE THING LEFT TO WORRY ABOUT.
... WHAT !?
MOLLIES.
ZURU (SLUMP)
DUNNO WHY I WASTED MY TIME LISTENING TO A DUMBASS LIKE YOU.
WHO YOU CALLING DUMB-ASS!?
THIS IS SERIOUS BUSINESS FOR US STRAY TOMS!
BUT I'M NOT GONNA LIE—NEKONAKI'S FOUR QUEENS HAVE FANS EVEN BEYOND OUR NECK OF THE WOODS.
HUH?

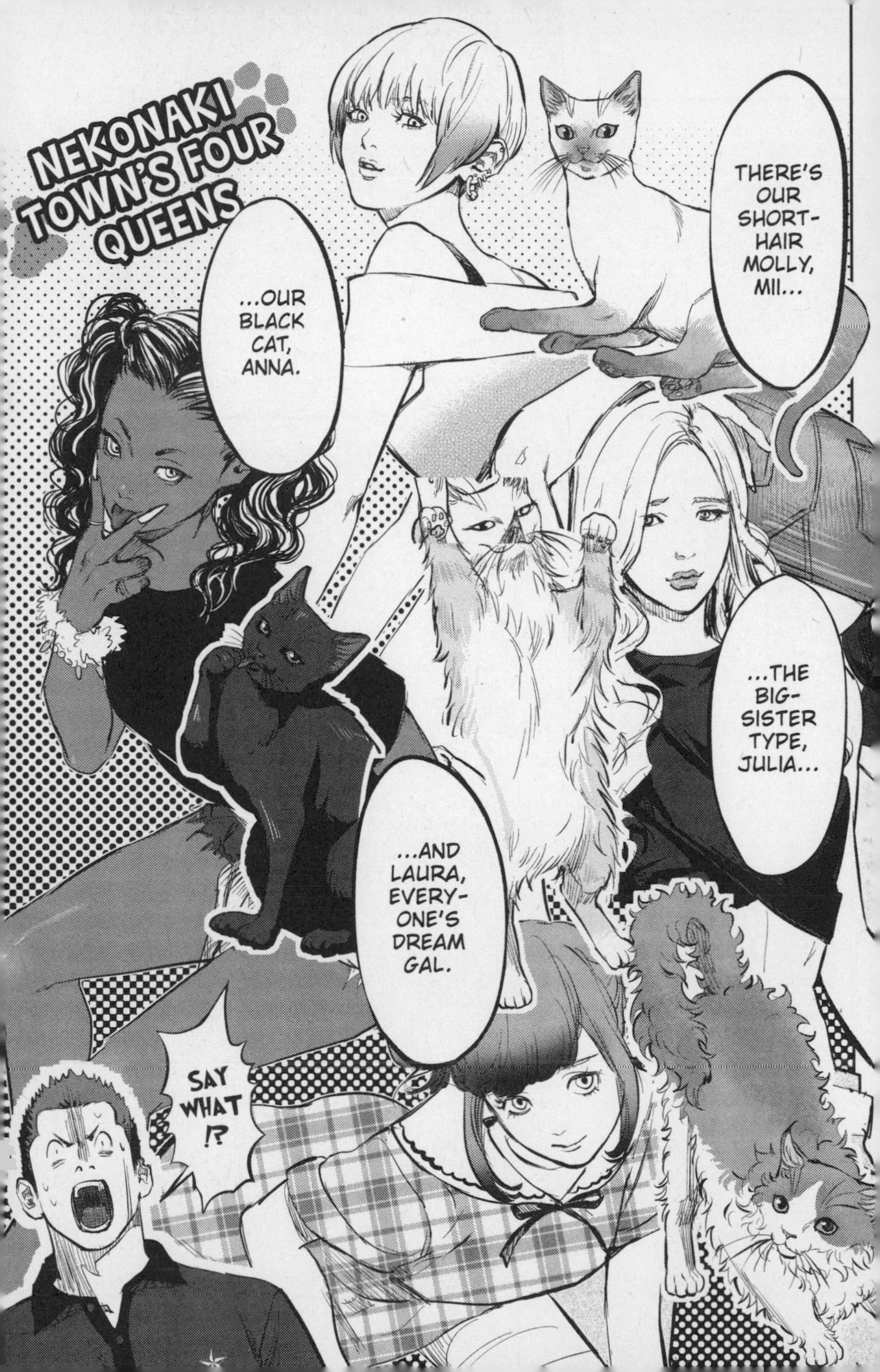
THERE'S OUR SHORT-HAIR MOLLY, MII...
NEKONAKI TOWN'S FOUR QUEENS
...OUR BLACK CAT, ANNA.
...THE BIG-SISTER TYPE, JULIA...
...AND LAURA, EVERY-ONE'S DREAM GAL.
SAY WHAT!?

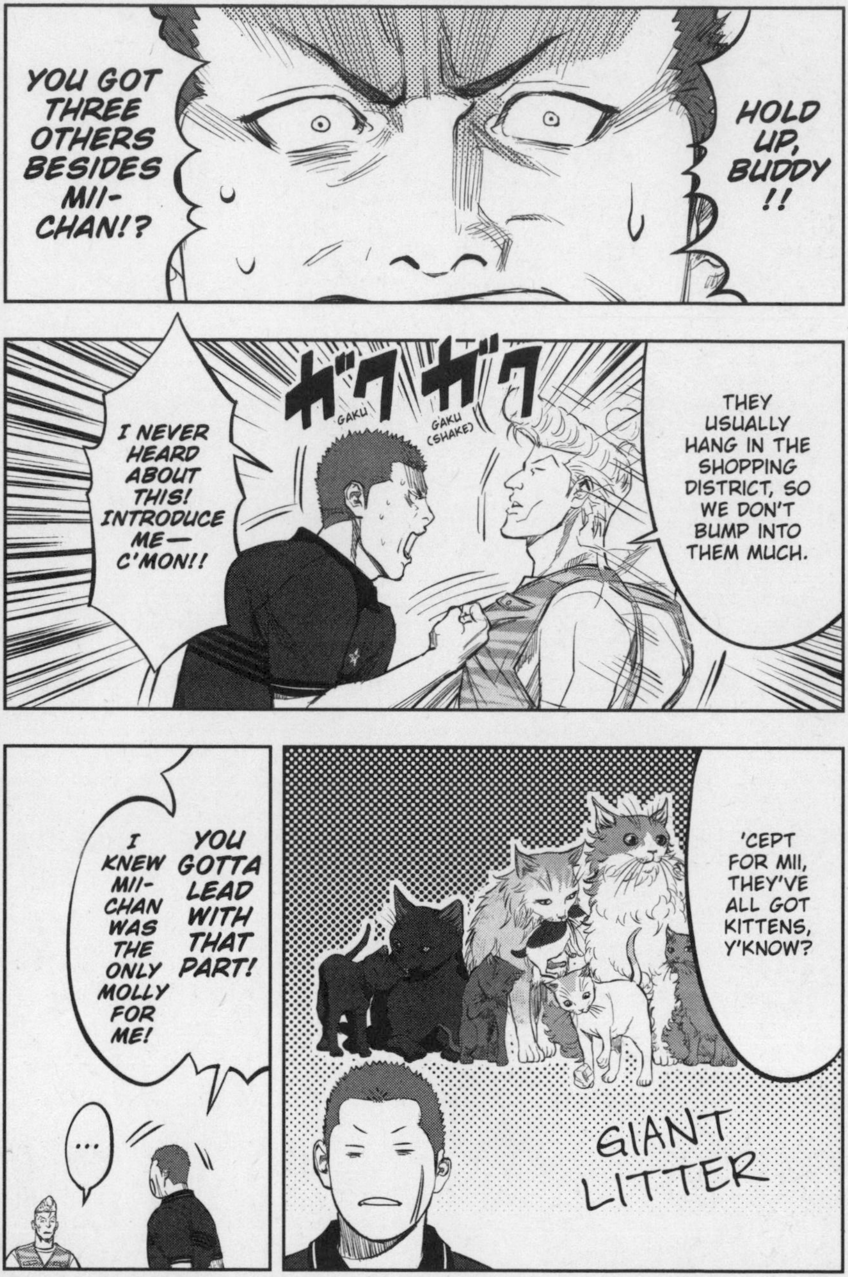
HOLD UP, BUDDY!!
YOU GOT THREE OTHERS BESIDES MII-CHAN!?
THEY USUALLY HANG IN THE SHOPPING DISTRICT, SO WE DON'T BUMP INTO THEM MUCH.
ガク ガク
GAKU GAKU (SHAKE)
I NEVER HEARD ABOUT THIS! INTRODUCE ME—C'MON!!
'CEPT FOR MII, THEY'VE ALL GOT KITTENS, Y'KNOW?
GIANT LITTER
YOU GOTTA LEAD WITH THAT PART!
I KNEW MII-CHAN WAS THE ONLY MOLLY FOR ME!
...

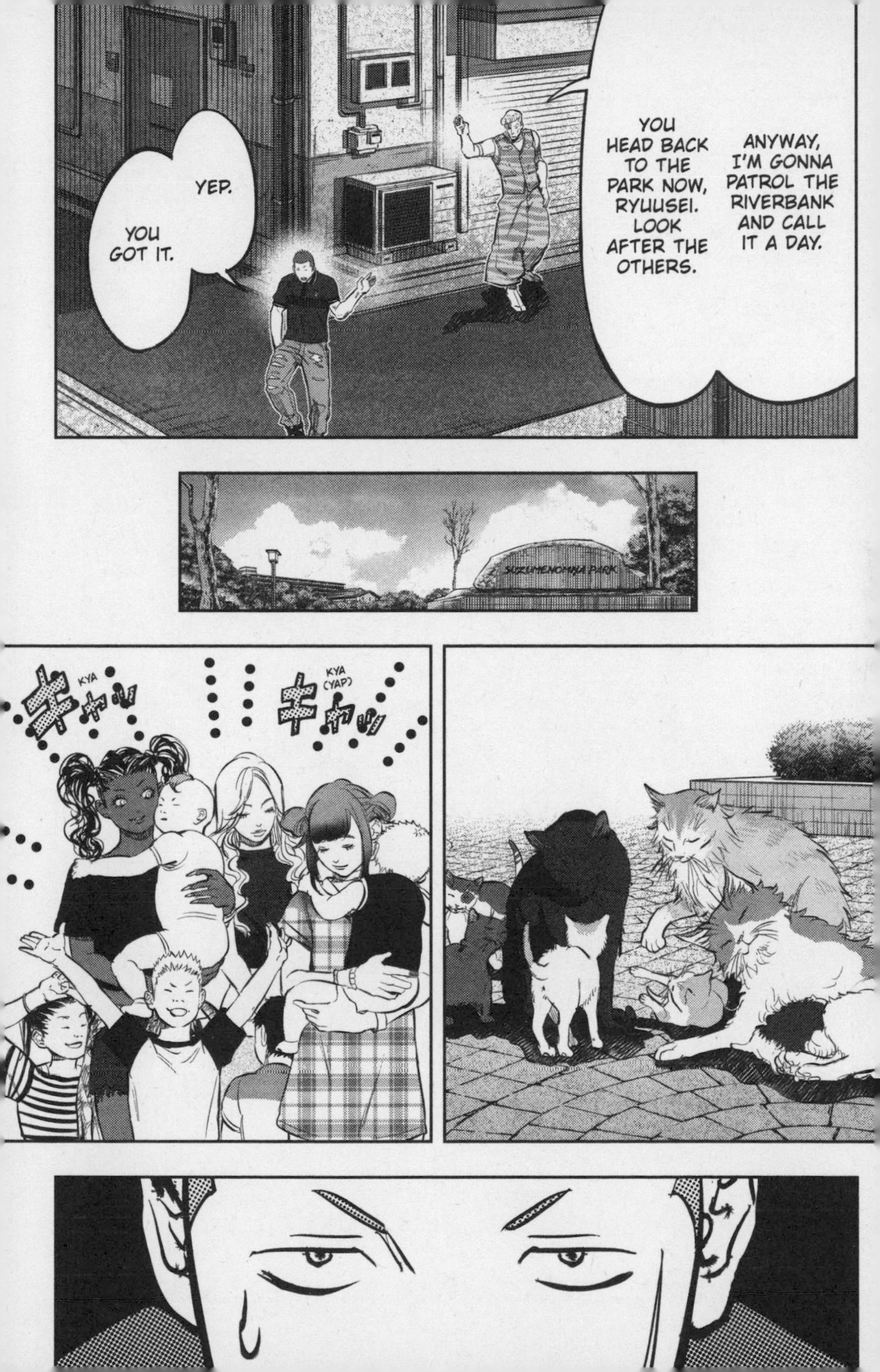
ANYWAY, I'M GONNA PATROL THE RIVERBANK AND CALL IT A DAY.
YOU HEAD BACK TO THE PARK NOW, RYUUSEI. LOOK AFTER THE OTHERS.
YEP.
YOU GOT IT.
SUZUMENOMIYA PARK
KYA (YAP)
KYA

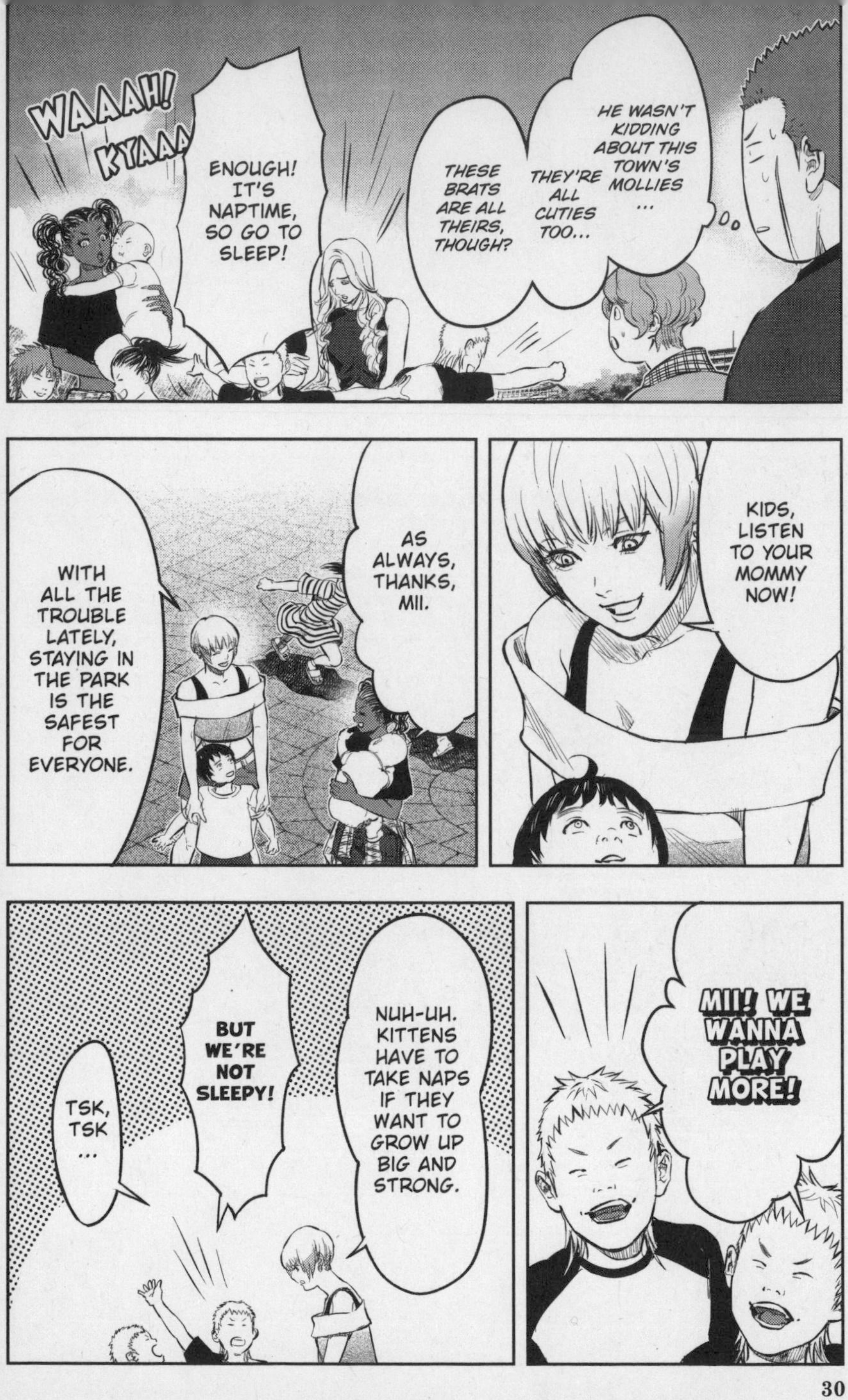
HE WASN'T KIDDING ABOUT THIS TOWN'S MOLLIES ...
THEY'RE ALL CUTIES TOO...
THESE BRATS ARE ALL THEIRS, THOUGH?
ENOUGH! IT'S NAPTIME, SO GO TO SLEEP!
KYAAA
WAAAH!
KIDS, LISTEN TO YOUR MOMMY NOW!
AS ALWAYS, THANKS, MII.
WITH ALL THE TROUBLE LATELY, STAYING IN THE PARK IS THE SAFEST FOR EVERYONE.
MII! WE WANNA PLAY MORE!
NUH-UH. KITTENS HAVE TO TAKE NAPS IF THEY WANT TO GROW UP BIG AND STRONG.
BUT WE'RE NOT SLEEPY!
TSK, TSK ...

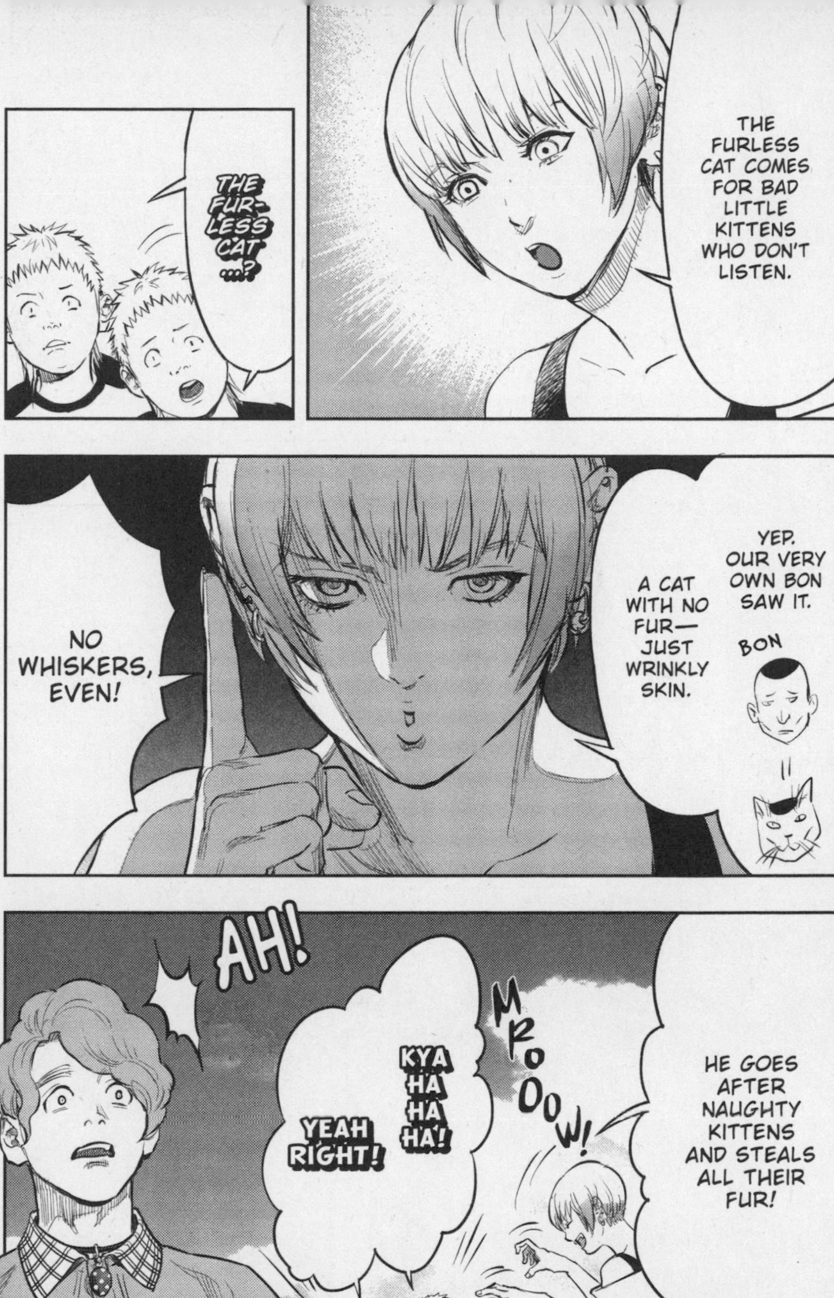
THE FURLESS CAT COMES FOR BAD LITTLE KITTENS WHO DON'T LISTEN.
THE FUR-LESS CAT ...?
YEP. OUR VERY OWN BON SAW IT.
BON
A CAT WITH NO FUR— JUST WRINKLY SKIN.
NO WHISKERS, EVEN!
HE GOES AFTER NAUGHTY KITTENS AND STEALS ALL THEIR FUR!
MROOOW!
KYA HA HA HA!
YEAH RIGHT!
AH!

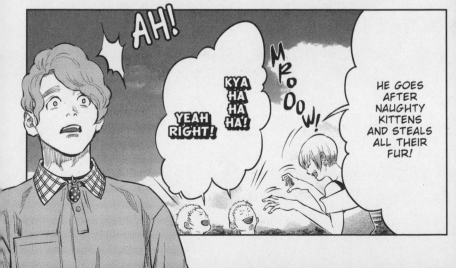

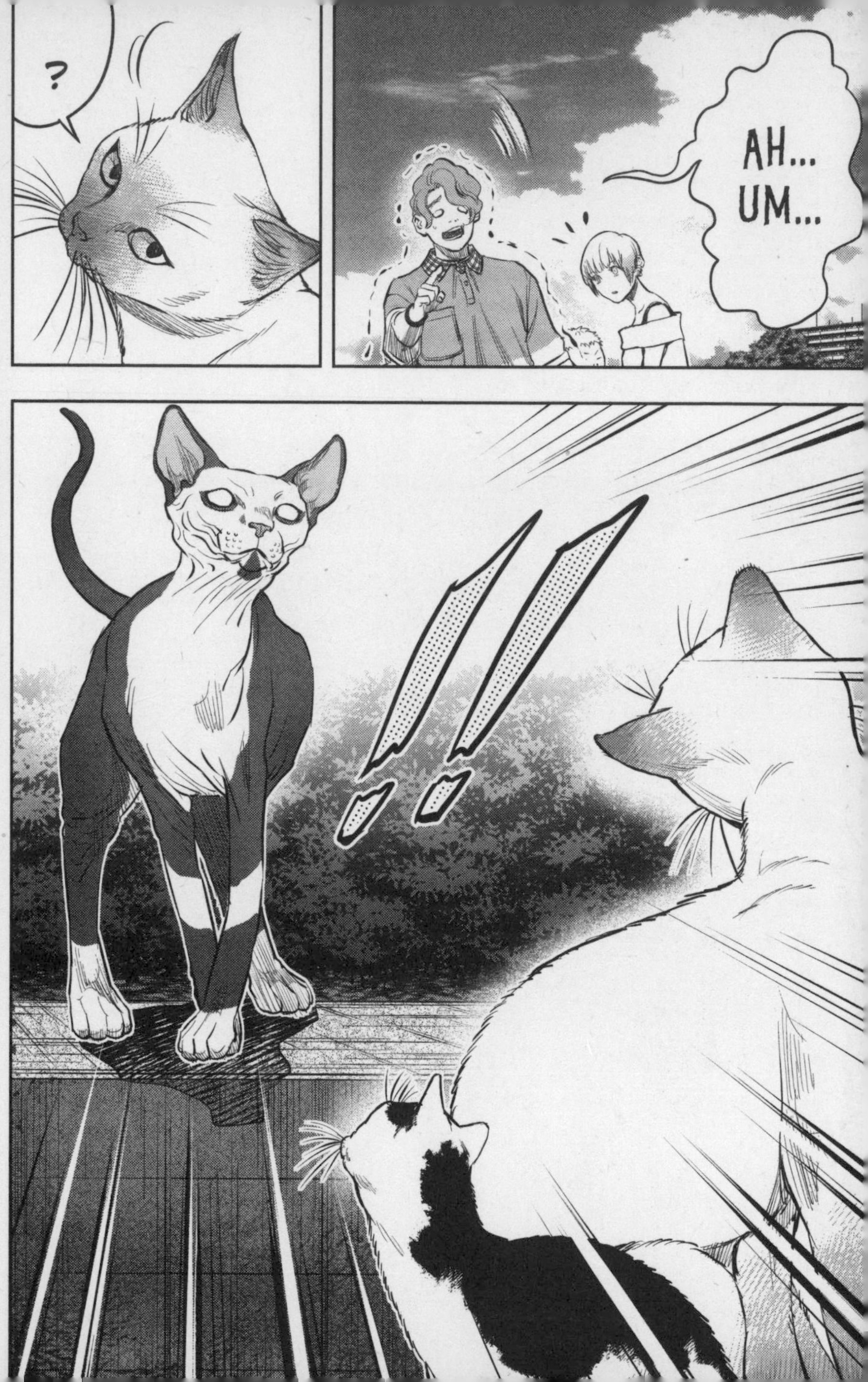
AH... UM...
?
!!

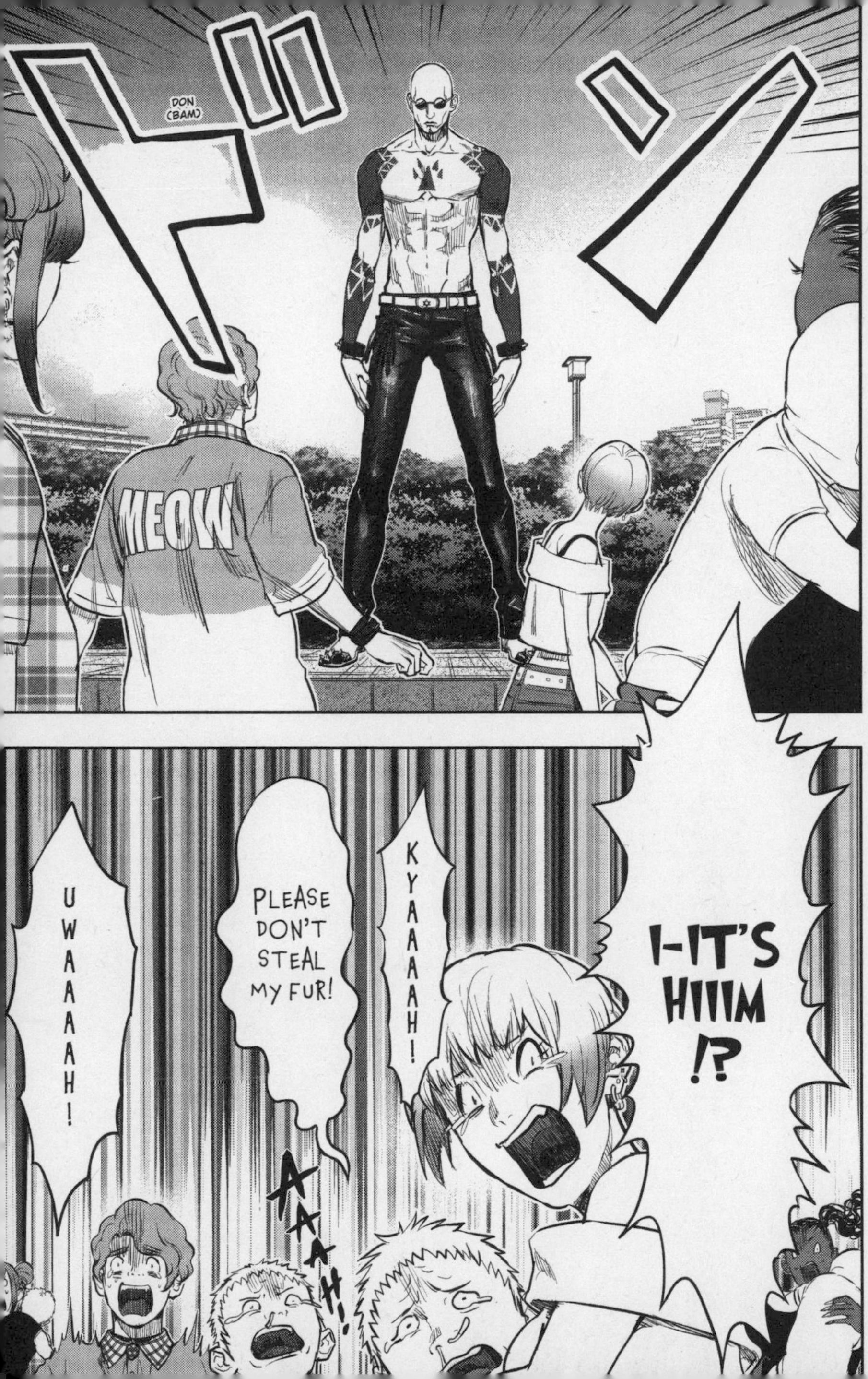
DON (BAM)
I-IT'S HIIIM!?
KYAAAAAH!
PLEASE DON'T STEAL MY FUR!
UWAAAAAH!
AAAAH!!

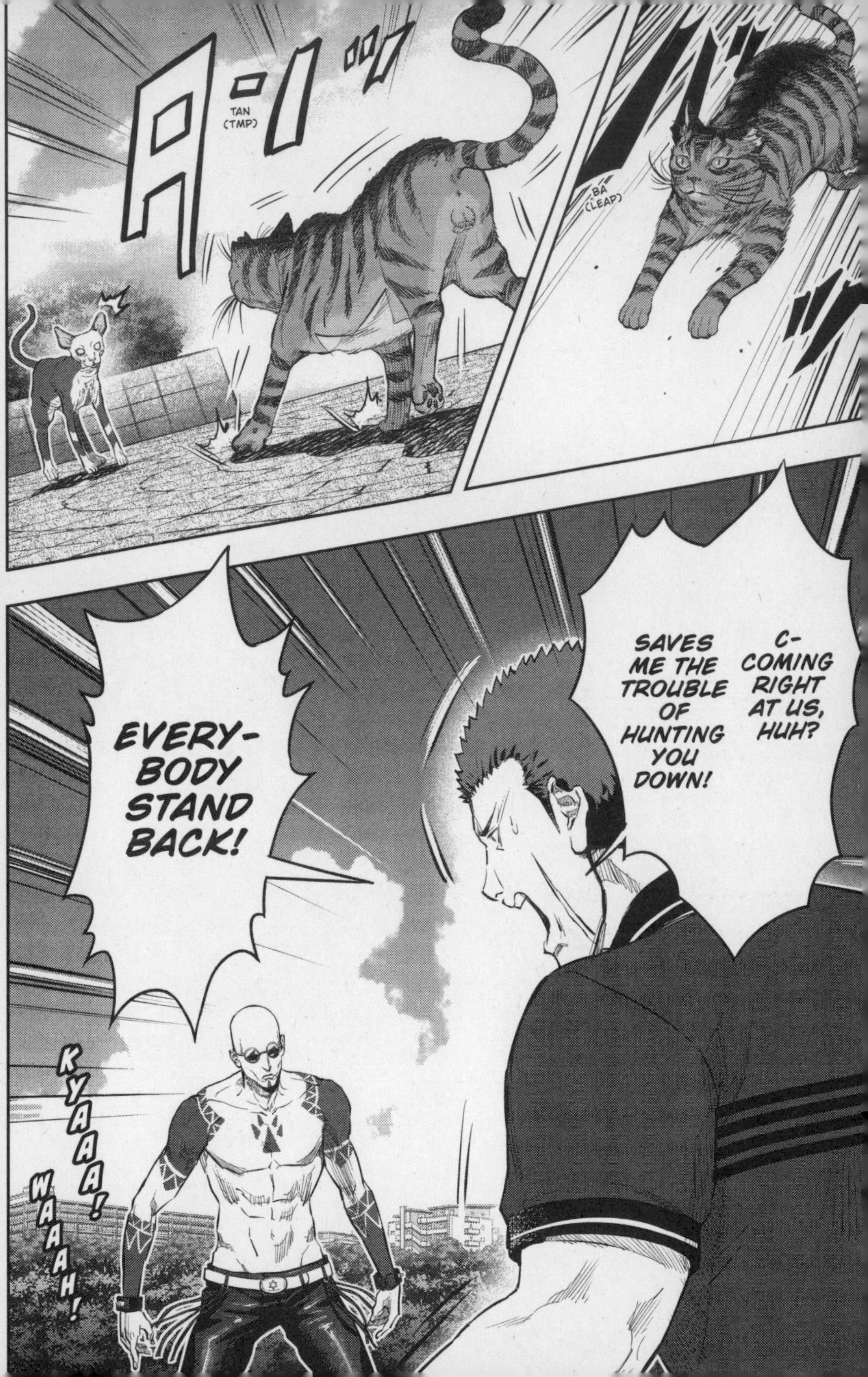
BA (LEAP)
TAN (TMP)
C-COMING RIGHT AT US, HUH?
SAVES ME THE TROUBLE OF HUNTING YOU DOWN!
EVERY-BODY STAND BACK!
KYAAAA!
WAAAAH!

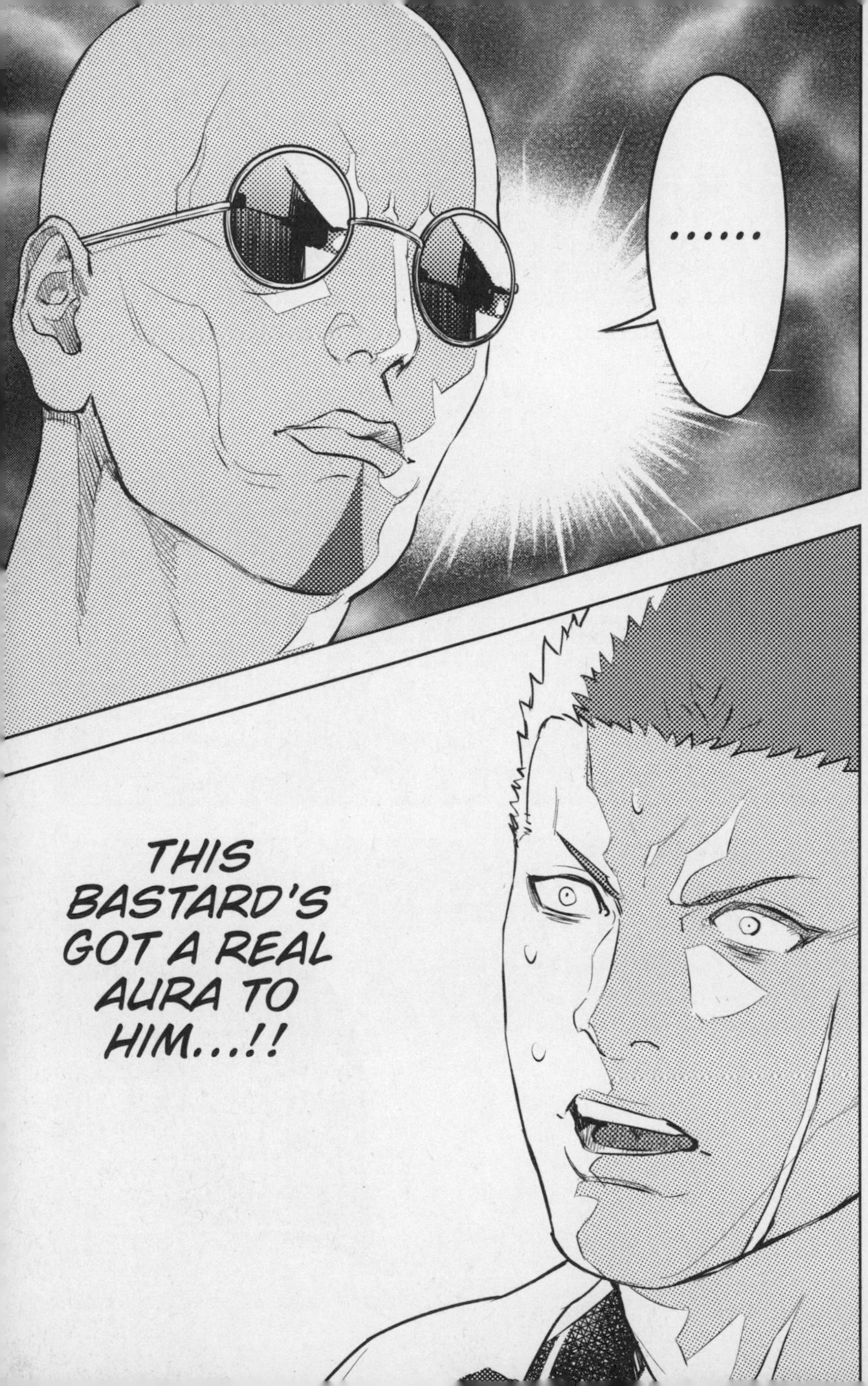
......
THIS BASTARD'S GOT A REAL AURA TO HIM...!!

NEKONAKI TOWN— BANKS OF NEKONAKI RIVER

PURU ブるっ ブる PURU (TREMBLE)

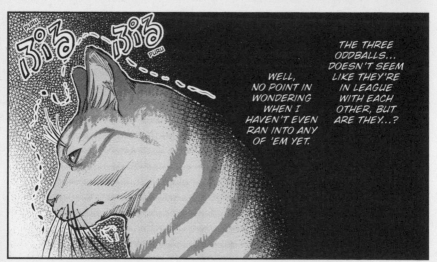

ブる ブる PURU PURU

THE THREE ODDBALLS... DOESN'T SEEM LIKE THEY'RE IN LEAGUE WITH EACH OTHER, BUT ARE THEY...?

WELL, NO POINT IN WONDERING WHEN I HAVEN'T EVEN RAN INTO ANY OF 'EM YET.

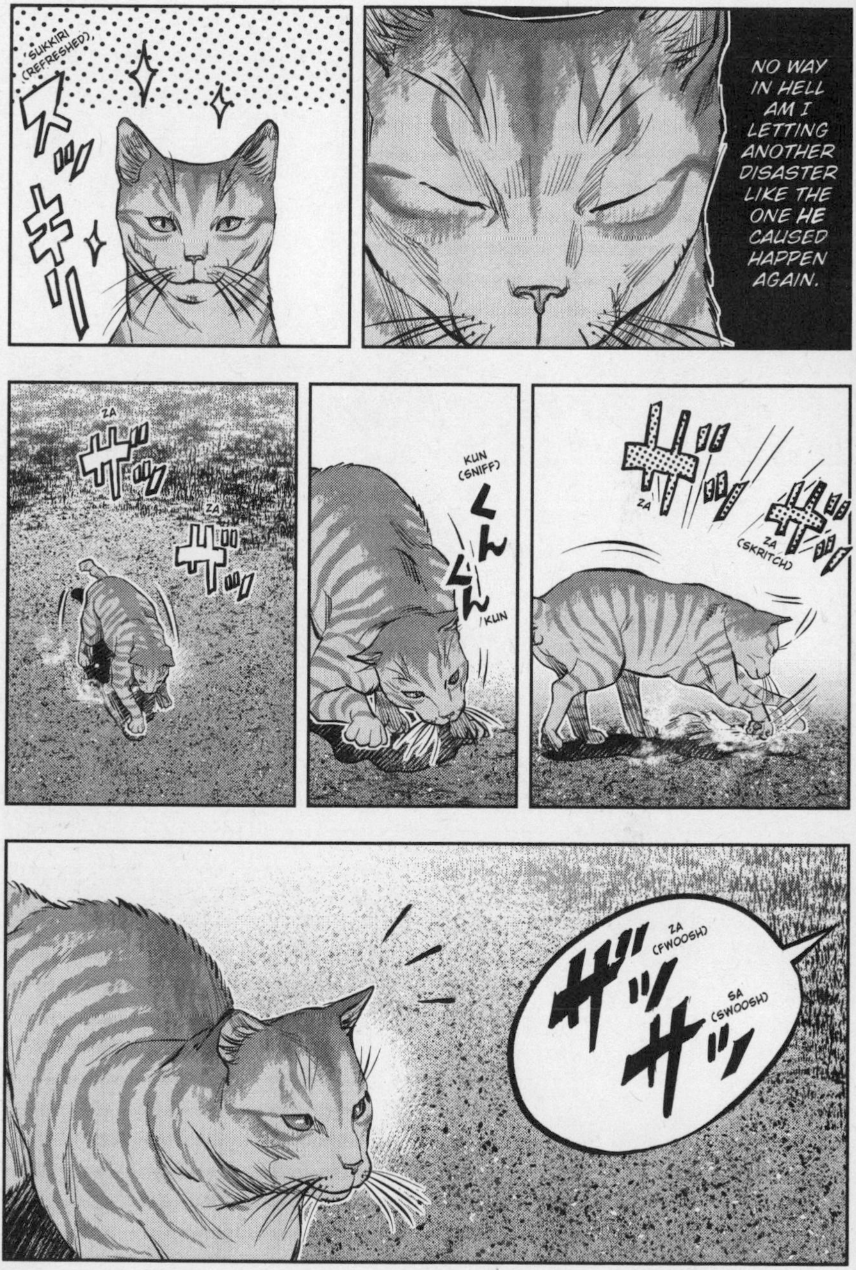
NO WAY IN HELL AM I LETTING ANOTHER DISASTER LIKE THE ONE HE CAUSED HAPPEN AGAIN.
SUKKIRI (REFRESHED)
ZA
ZA (SKRITCH)
KUN (SNIFF)
KUN
ZA
ZA
ZA (FWOOSH)
SA (SWOOSH)

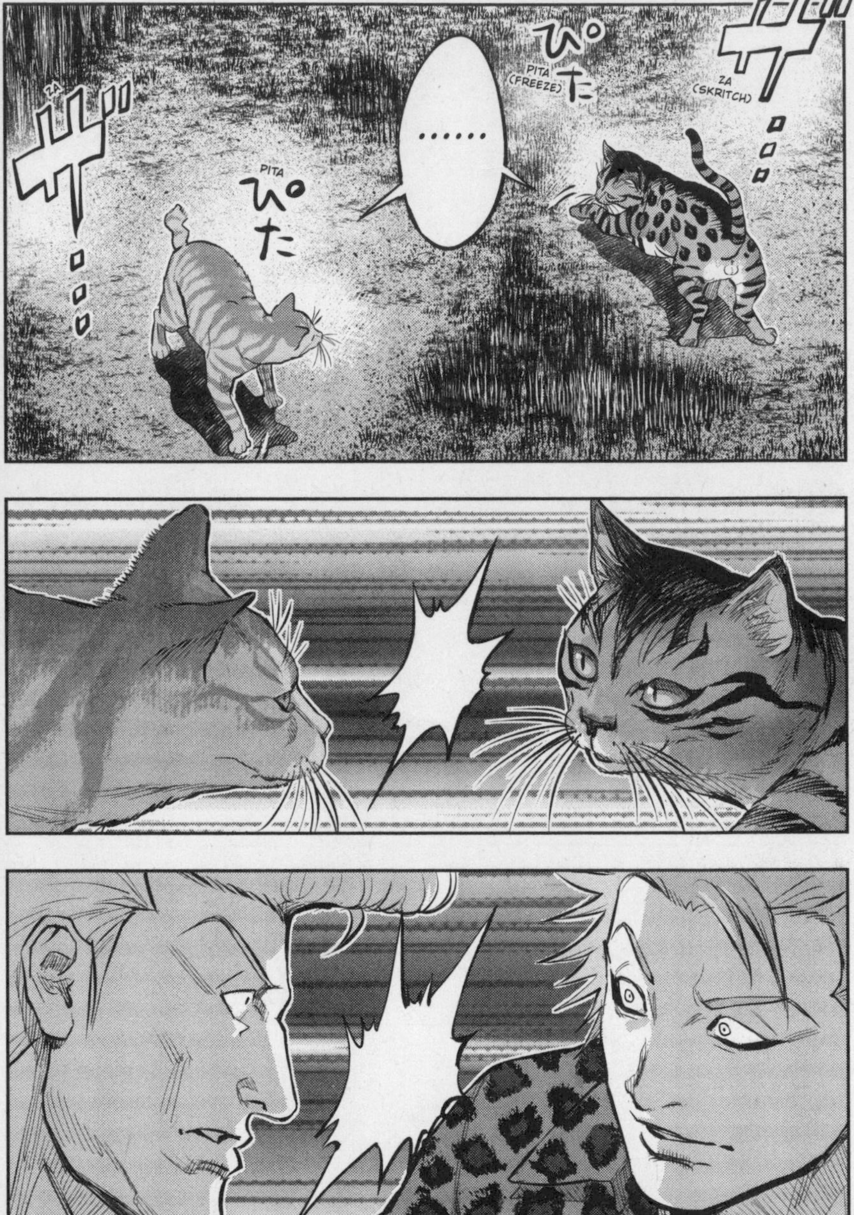
ZA (SKRITCH)
ぴた
PITA (FREEZE)
......
ぴた
PITA
ZA

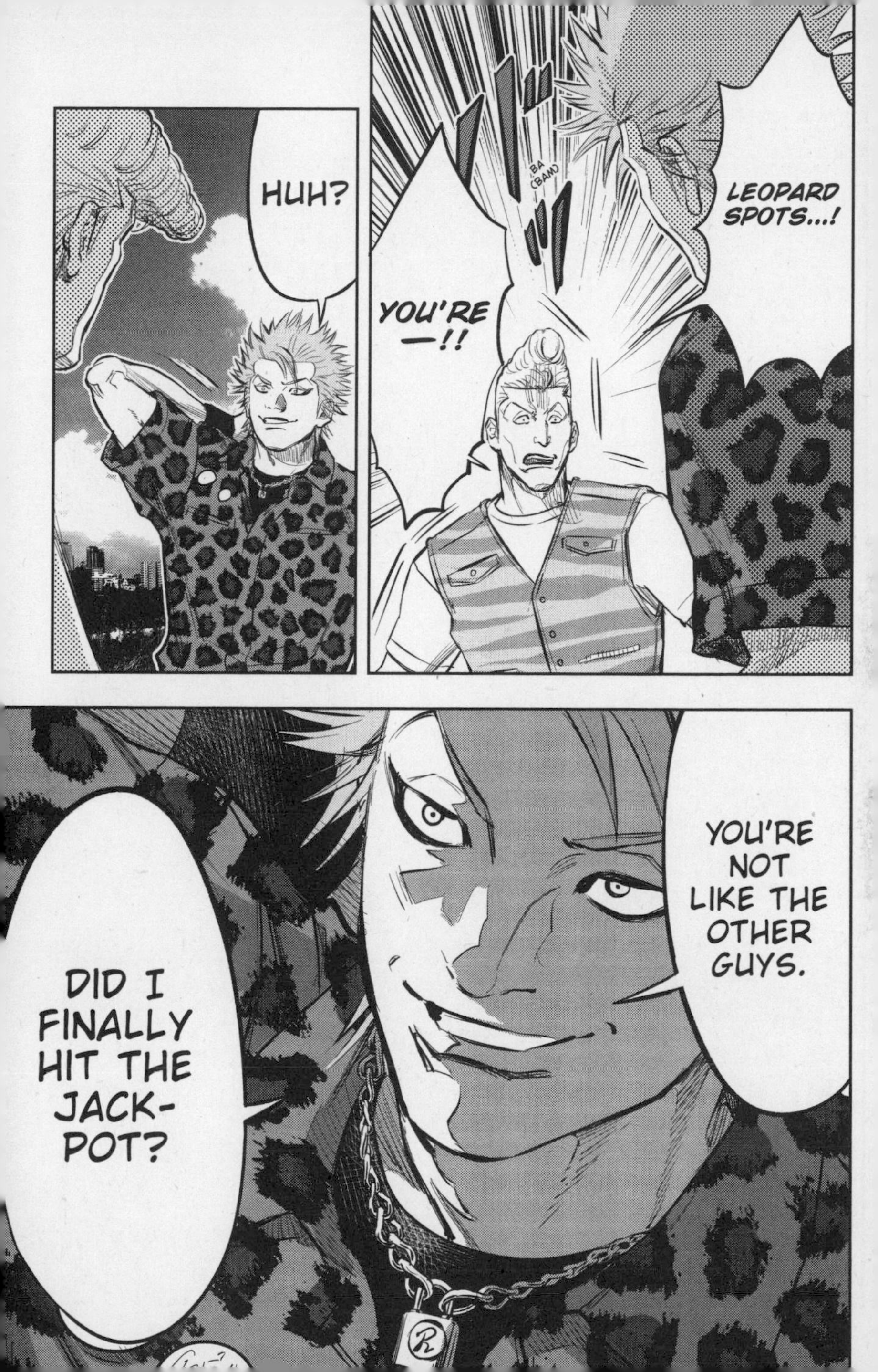
LEOPARD SPOTS...!
BA (BAM)
YOU'RE —!!
HUH?
YOU'RE NOT LIKE THE OTHER GUYS.
DID I FINALLY HIT THE JACK-POT?

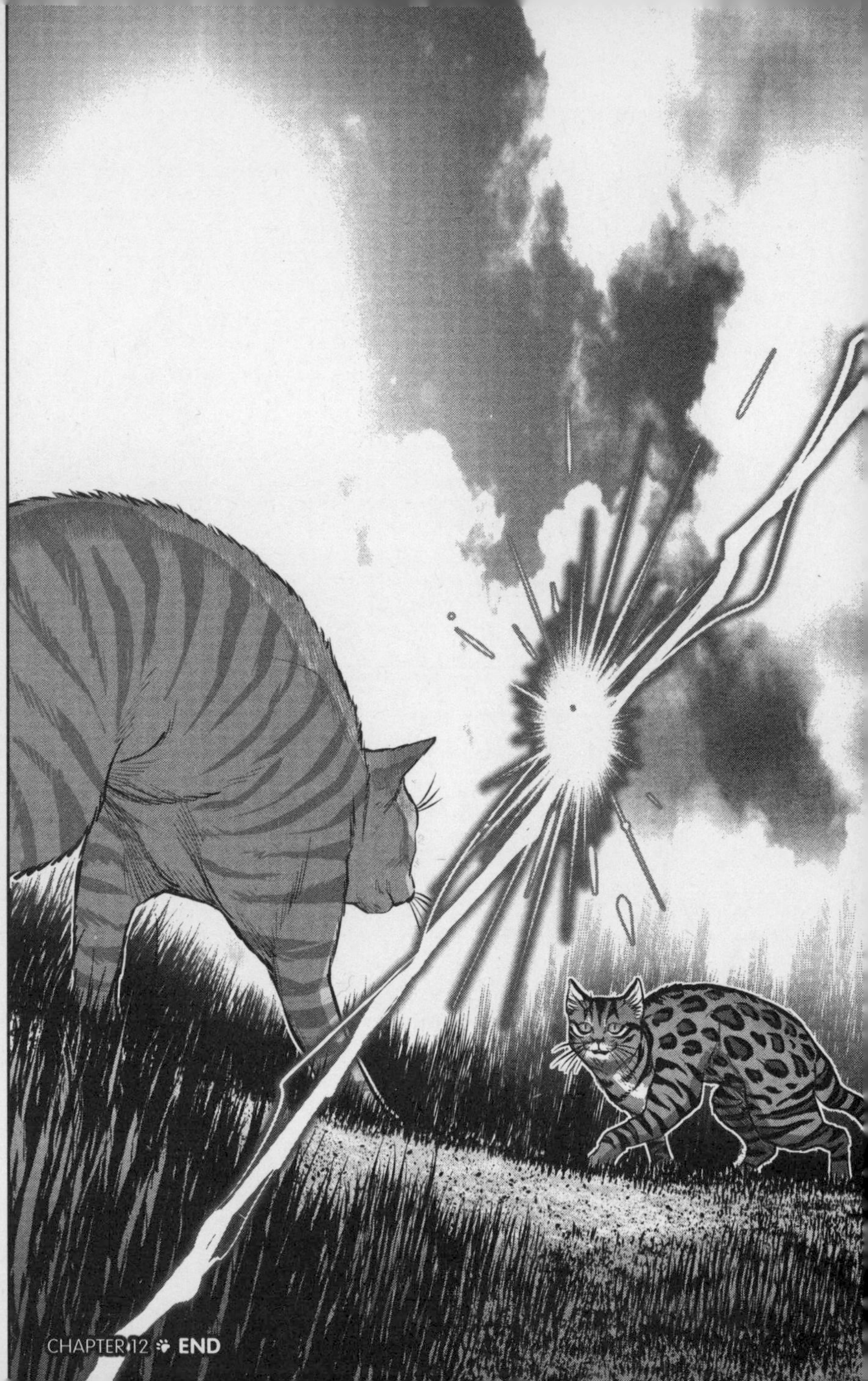
CHAPTER 12 END

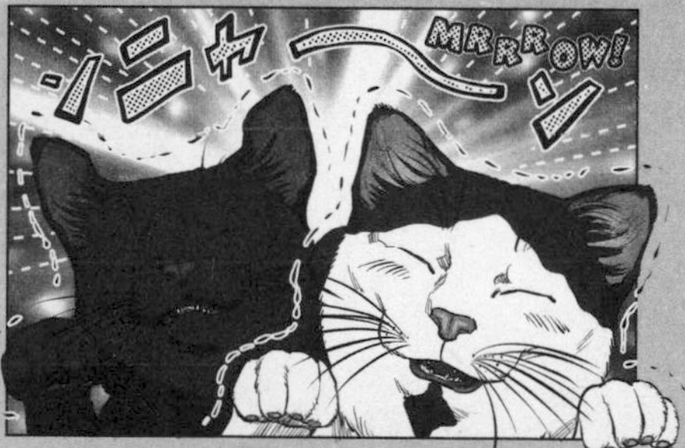
MRRROW!

NYANKEES

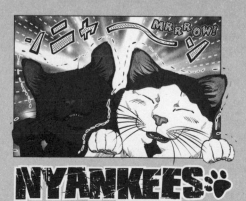

NYANKEES:🐾

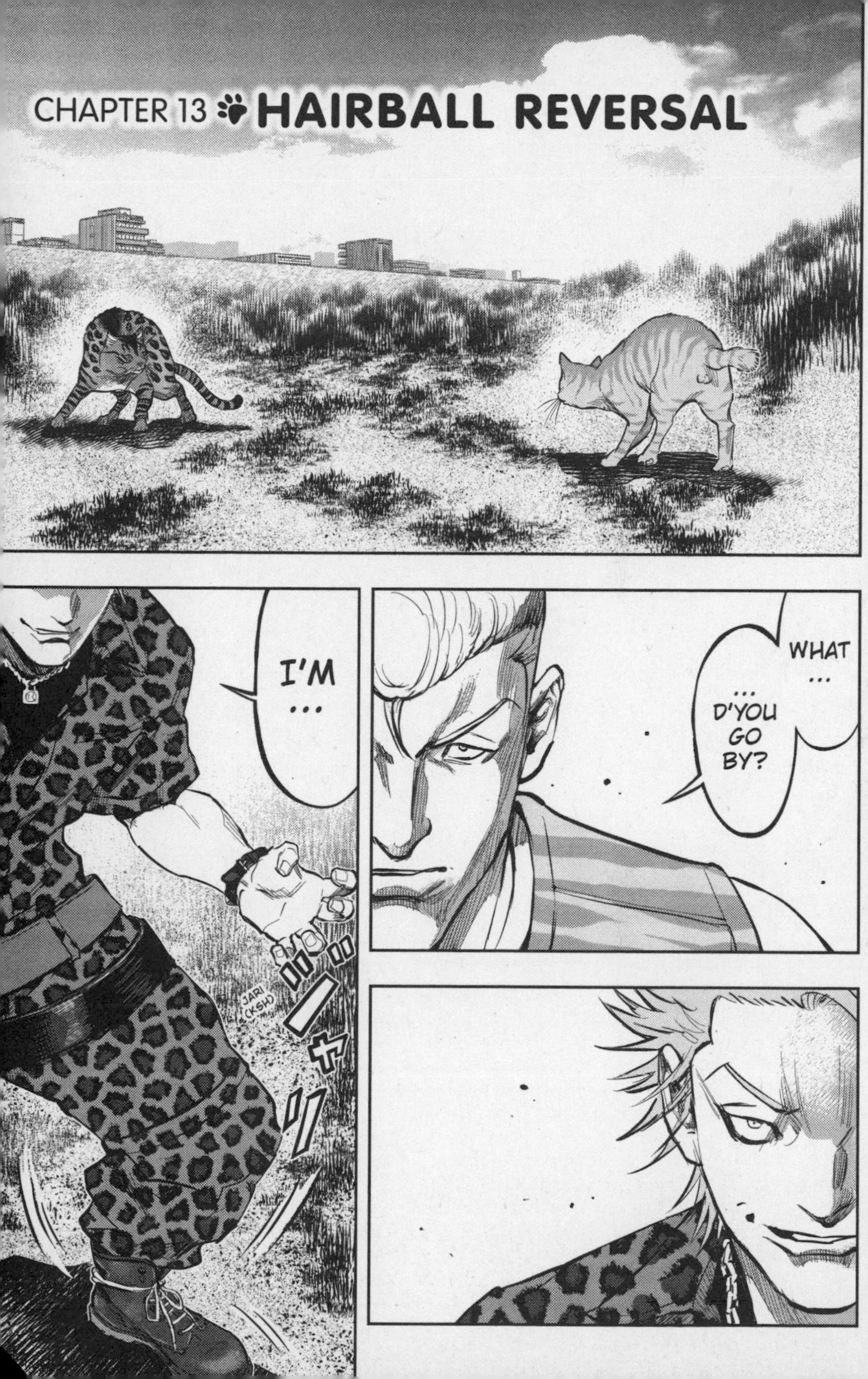
CHAPTER 13 HAIRBALL REVERSAL
WHAT ... ... D'YOU GO BY?
I'M ...
JARI (KSH)

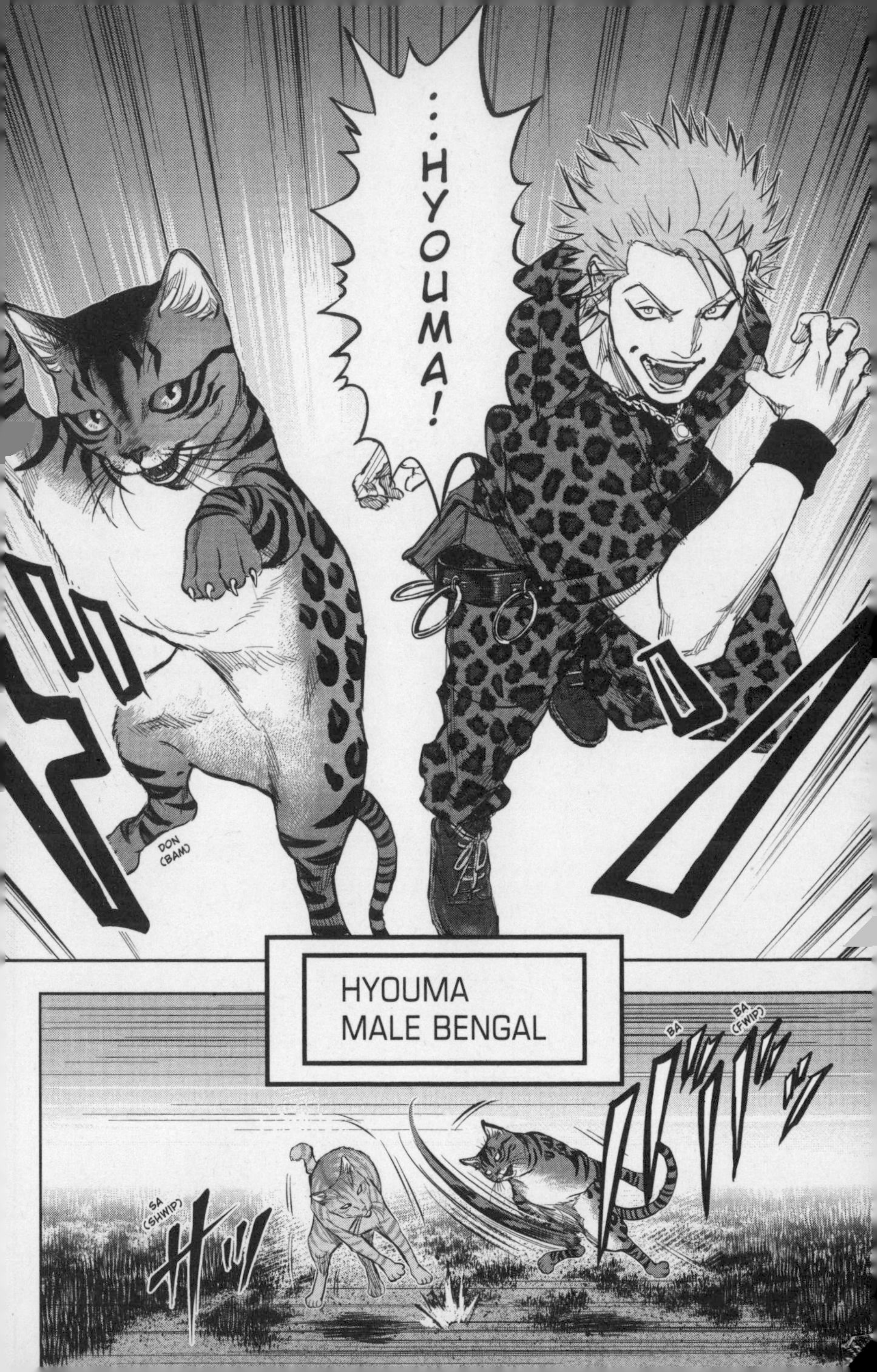
...HYOUMA!
DON (BAM)
HYOUMA
MALE BENGAL
BA (FWIP)
BA
SA (SHWIP)

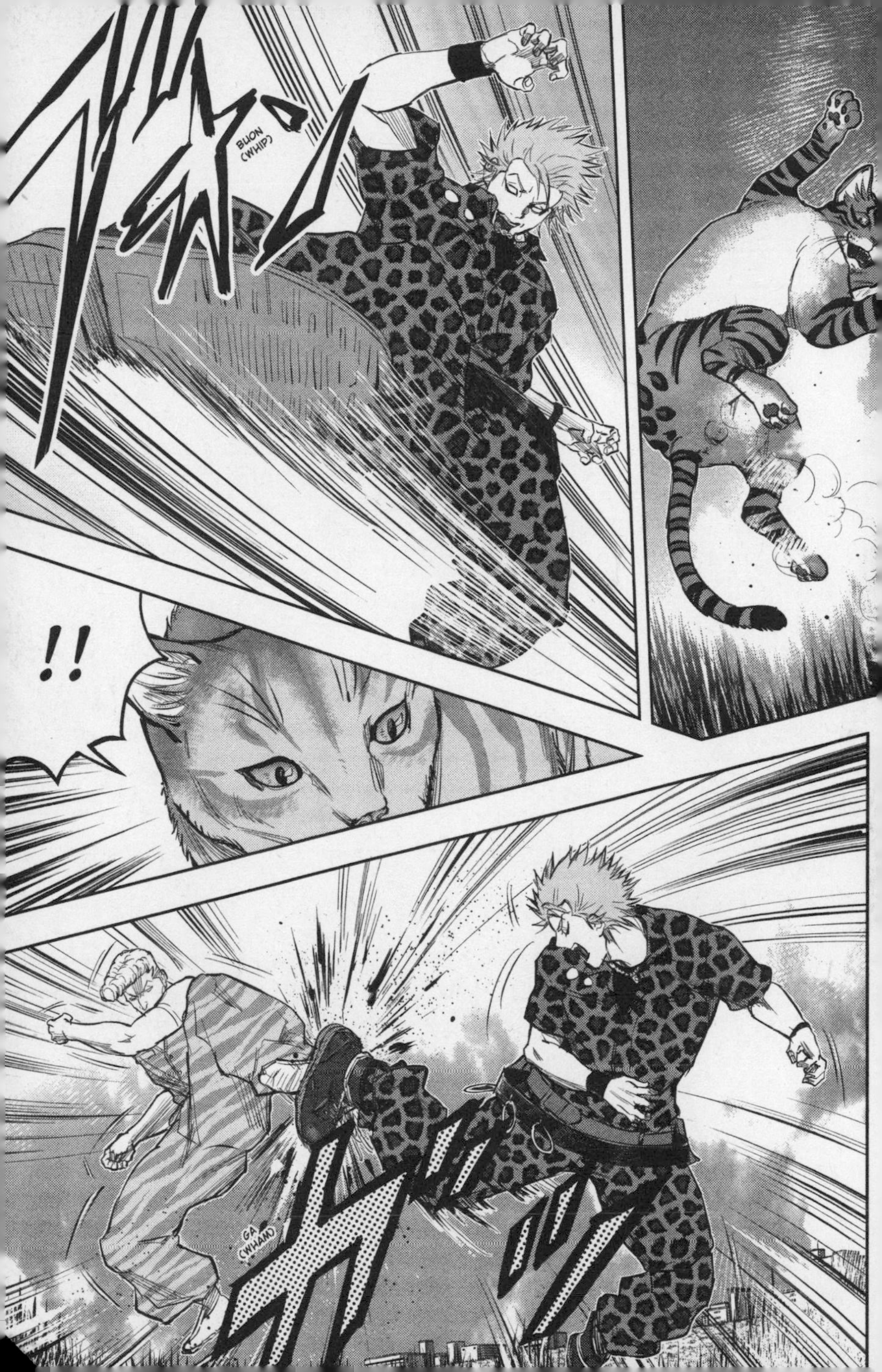
BUON (WHIP)
!!
GA (WHAM)

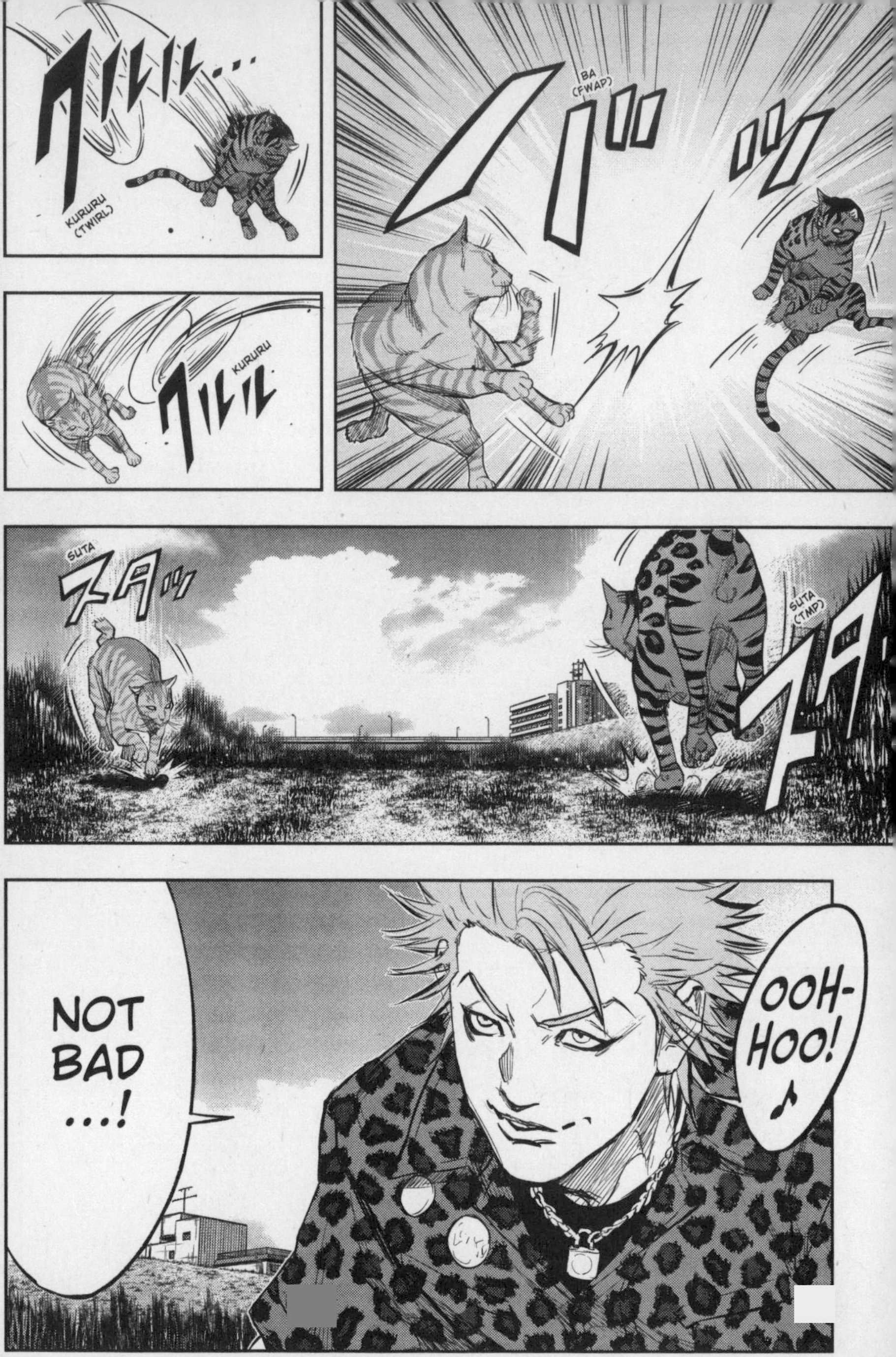
BA
(FWAP)
KURURU
(TWIRL)
KURURU
SUTA
(TMP)
SUTA
OOH-HOO! ♪
NOT BAD ...!

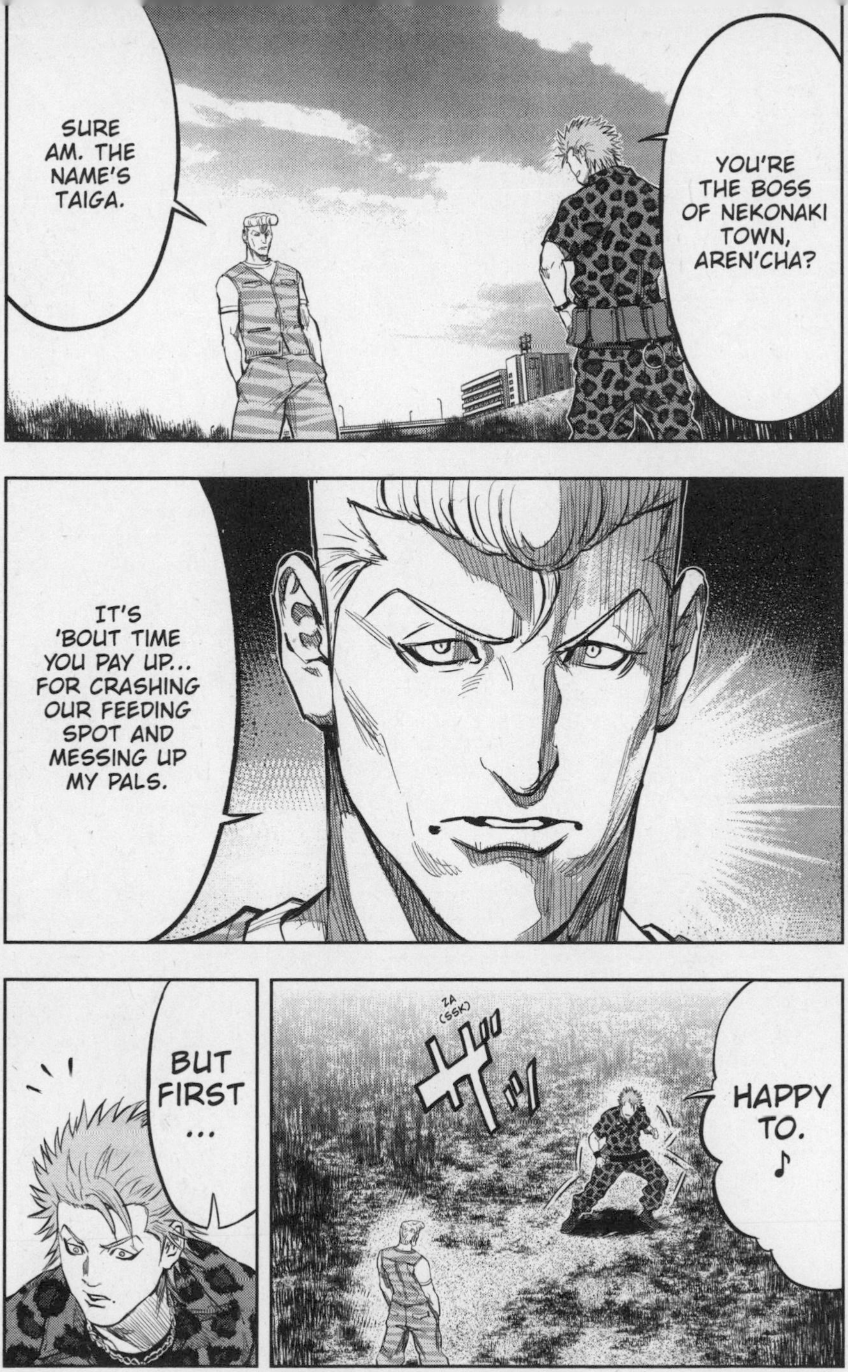
YOU'RE THE BOSS OF NEKONAKI TOWN, AREN'CHA?
SURE AM. THE NAME'S TAIGA.
IT'S 'BOUT TIME YOU PAY UP... FOR CRASHING OUR FEEDING SPOT AND MESSING UP MY PALS.
HAPPY TO. ♪
ZA (SSK)
BUT FIRST ...

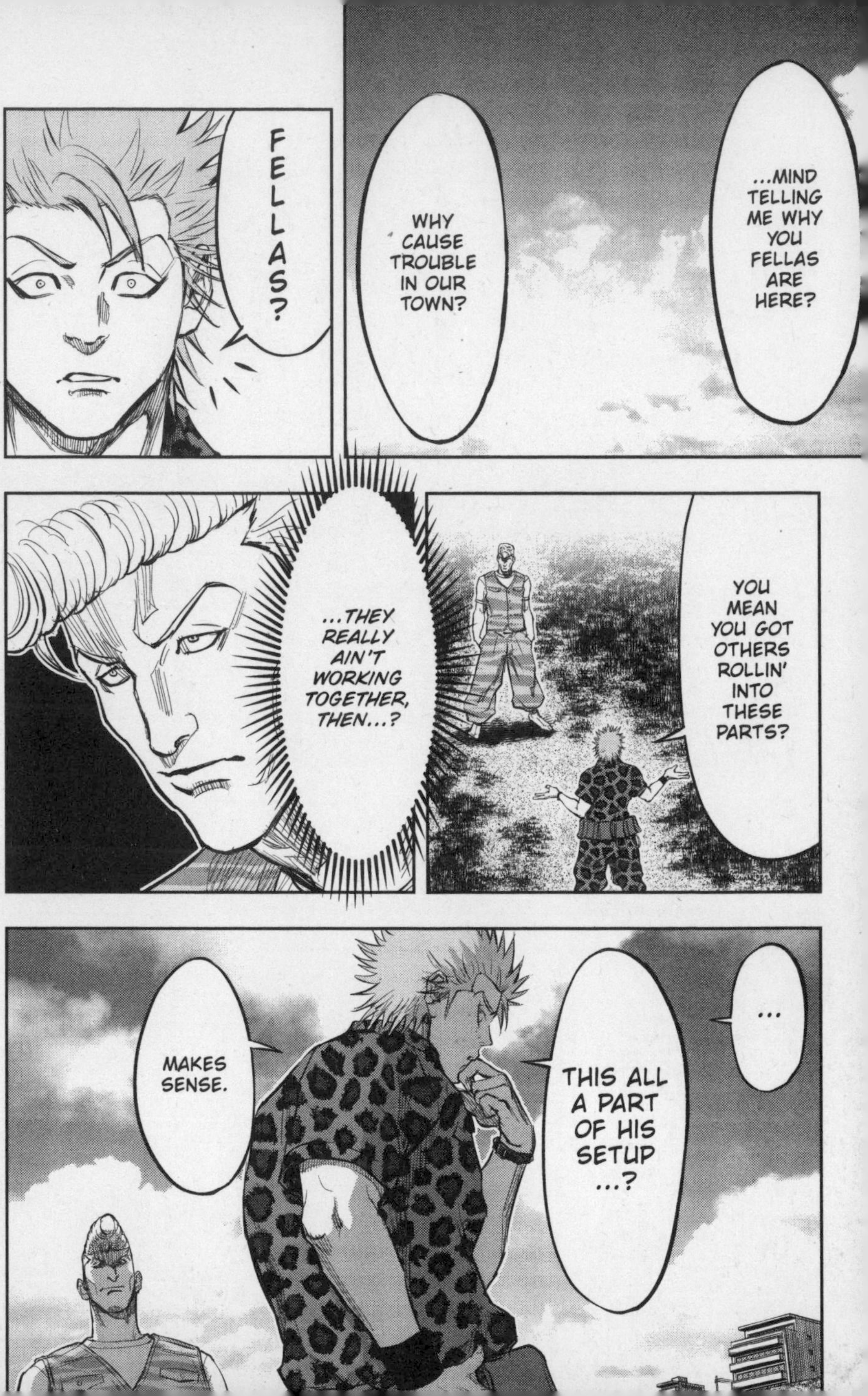
...MIND TELLING ME WHY YOU FELLAS ARE HERE?
WHY CAUSE TROUBLE IN OUR TOWN?
FELLAS?
YOU MEAN YOU GOT OTHERS ROLLIN' INTO THESE PARTS?
...THEY REALLY AIN'T WORKING TOGETHER, THEN...?
...
THIS ALL A PART OF HIS SETUP ...?
MAKES SENSE.

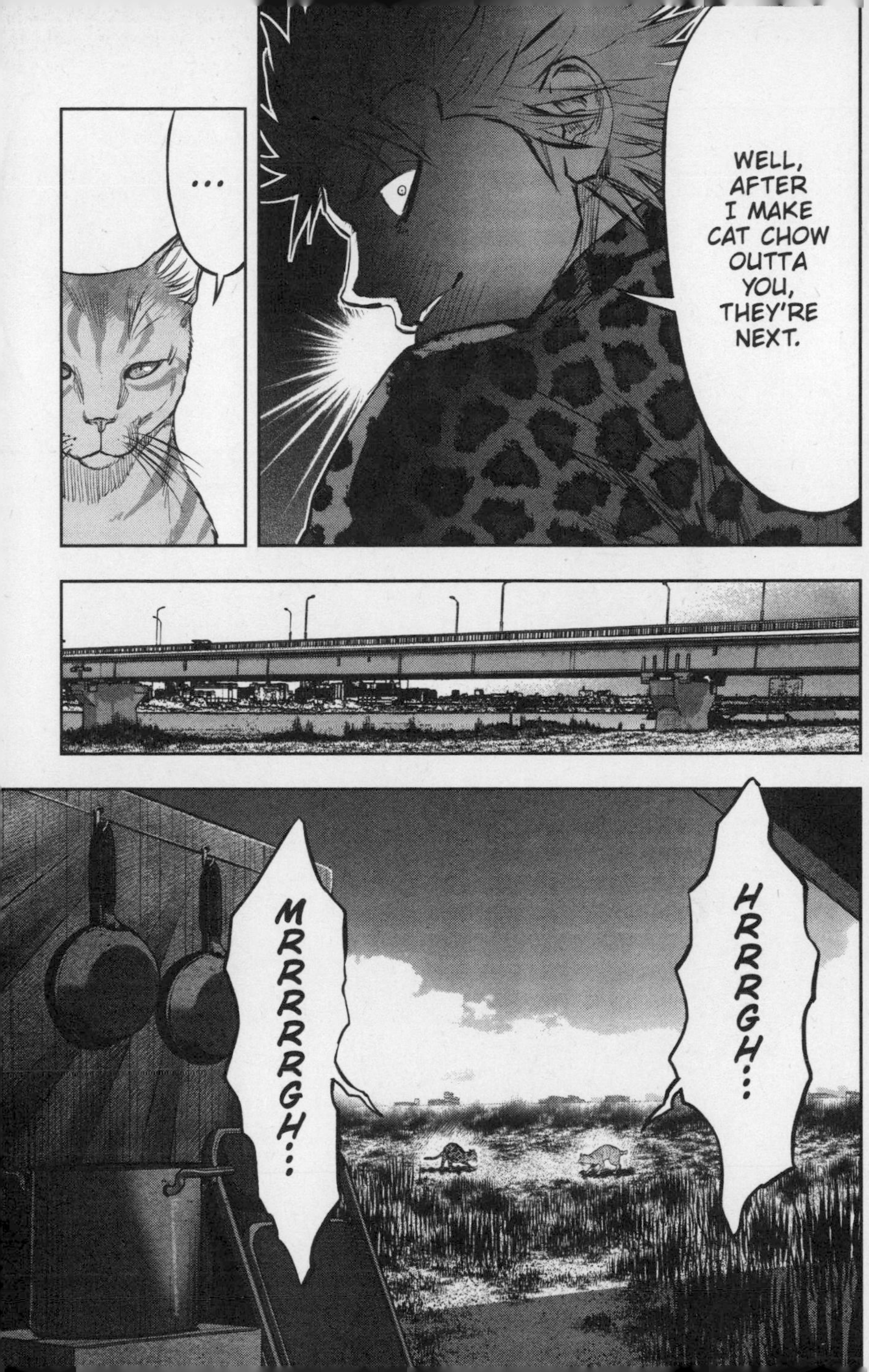
WELL, AFTER I MAKE CAT CHOW OUTTA YOU, THEY'RE NEXT.
...
HRRRGH...
MRRRRRGH...

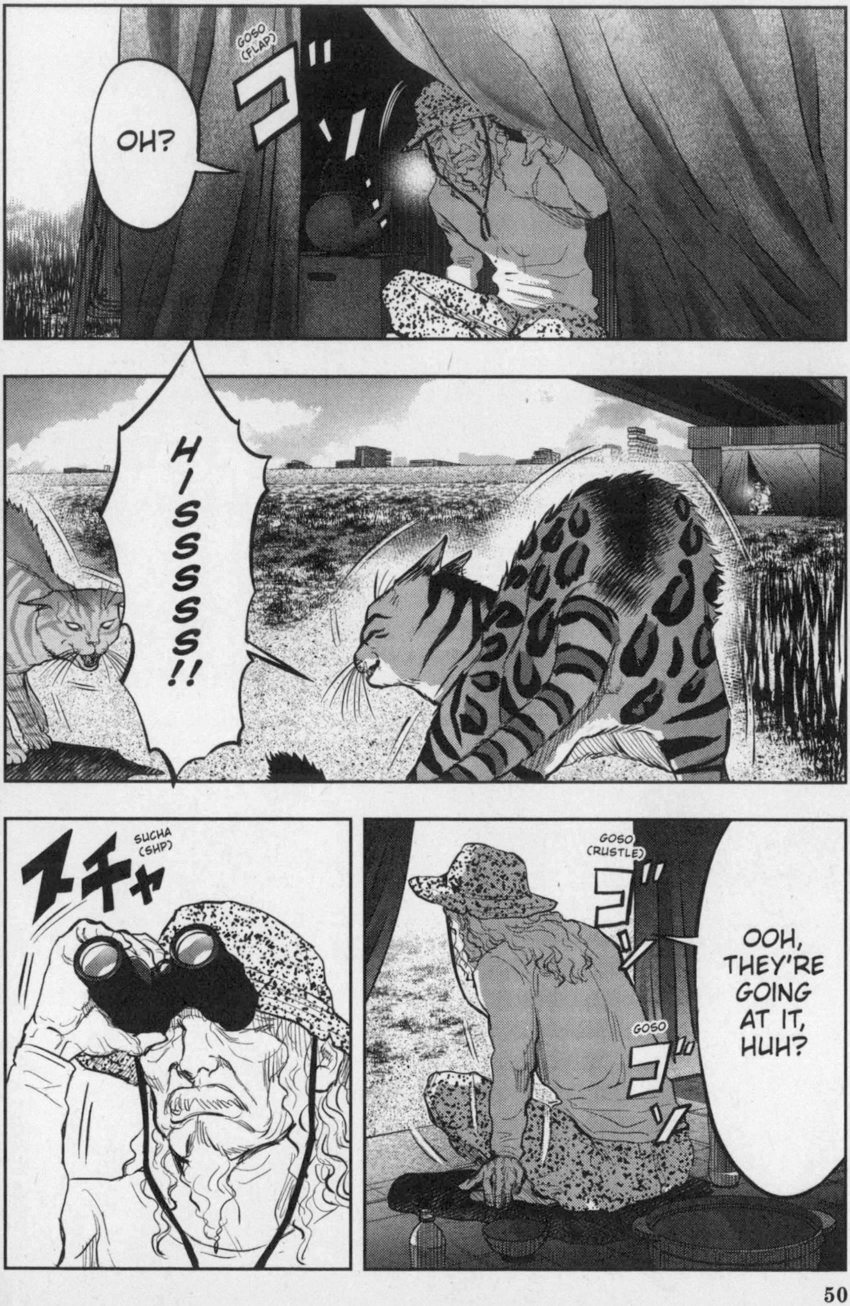
GOSO (FLAP)
OH?
HISSSSSS!!
GOSO (RUSTLE)
OOH, THEY'RE GOING AT IT, HUH?
GOSO
SUCHA (SHP)

LEOPARD SPOTS OVER THERE'S A NEWCOMER, THOUGH. RARE SORTA PATTERN ON HIM.

HMMM?

THAT ORANGE TABBY'S NEKO-NAKI'S BOSS.

OH-HO.

BUN (WAG)

BUN

MRROOOW! MROW! MROW!!

BA (FWIP)

BA

BA

BA

BA

OLD GEN
OBSERVER OF CAT FIGHTS AT THE RIVER BANK FOR HALF A CENTURY

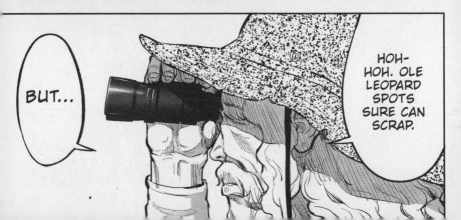

BUT...

HOH-HOH. OLE LEOPARD SPOTS SURE CAN SCRAP.

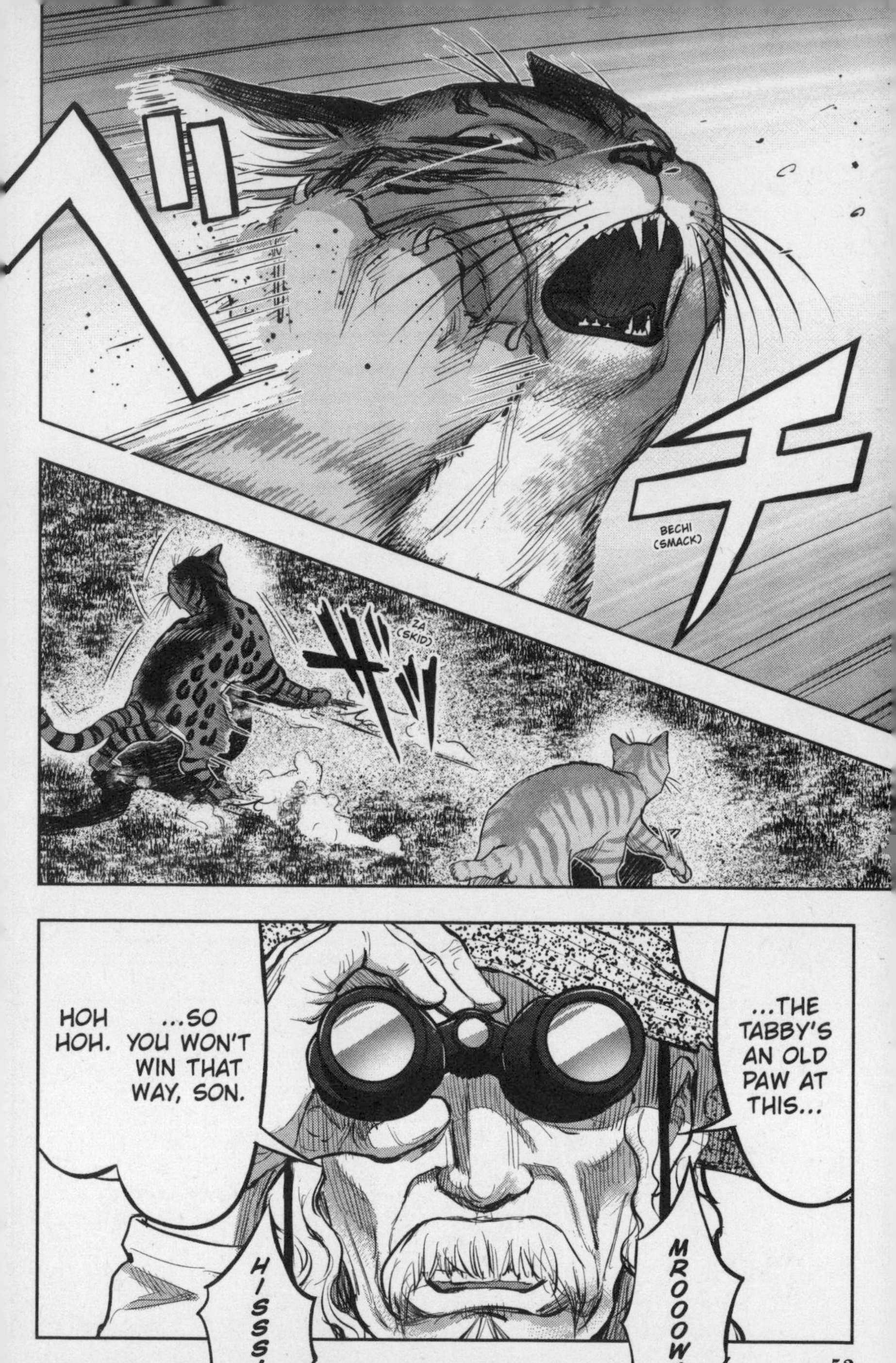
BECHI (SMACK)
ZA (SKID)
...THE TABBY'S AN OLD PAW AT THIS...
...SO YOU WON'T WIN THAT WAY, SON.
HOH HOH.
MROOOOW!
HISSS!

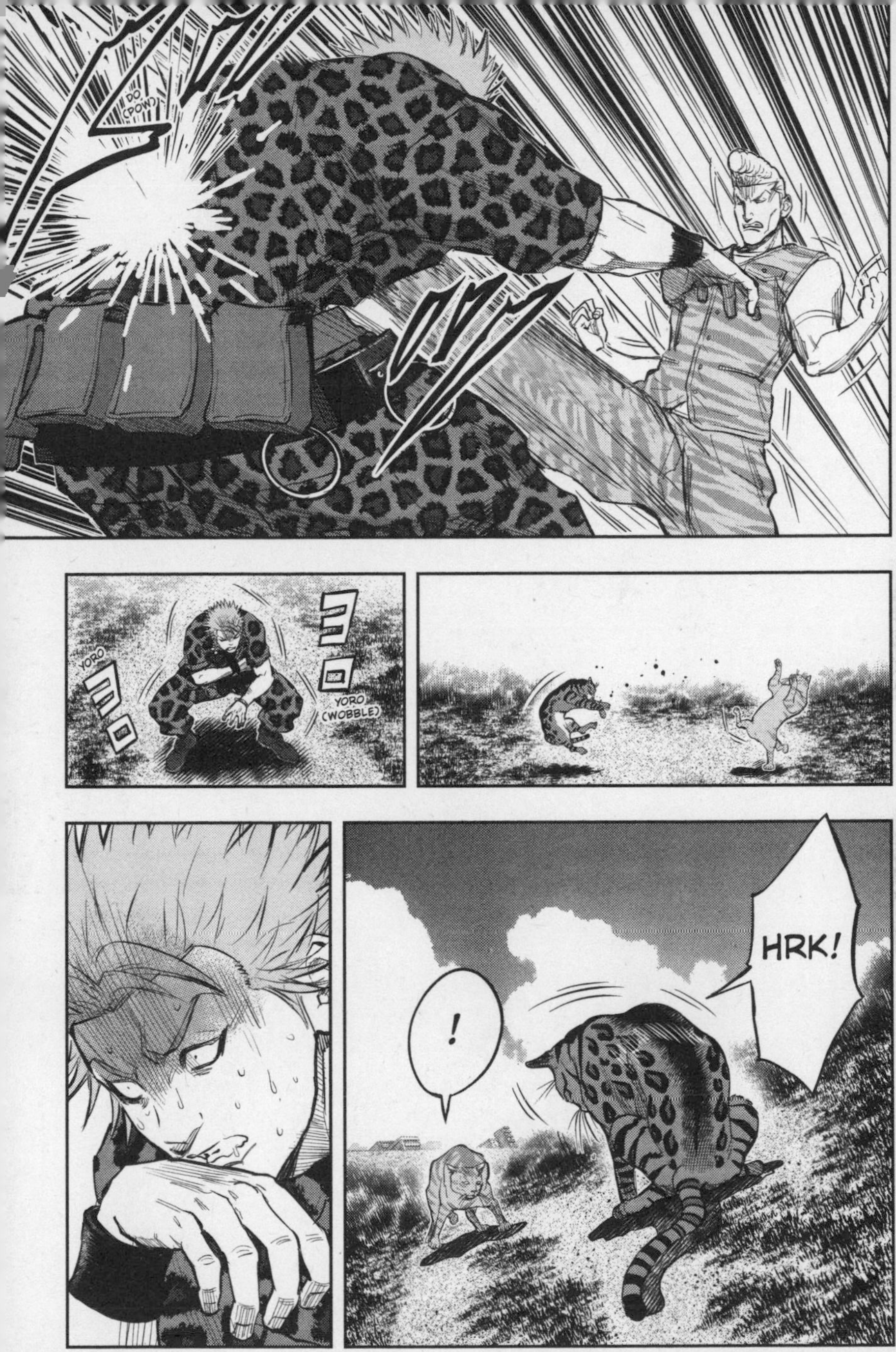
DO (POW)
YORO
YORO (WOBBLE)
HRK!
!

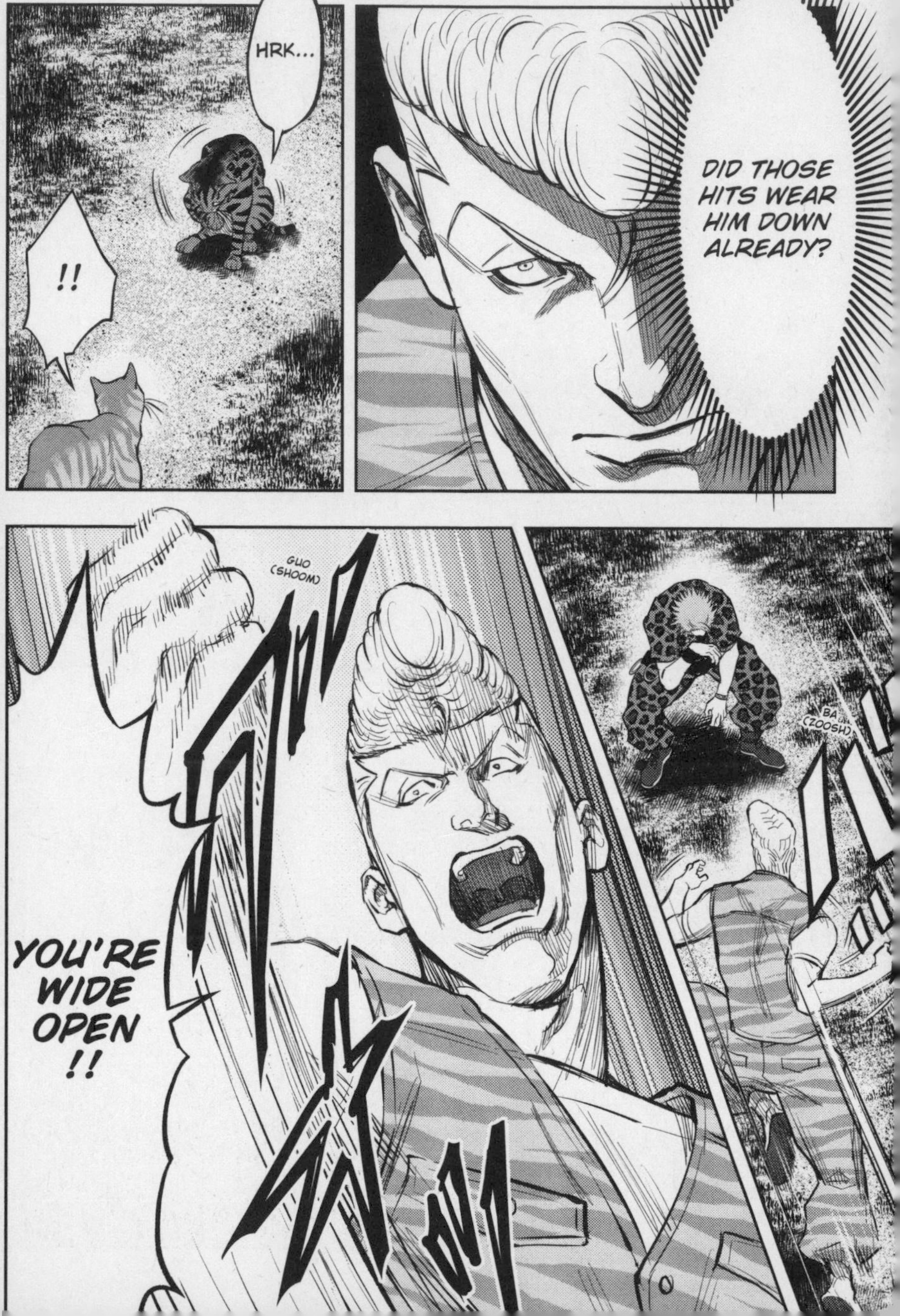
DID THOSE HITS WEAR HIM DOWN ALREADY?
HRK...
!!
BA (ZOOSH)
GUO (SHOOM)
YOU'RE WIDE OPEN !!

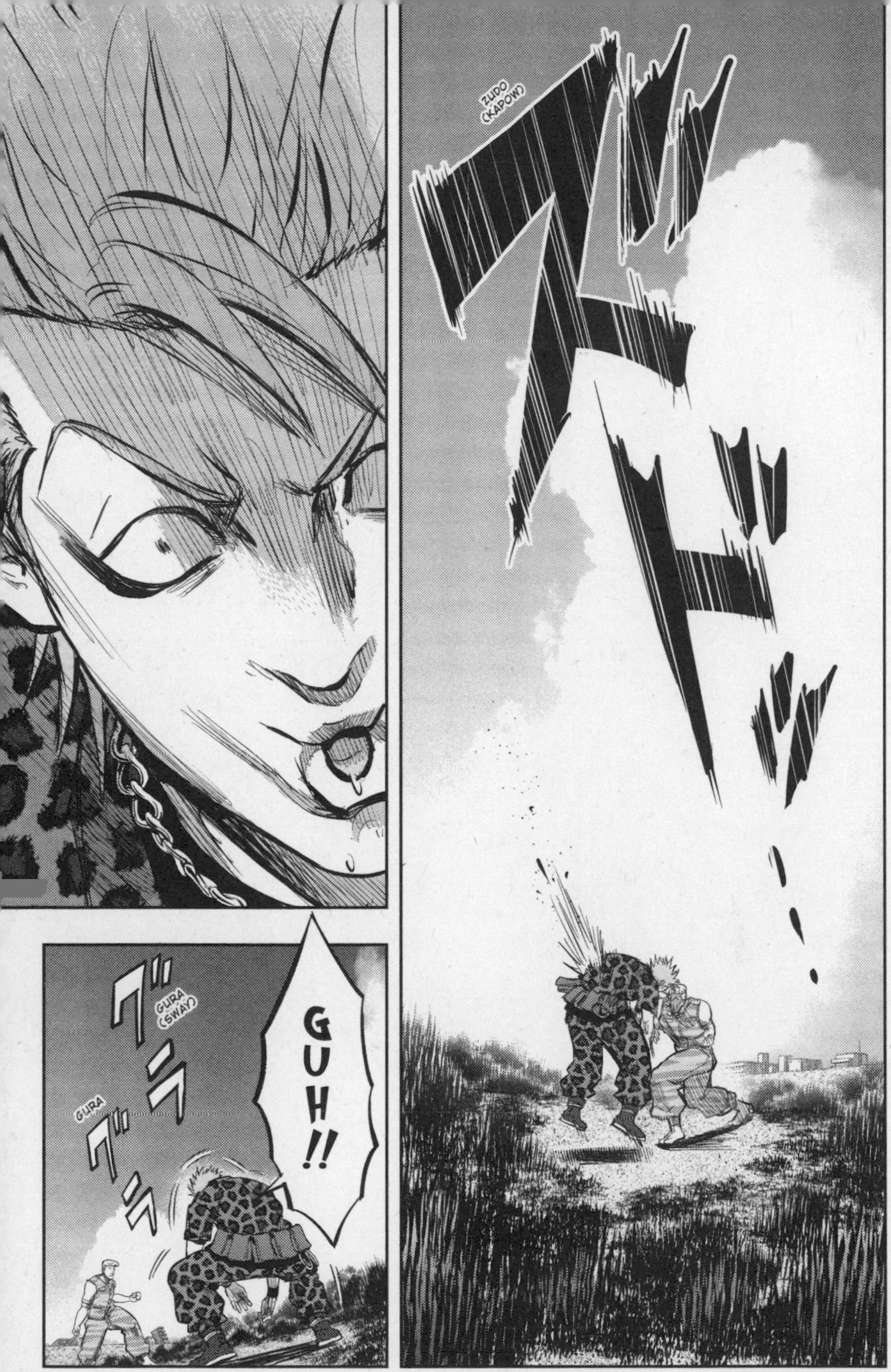
ZUDO (KAPOW)
GUH!!
GURA (SWAY)
GURA

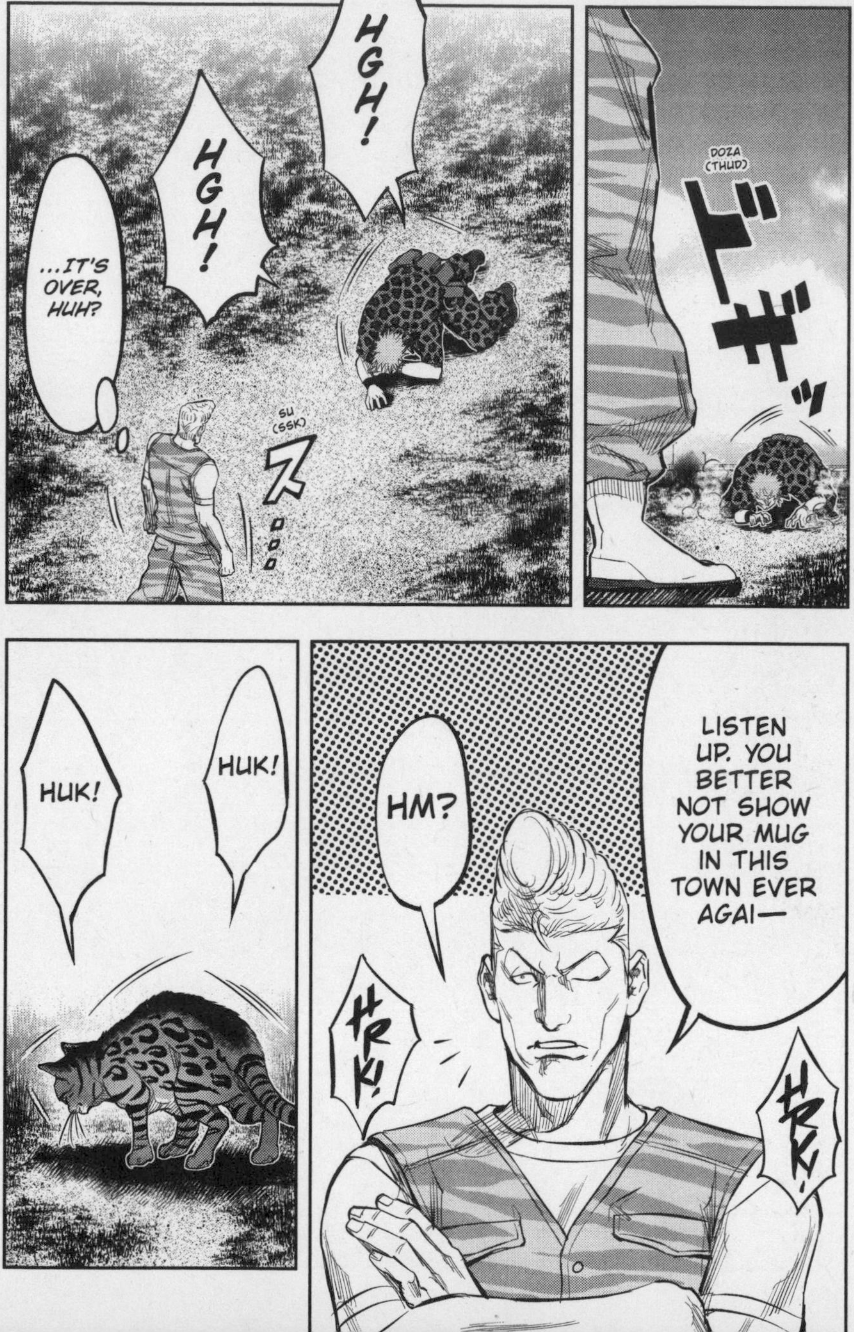

DOZA (THUD)
ドザッ
HGH!
HGH!
...IT'S OVER, HUH?
SU (SSK)
ス
LISTEN UP. YOU BETTER NOT SHOW YOUR MUG IN THIS TOWN EVER AGAI—
HM?
HRK!
HRK!
HUK!
HUK!

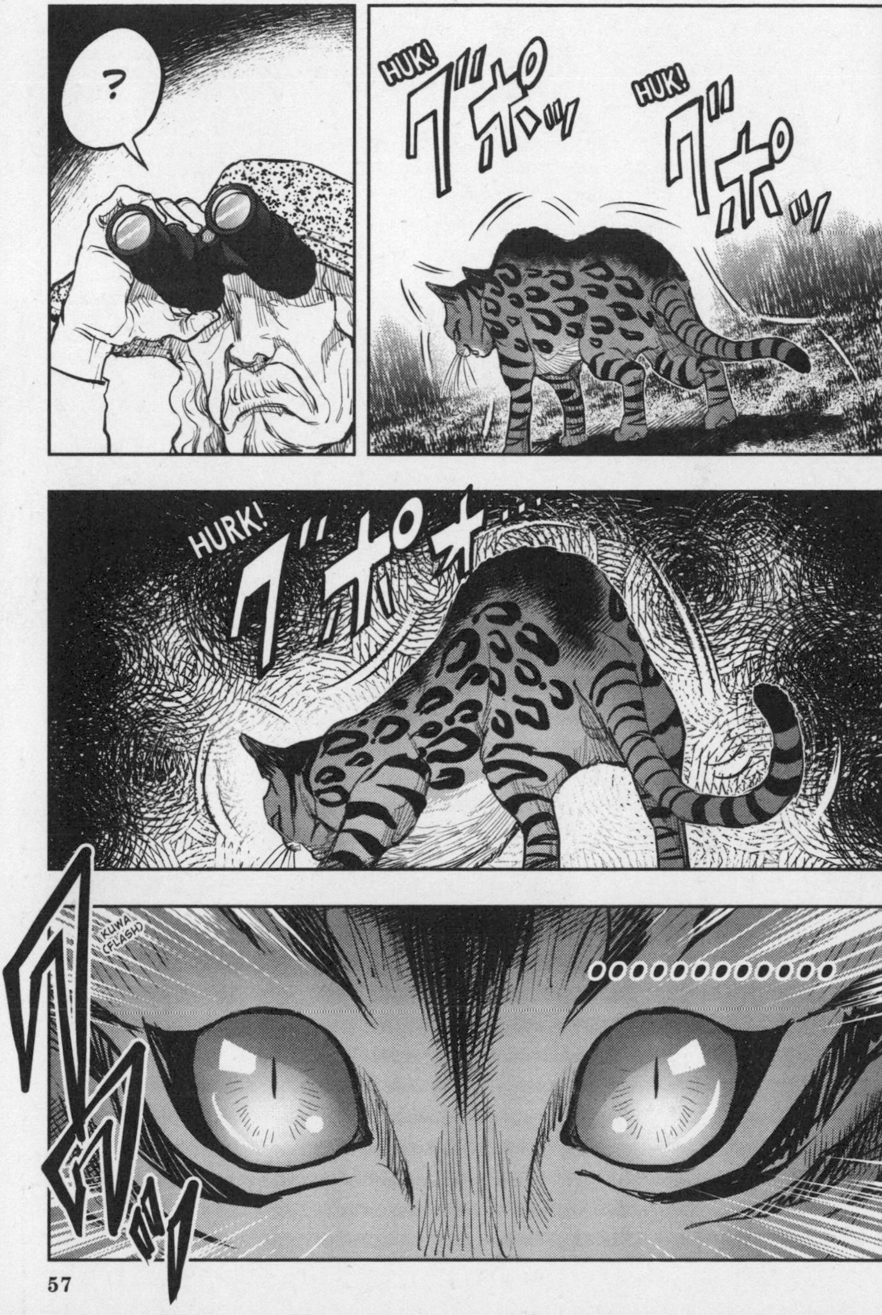
HUK!
グポッ
HUK!
グポッ
?
HURK!
グポォ…
KUWA (FLASH)
クワッ
OOOOOOOOOOOOO

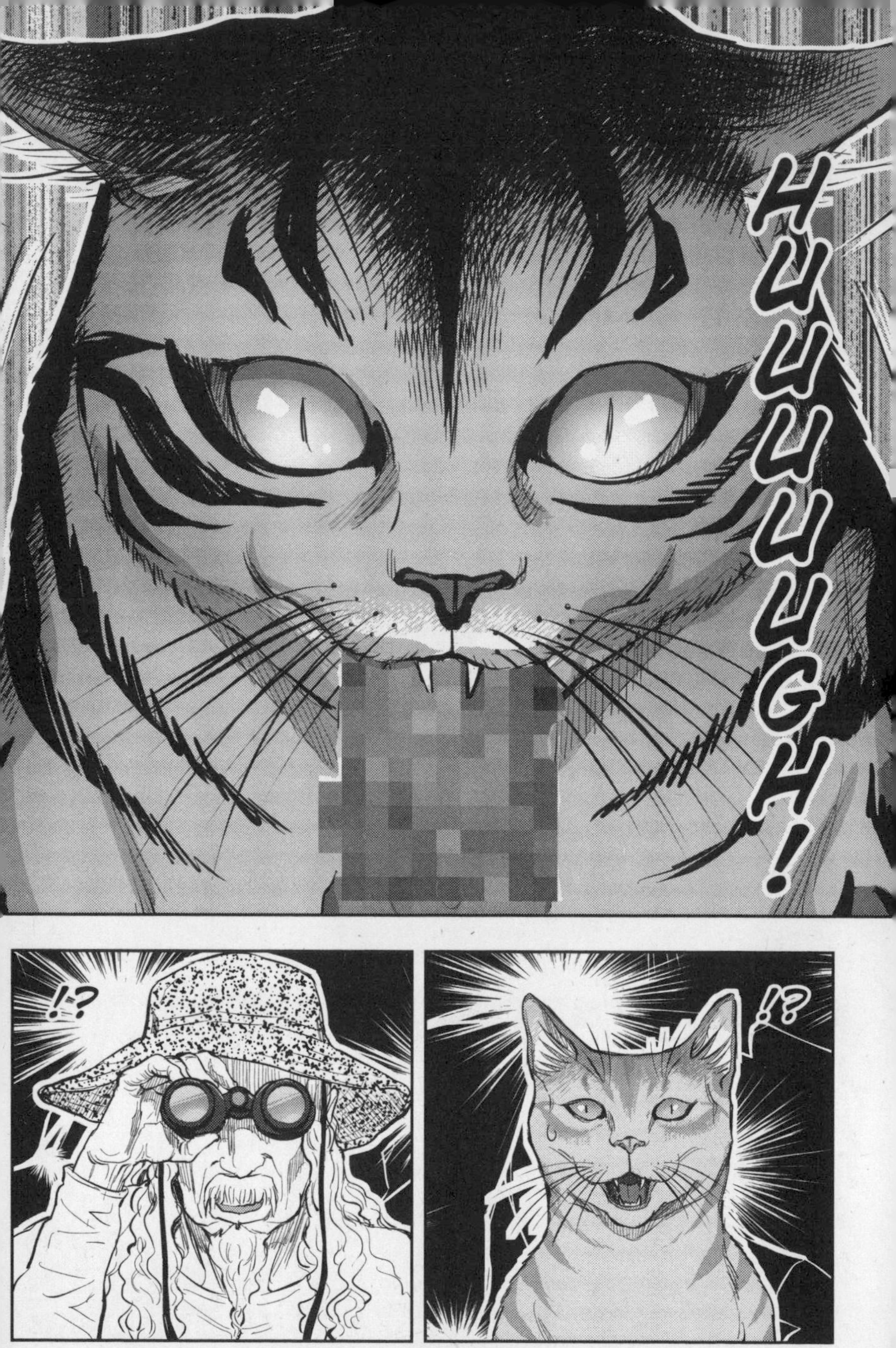
HUUUUUGH!
!?
!?

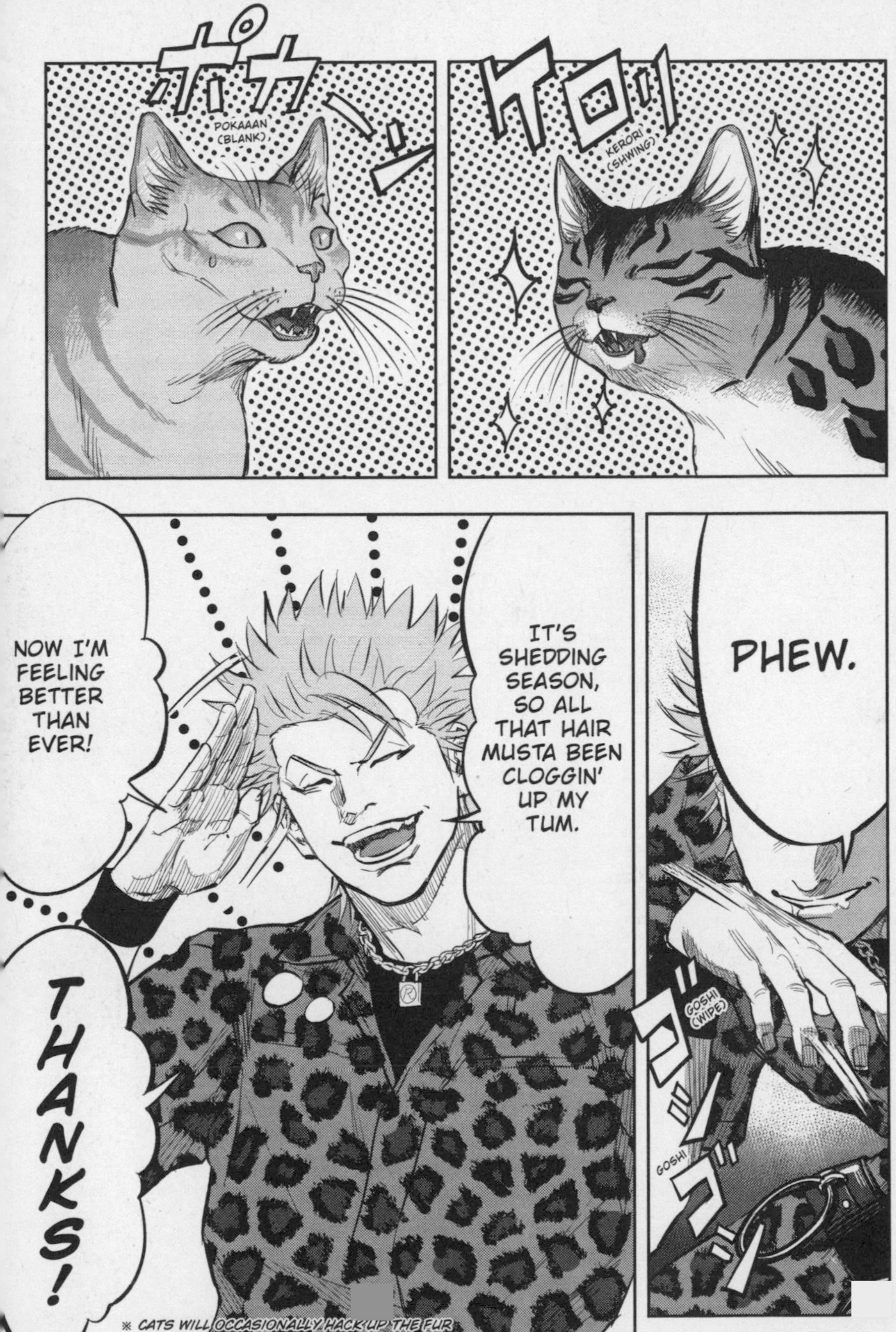
KERORI (SHWING)
POKAAAN (BLANK)
PHEW.
GOSHI (WIPE)
GOSHI
IT'S SHEDDING SEASON, SO ALL THAT HAIR MUSTA BEEN CLOGGIN' UP MY TUM.
NOW I'M FEELING BETTER THAN EVER!
THANKS!
※ CATS WILL OCCASIONALLY HACK UP THE FUR THEY SWALLOW WHILE GROOMING THEMSELVES.

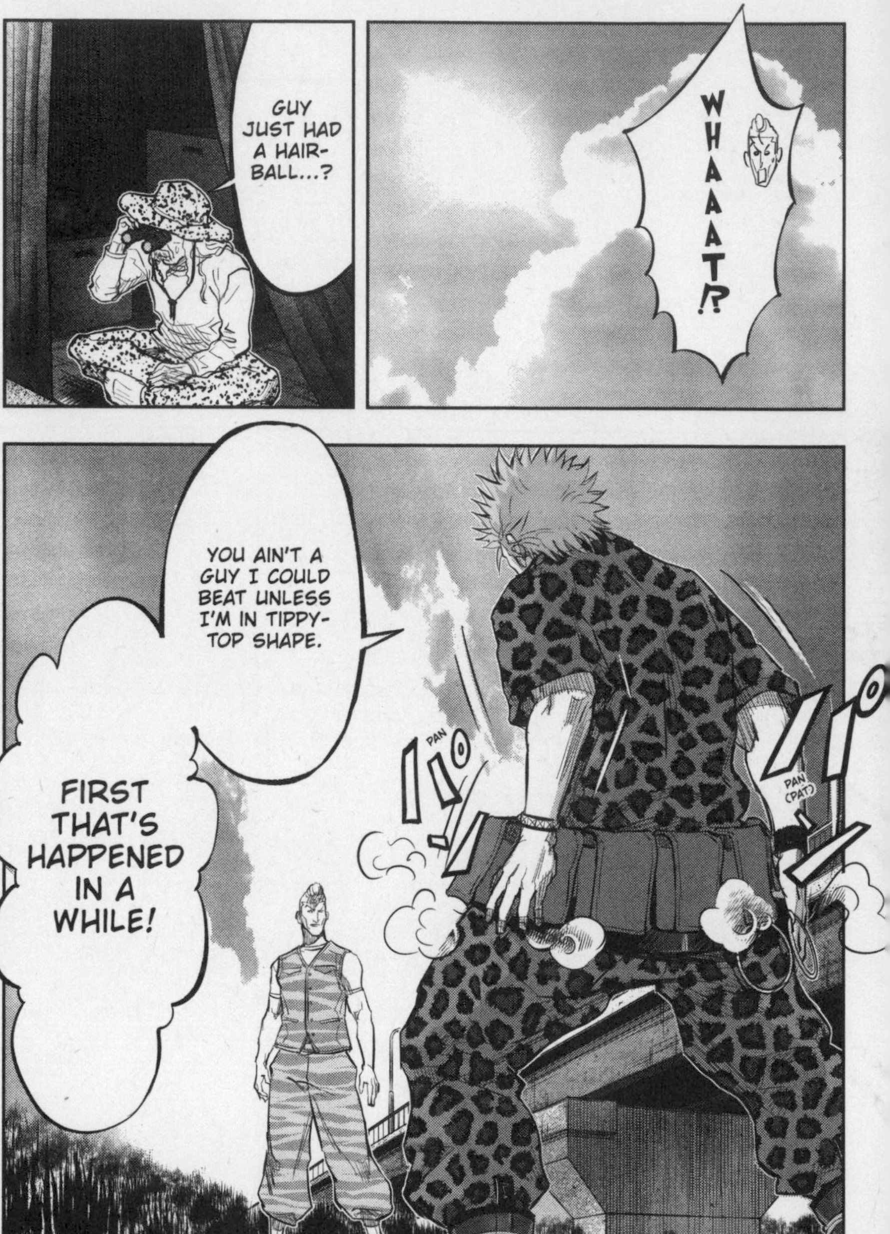
WHAAAT!?
GUY JUST HAD A HAIR-BALL...?
YOU AIN'T A GUY I COULD BEAT UNLESS I'M IN TIPPY-TOP SHAPE.
PAN (PAT)
PAN
FIRST THAT'S HAPPENED IN A WHILE!

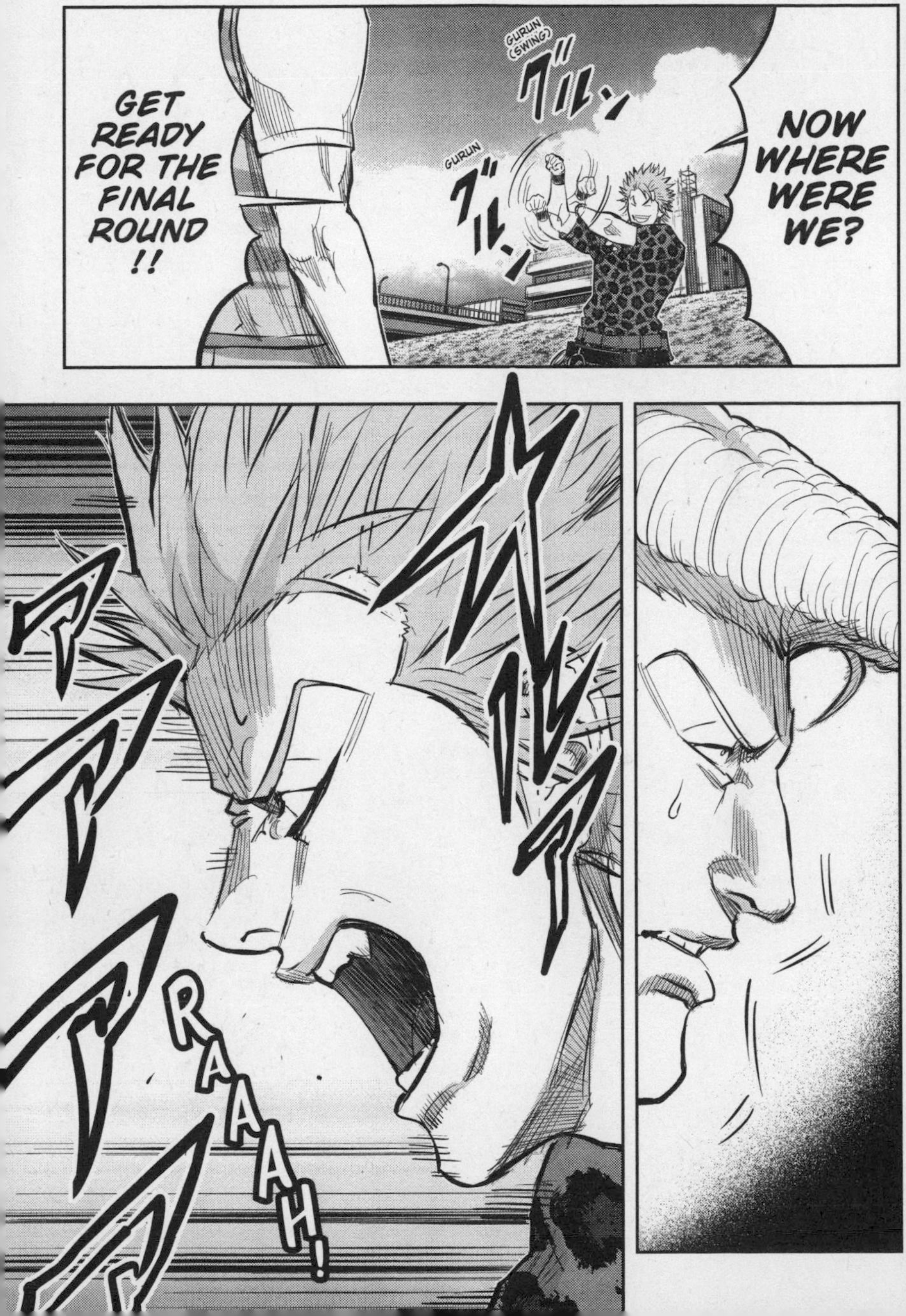
NOW WHERE WERE WE?
GURUN (SWING)
GURUN
GET READY FOR THE FINAL ROUND!!
RAAAAH!

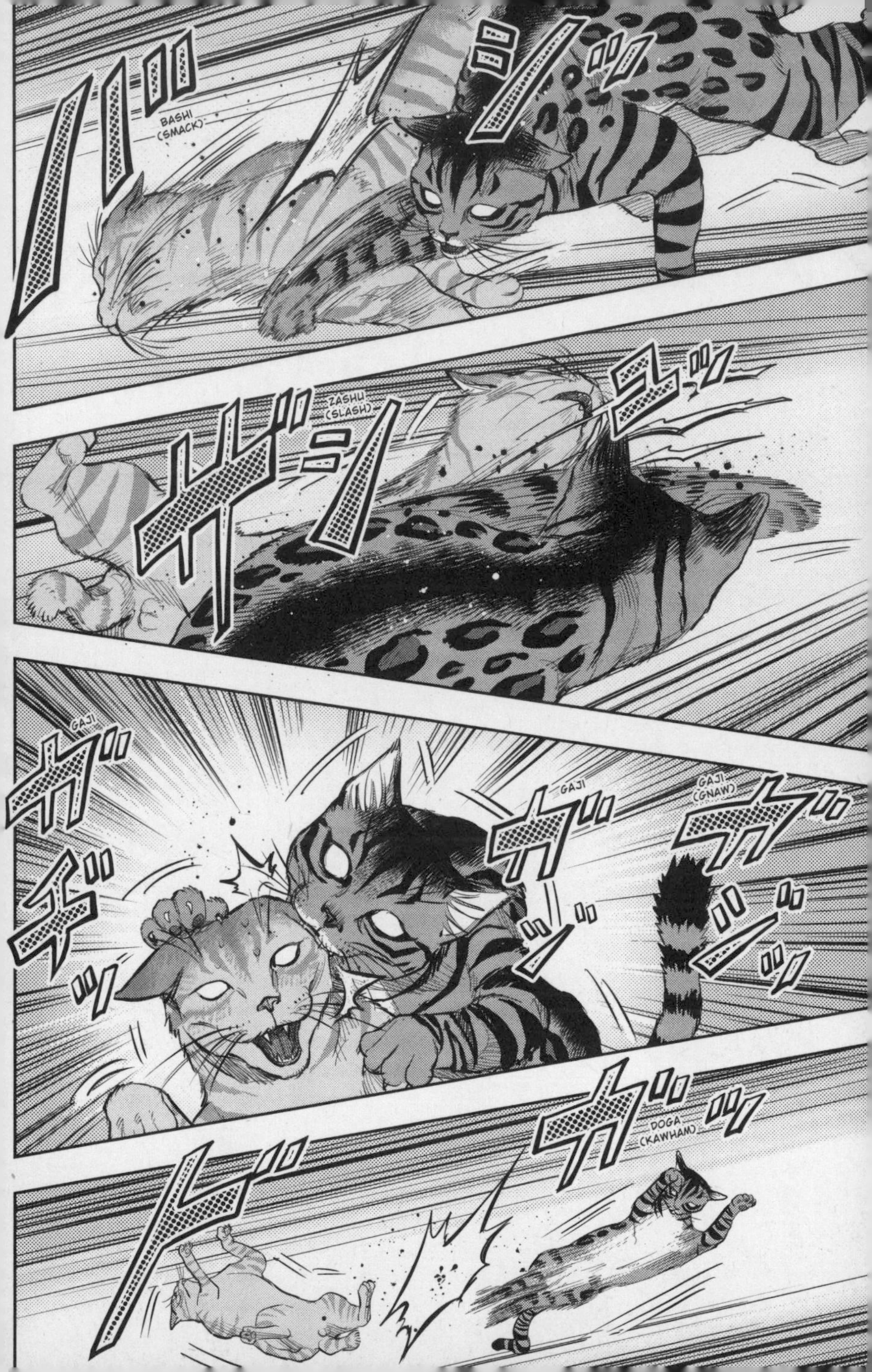
BASHI
(SMACK)
ZASHU
(SLASH)
GAJI
(GNAW)
GAJI
GAJI
DOGA
(KAWHAM)

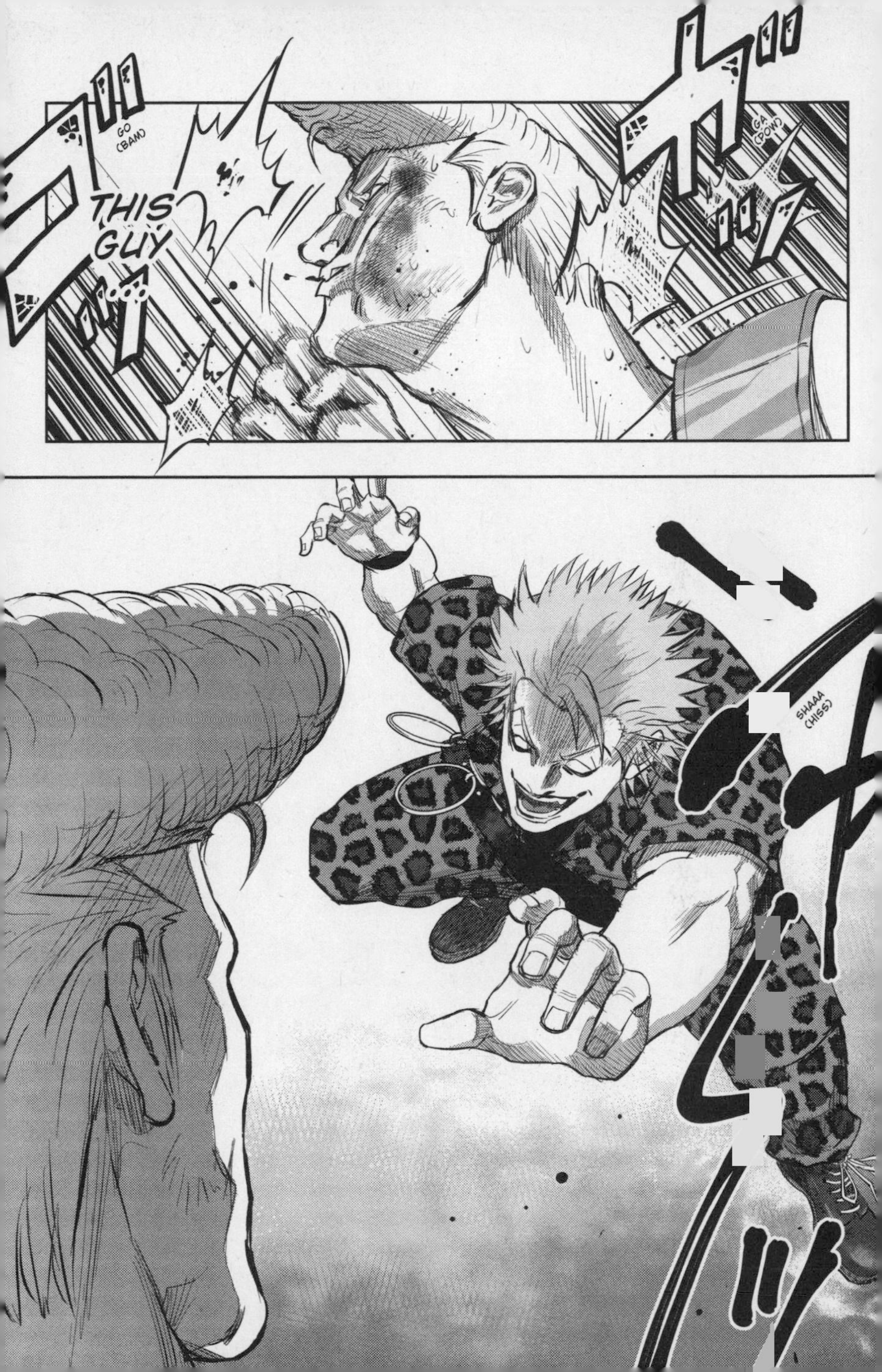
GA (POW)
GO (BAM)
THIS GUY...
SHAAA (HISS)

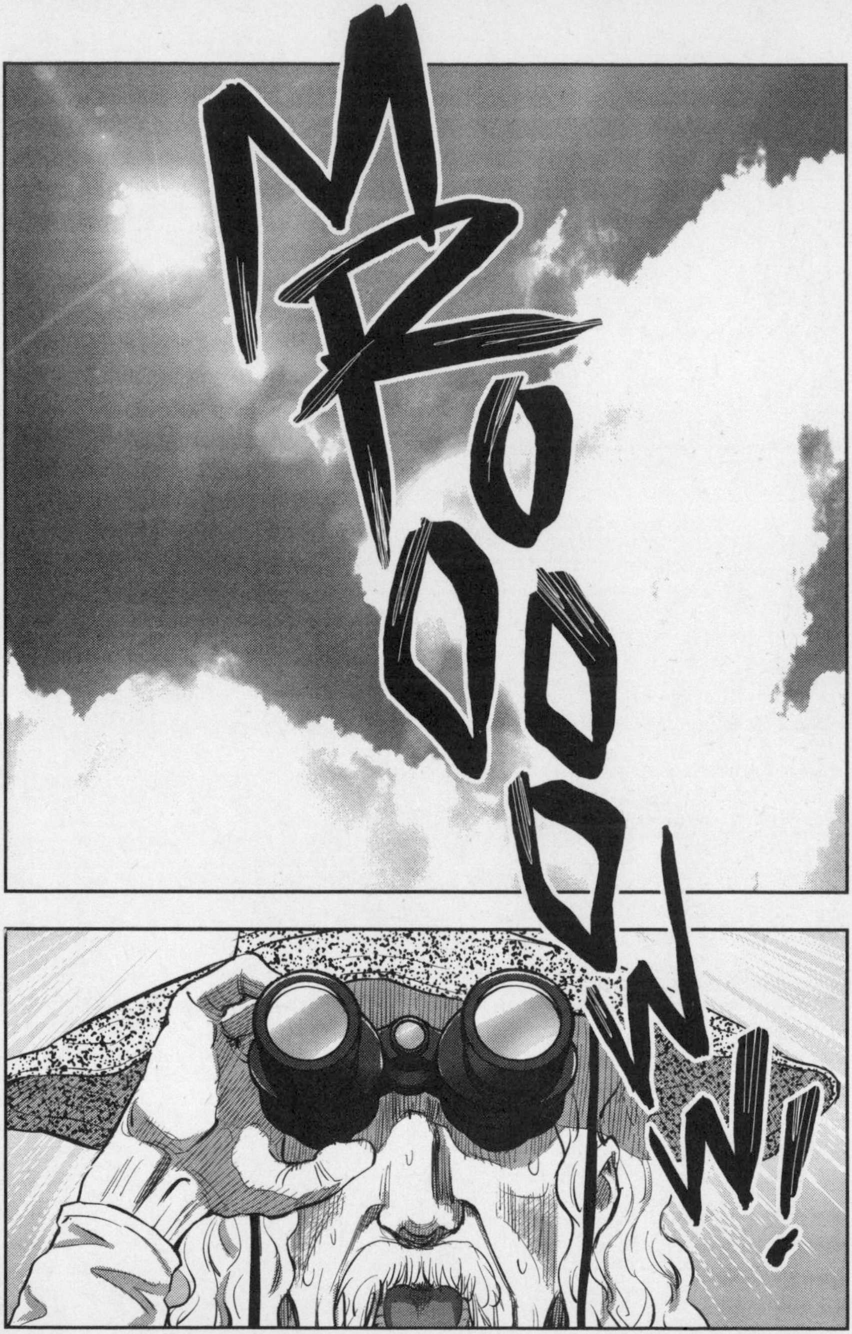
MROOOOWW!!

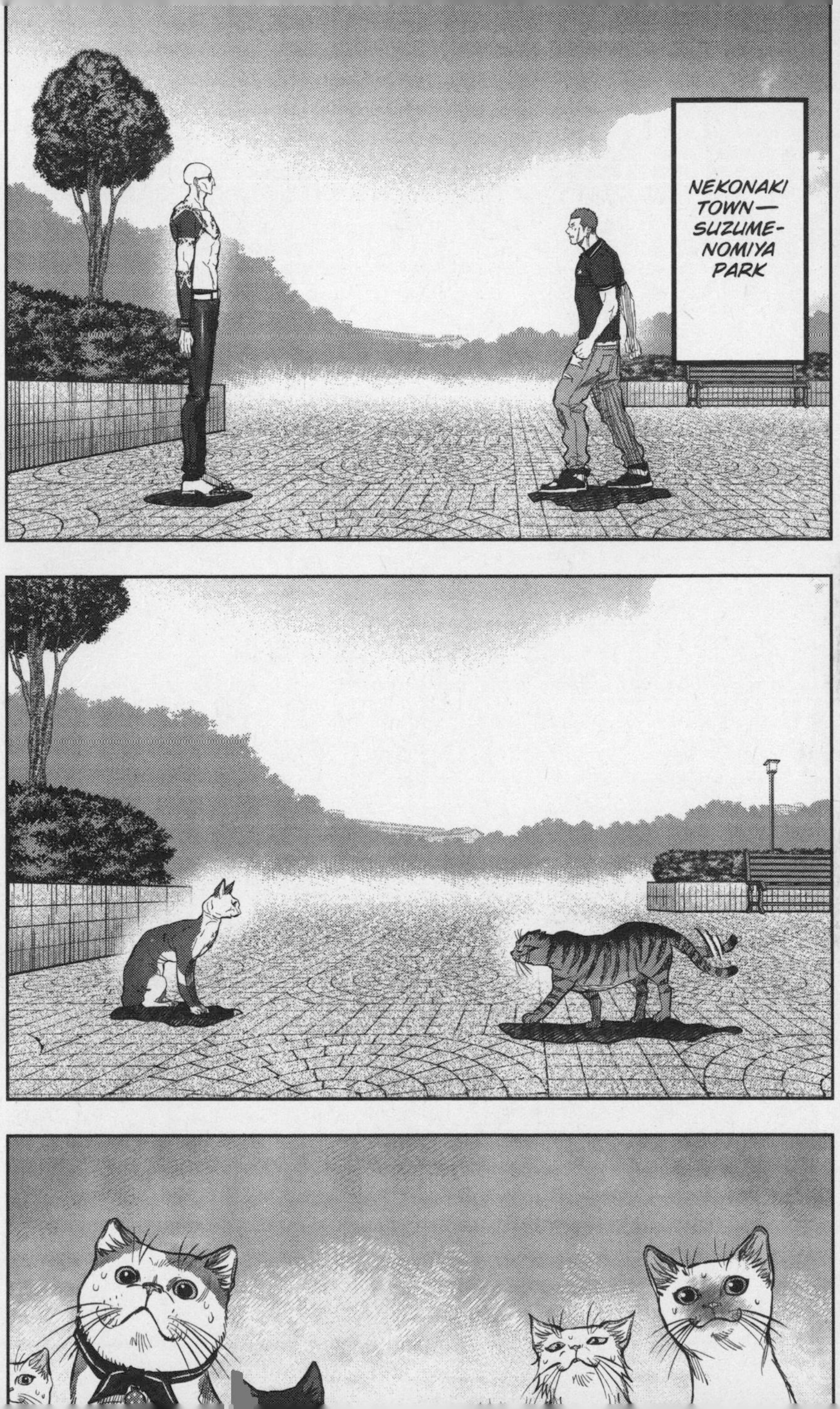
NEKONAKI TOWN—SUZUME-NOMIYA PARK

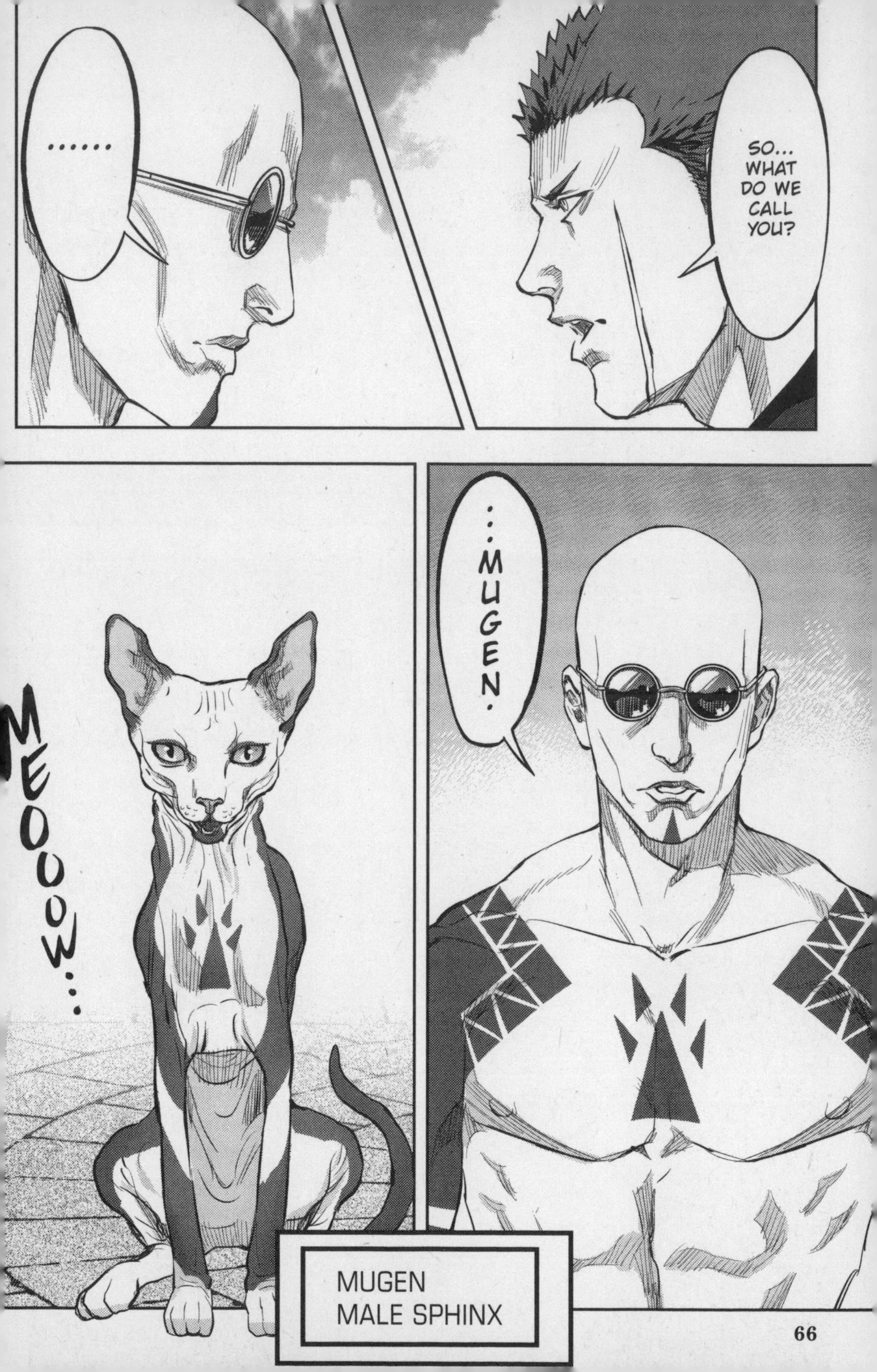
SO... WHAT DO WE CALL YOU?
......
...MUGEN.
MEOUUW...
MUGEN
MALE SPHINX

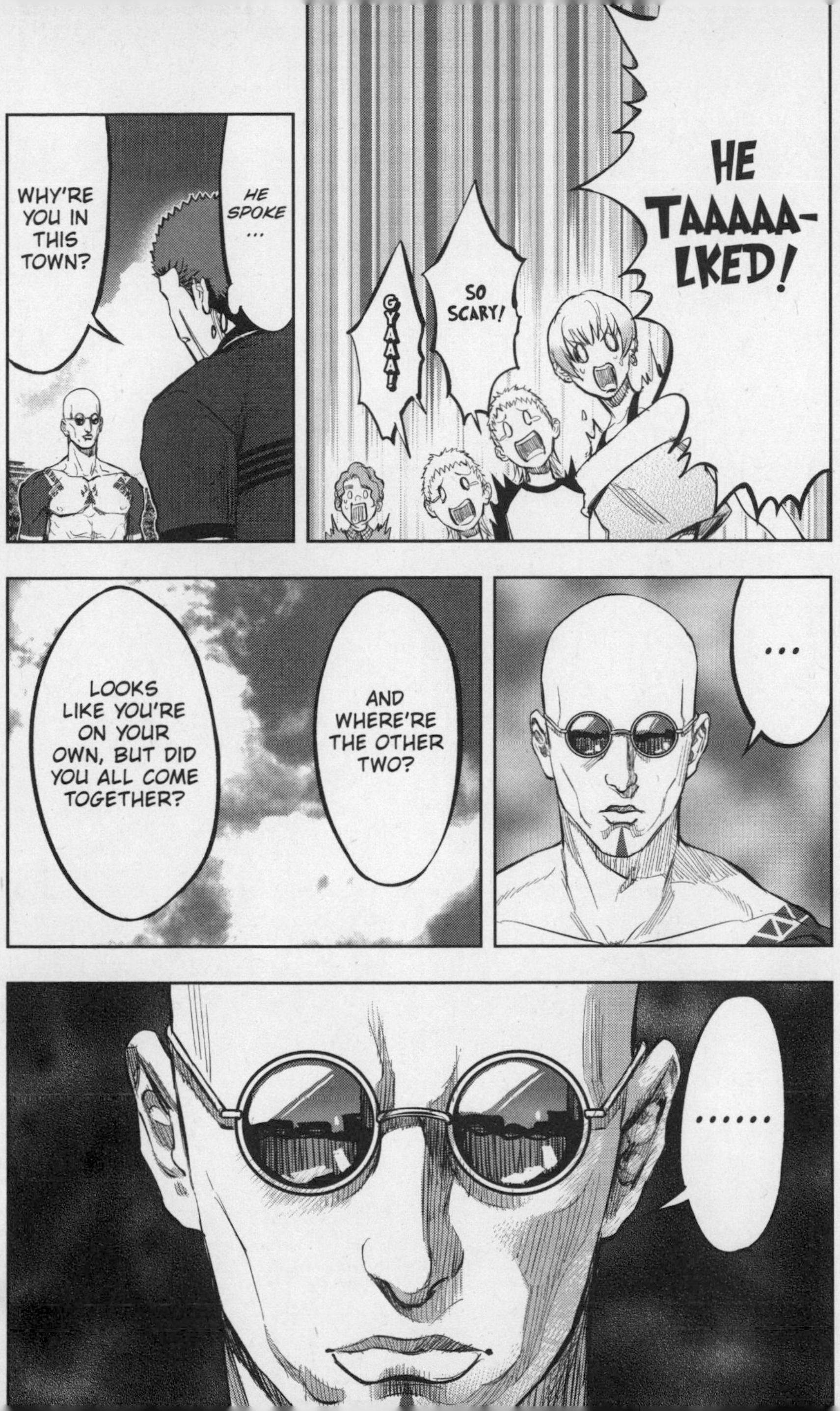
HE TAAAAA-LKED!
SO SCARY!
GYAAA!
HE SPOKE ...
WHY'RE YOU IN THIS TOWN?
...
LOOKS LIKE YOU'RE ON YOUR OWN, BUT DID YOU ALL COME TOGETHER?
AND WHERE'RE THE OTHER TWO?
......

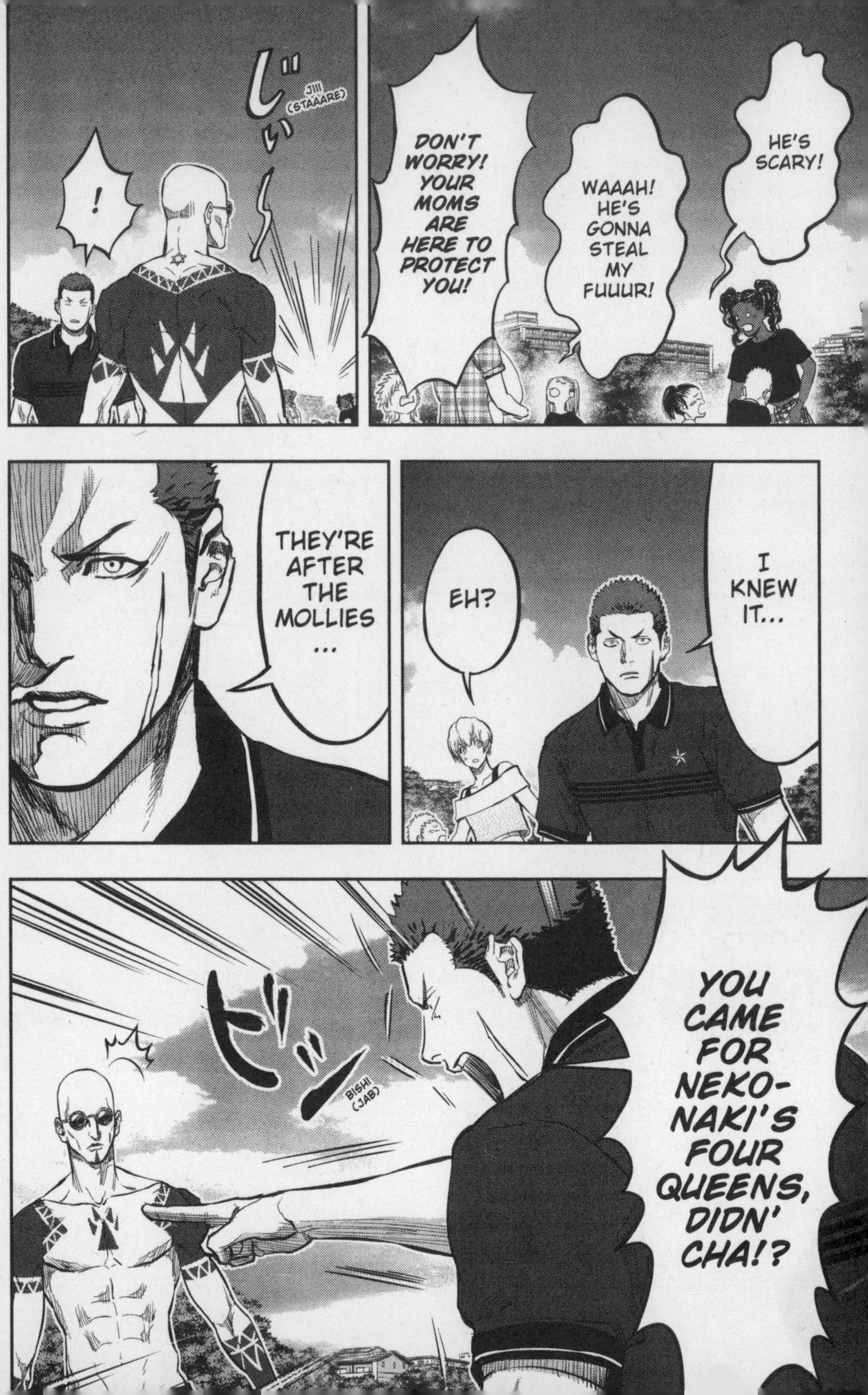
HE'S SCARY!
WAAAH! HE'S GONNA STEAL MY FUUUR!
DON'T WORRY! YOUR MOMS ARE HERE TO PROTECT YOU!
JIII (STAAARE)
!
I KNEW IT...
EH?
THEY'RE AFTER THE MOLLIES ...
YOU CAME FOR NEKO-NAKI'S FOUR QUEENS, DIDN' CHA!?
BISHI (JAB)

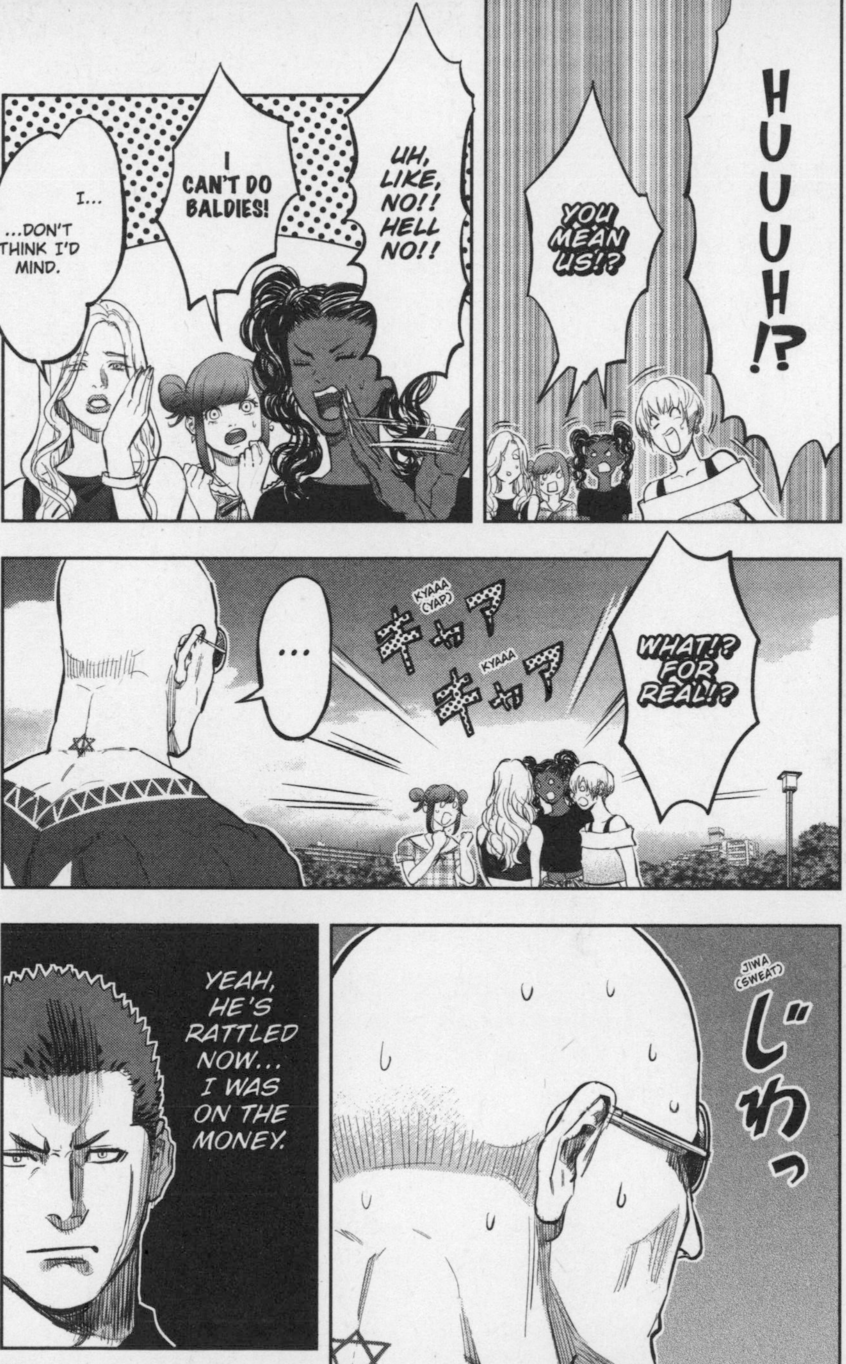
HUUUH!?
YOU MEAN US!?
UH, LIKE, NO!! HELL NO!!
I CAN'T DO BALDIES!
I... ...DON'T THINK I'D MIND.
WHAT!? FOR REAL!?
KYAAA (YAP)
キャア
KYAAA
キャア
...
JIWA (SWEAT)
じわっ
YEAH, HE'S RATTLED NOW... I WAS ON THE MONEY.

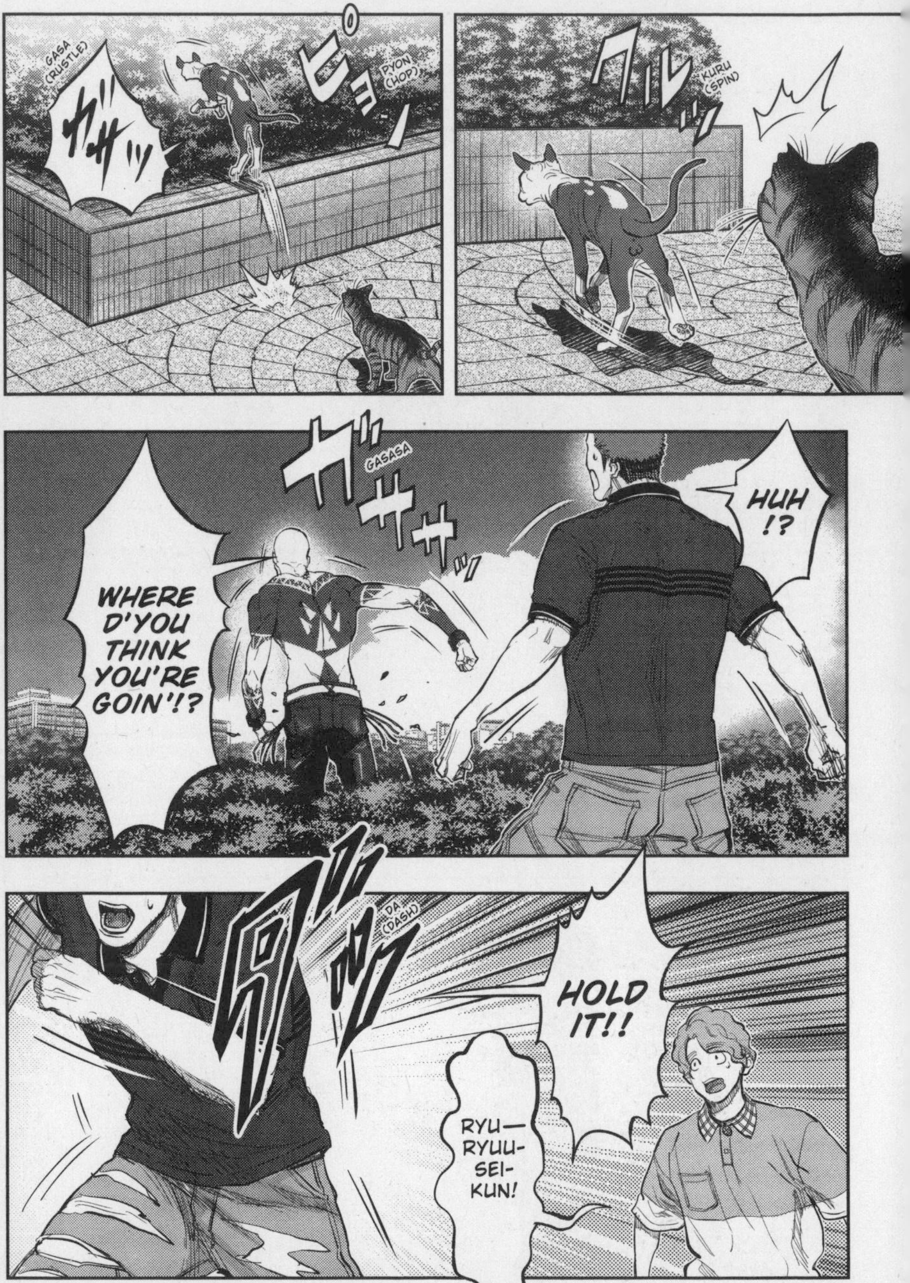
KURU (SPIN)
PYON (HOP)
GASA (RUSTLE)
HUH!?
GASASA
WHERE D'YOU THINK YOU'RE GOIN'!?
HOLD IT!!
DA (DASH)
RYU— RYUU-SEI-KUN!

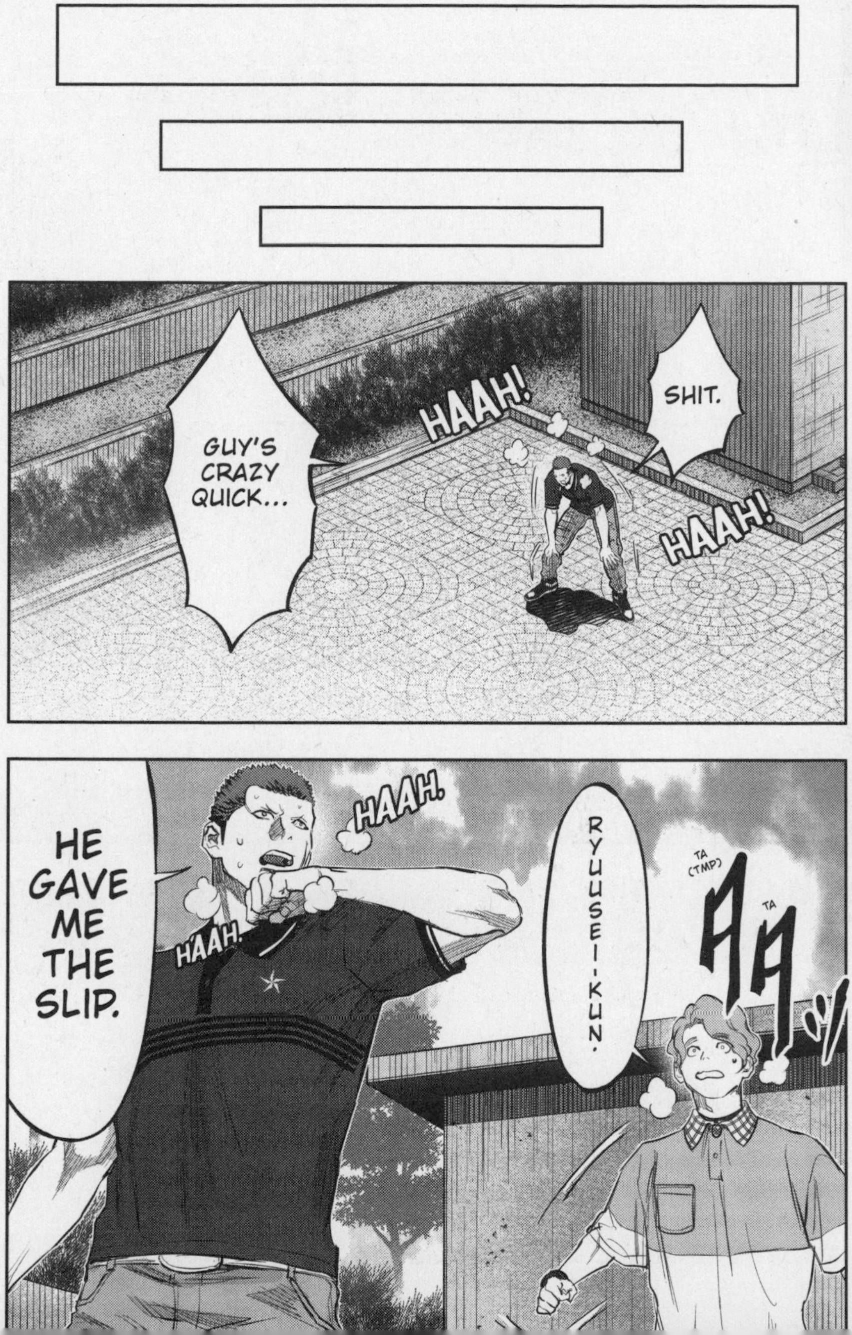
SHIT.
HAAH!
HAAH!
GUY'S CRAZY QUICK...
TA (TMP) TA
RYUUSEI-KUN.
HAAH.
HAAH...
HE GAVE ME THE SLIP.

...HMM?

NO TRACE OF HIS SCENT EITHER...

ヒクヒク
HIKU (SNIFF)

モワ～
MOWAAAN (WAFT)

THIS SMELL...

MEOW

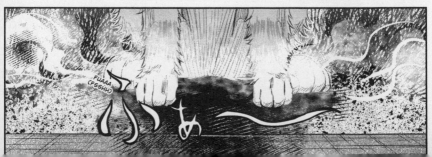

フアァ
FUAAA (FSSHH)

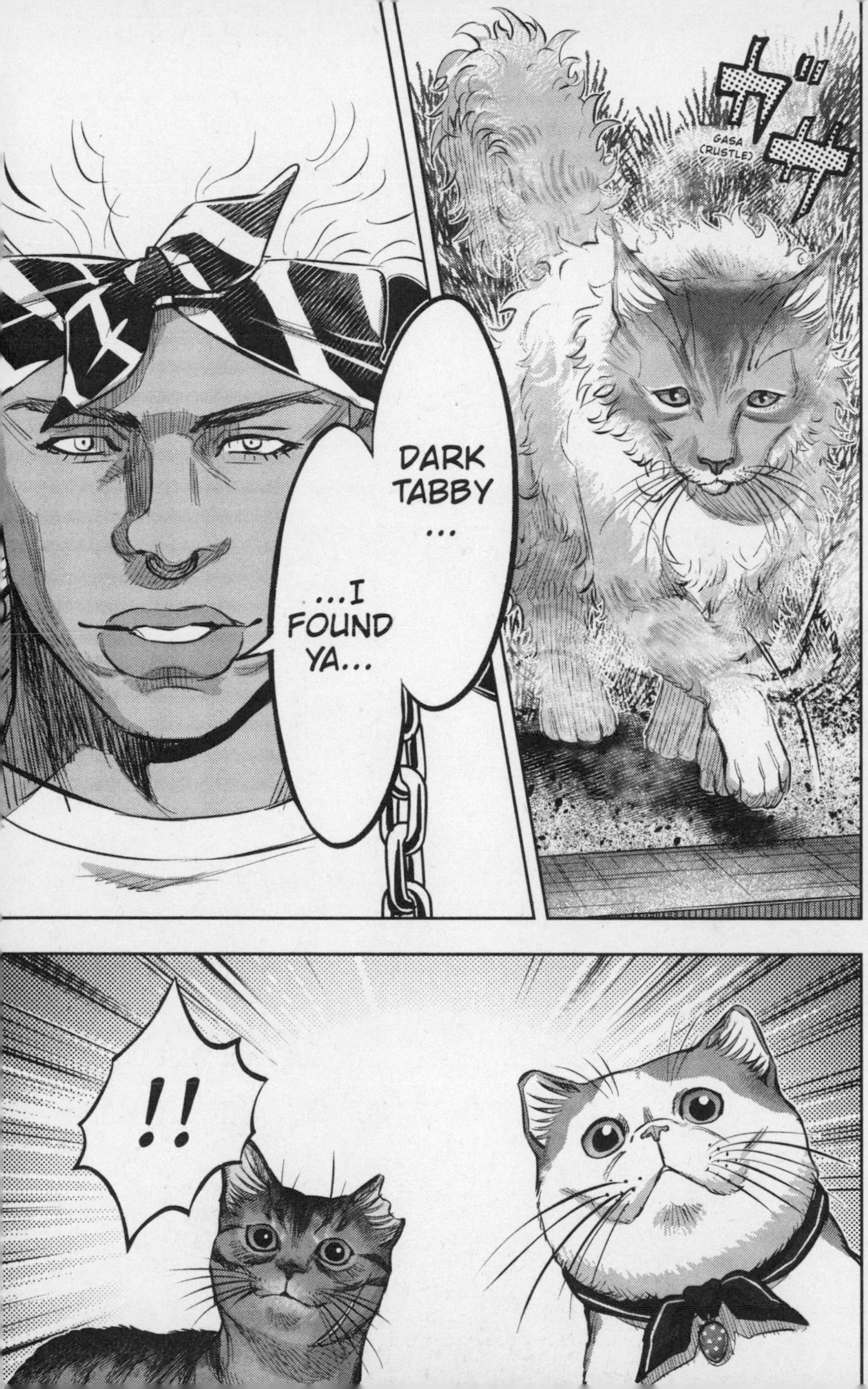
GASA (RUSTLE)
DARK TABBY ...
...I FOUND YA...
!!

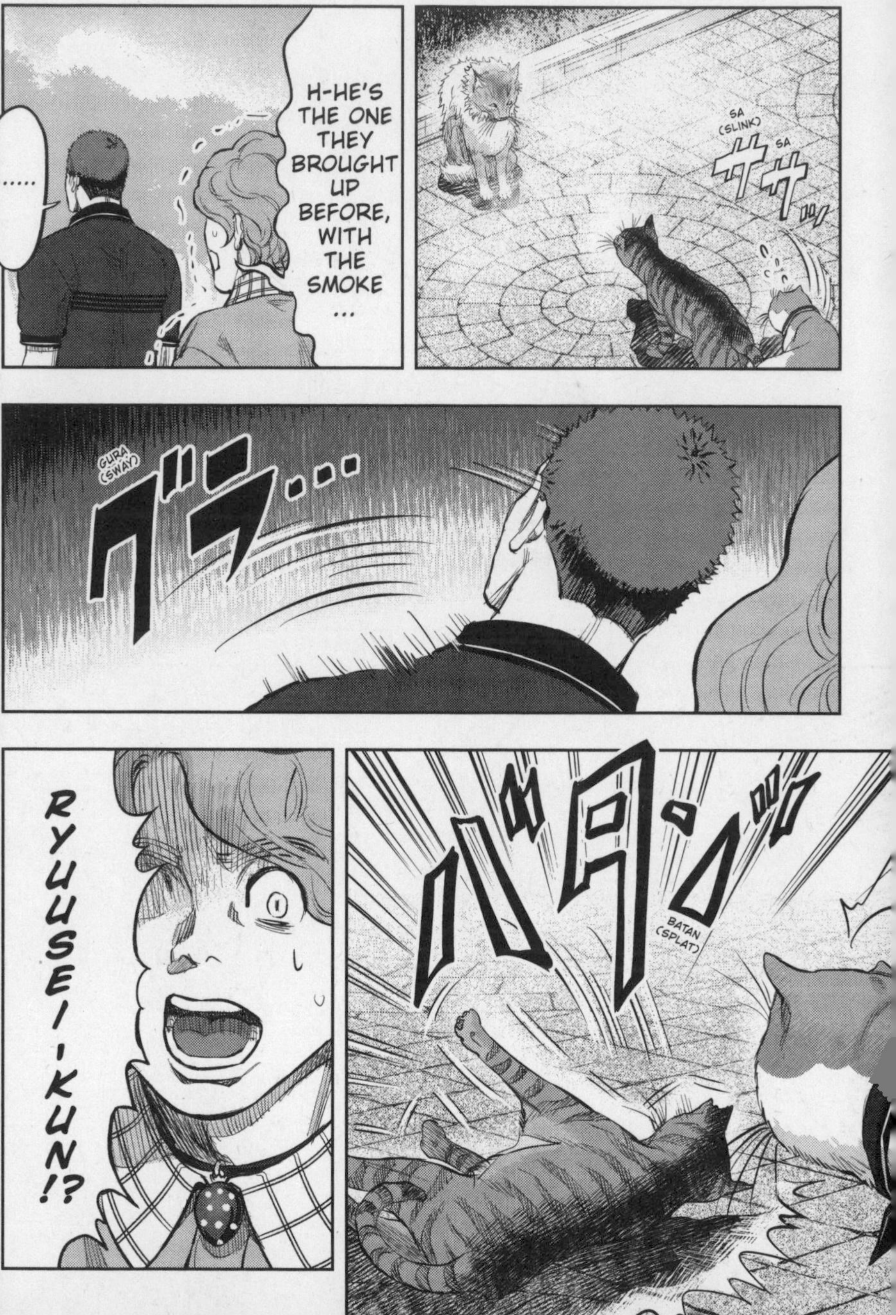
SA (SLINK)
SA
H-HE'S THE ONE THEY BROUGHT UP BEFORE, WITH THE SMOKE...
......
GURA (SWAY)
BATAN (SPLAT)
RYUUSEI-KUN!?

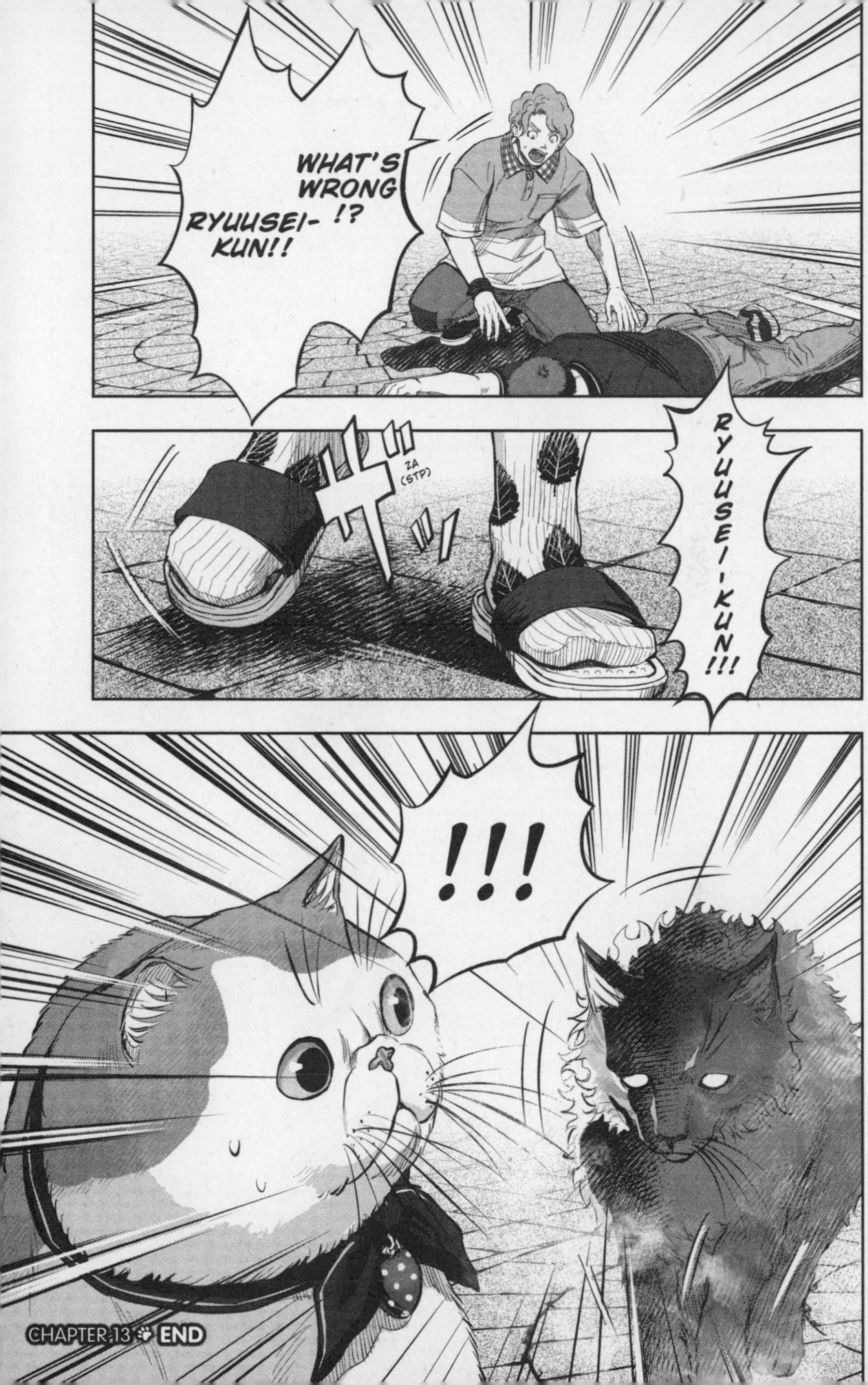
WHAT'S WRONG!? RYUUSEI-KUN!!
RYUUSEI-KUN!!!
ZA (STP)
!!!
CHAPTER 13 END

NYANKEES

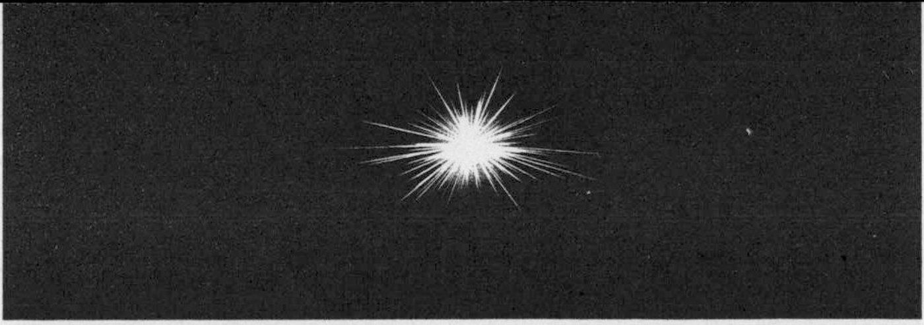
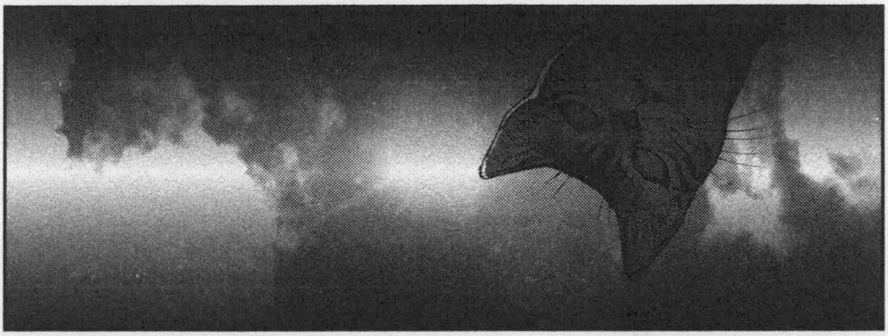
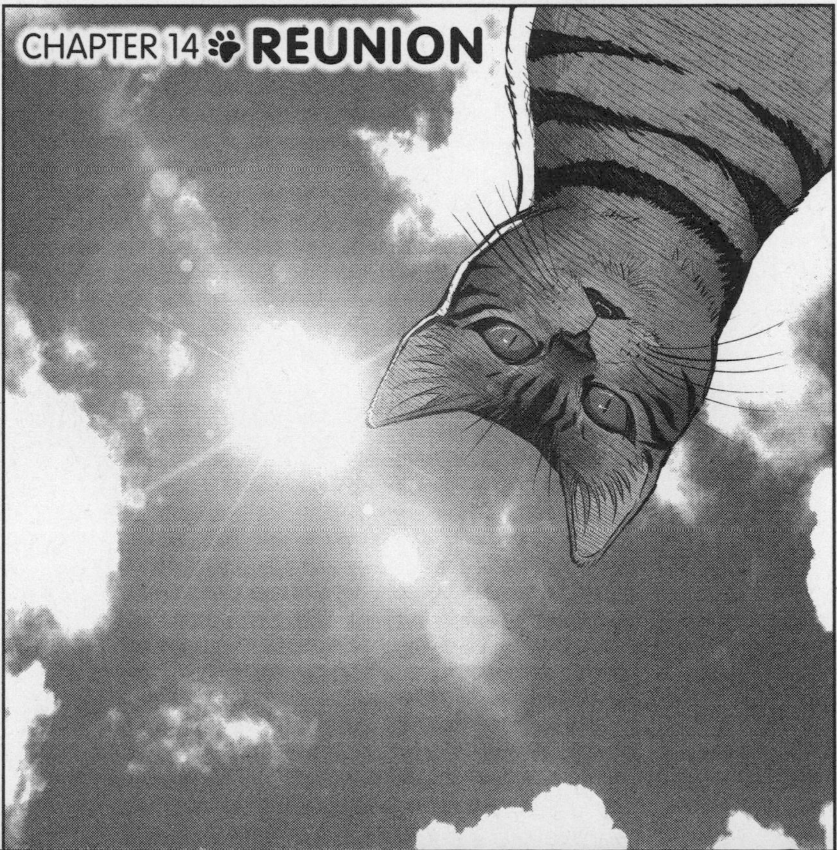
CHAPTER 14 REUNION

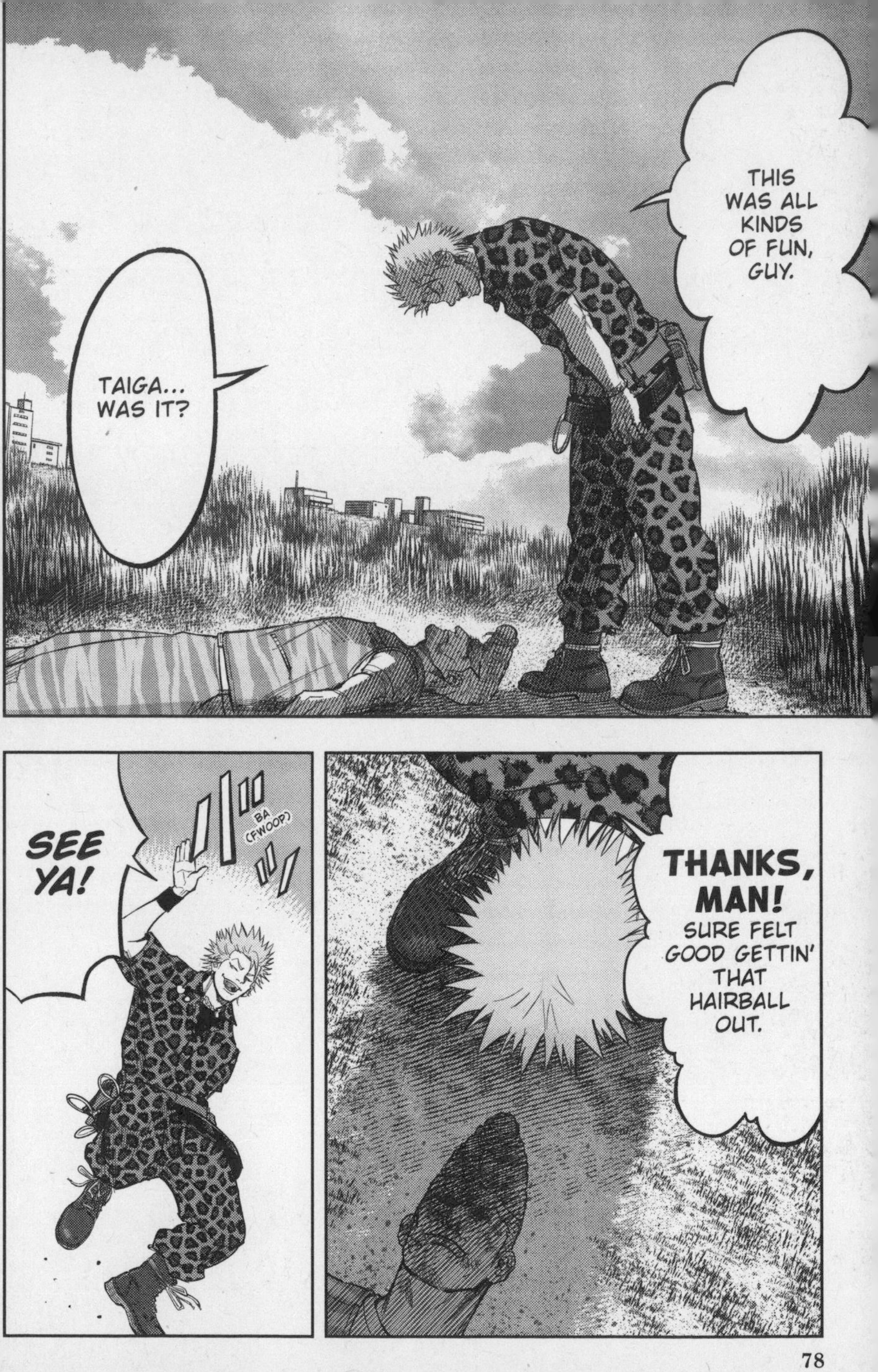
THIS WAS ALL KINDS OF FUN, GUY.
TAIGA... WAS IT?
THANKS, MAN! SURE FELT GOOD GETTIN' THAT HAIRBALL OUT.
BA (FWOOP)
SEE YA!

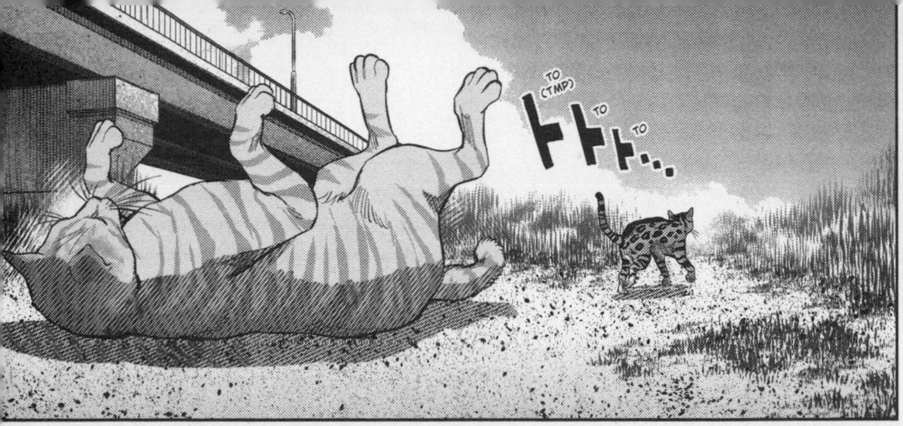
TO
(TMP)
トトト...
TO
TO

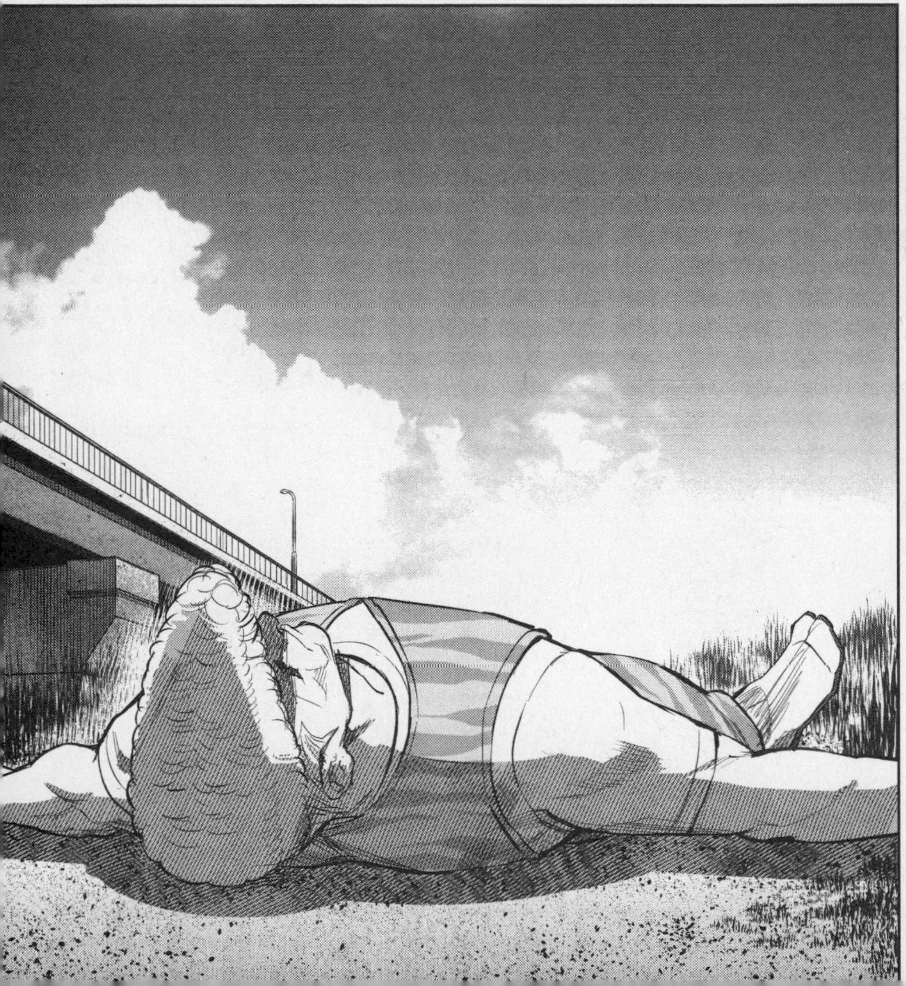

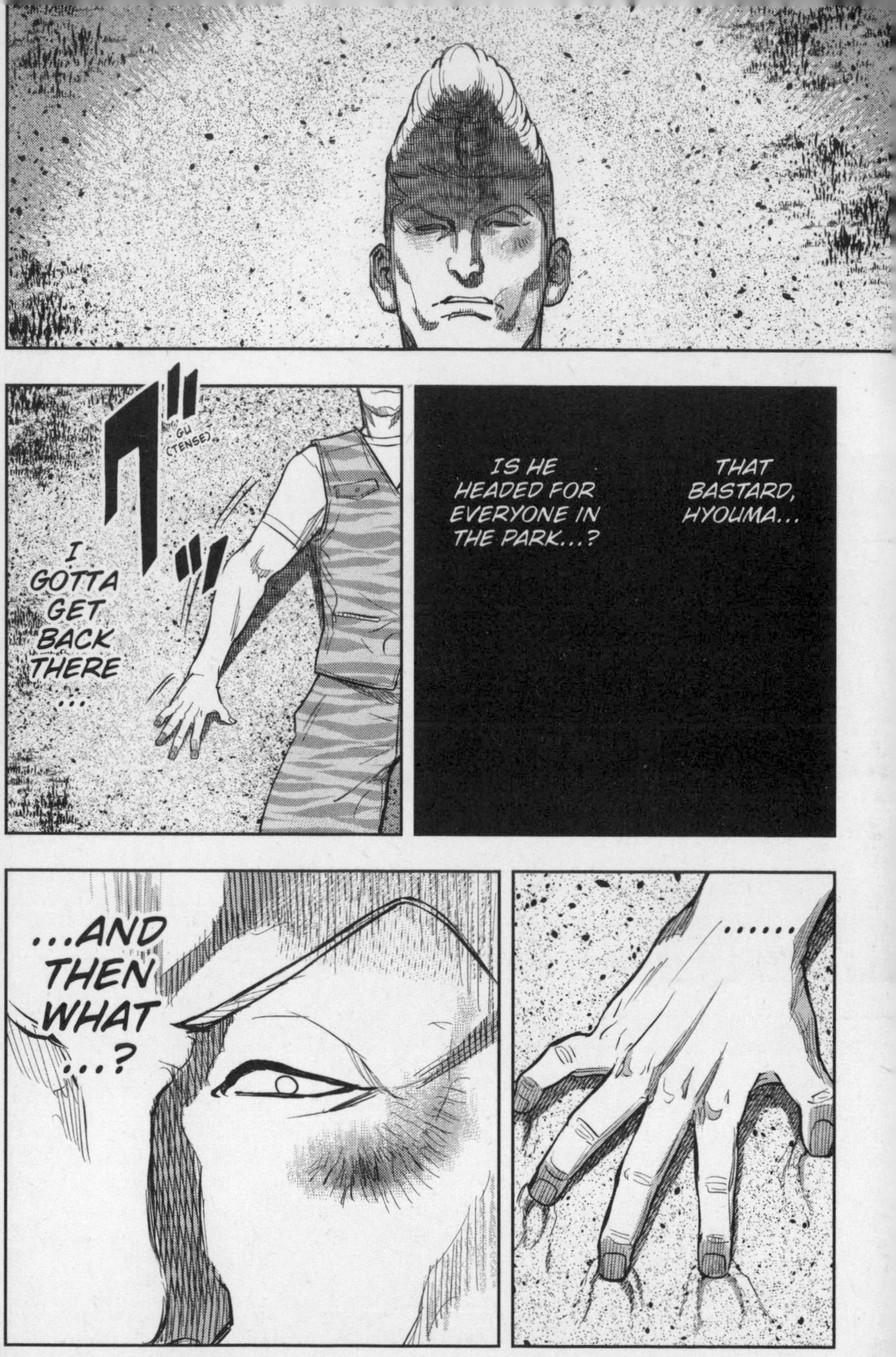
THAT BASTARD, HYOUMA...
IS HE HEADED FOR EVERYONE IN THE PARK...?
GU (TENSE)
I GOTTA GET BACK THERE...
......
...AND THEN WHAT...?

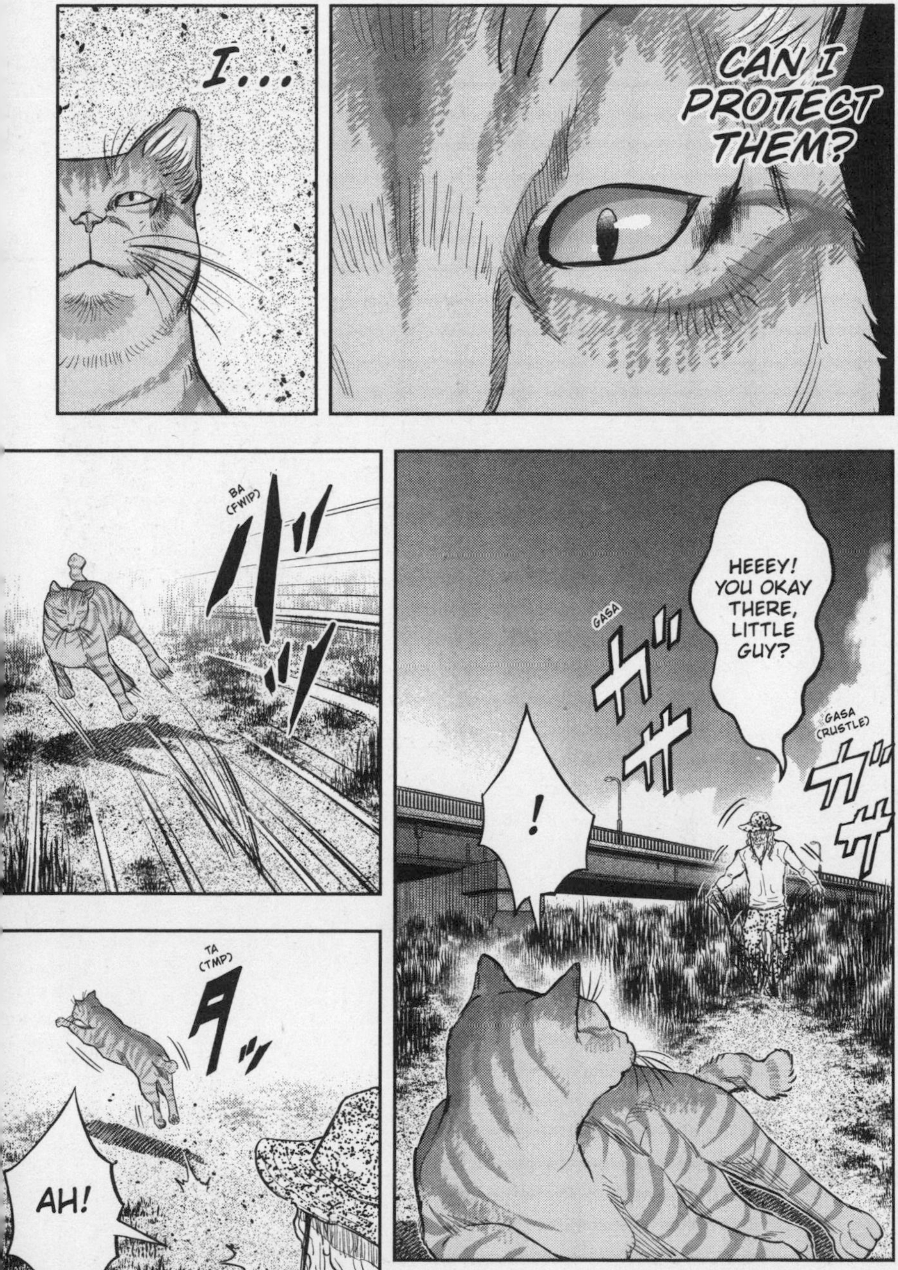
CAN I PROTECT THEM?
I...
HEEEY! YOU OKAY THERE, LITTLE GUY?
GASA (RUSTLE)
GASA
!
BA (FWIP)
TA (TMP)
AH!

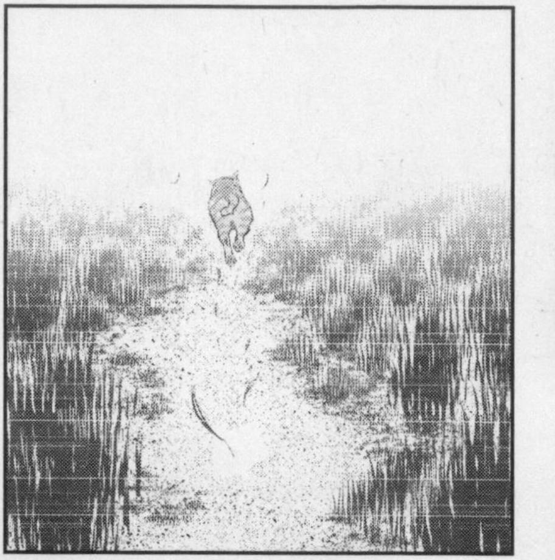

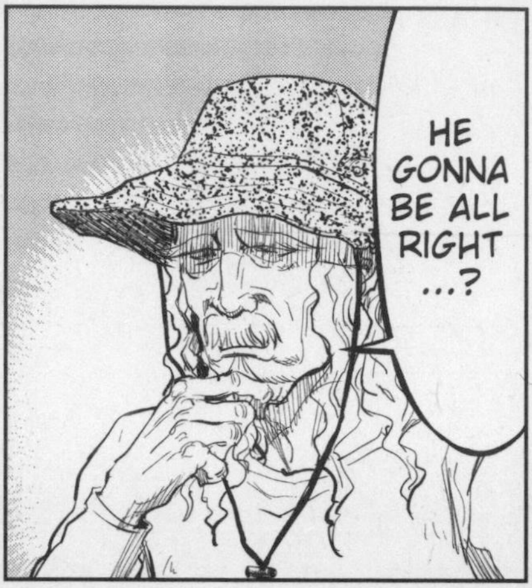
HE GONNA BE ALL RIGHT ...?

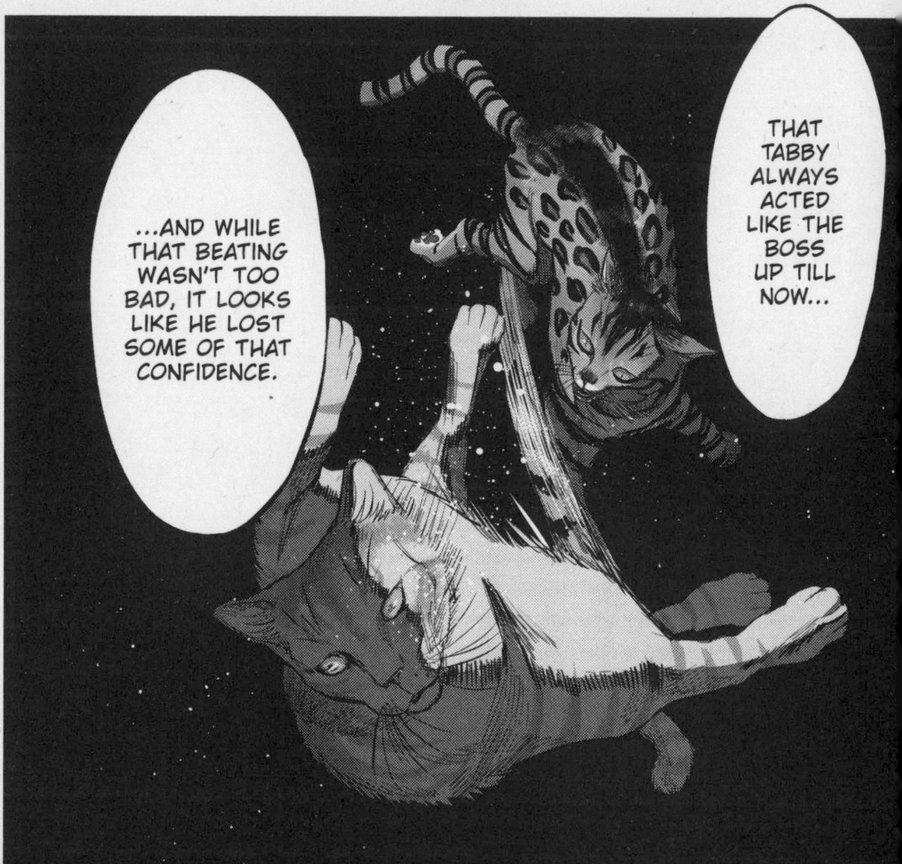
THAT TABBY ALWAYS ACTED LIKE THE BOSS UP TILL NOW...
...AND WHILE THAT BEATING WASN'T TOO BAD, IT LOOKS LIKE HE LOST SOME OF THAT CONFIDENCE.

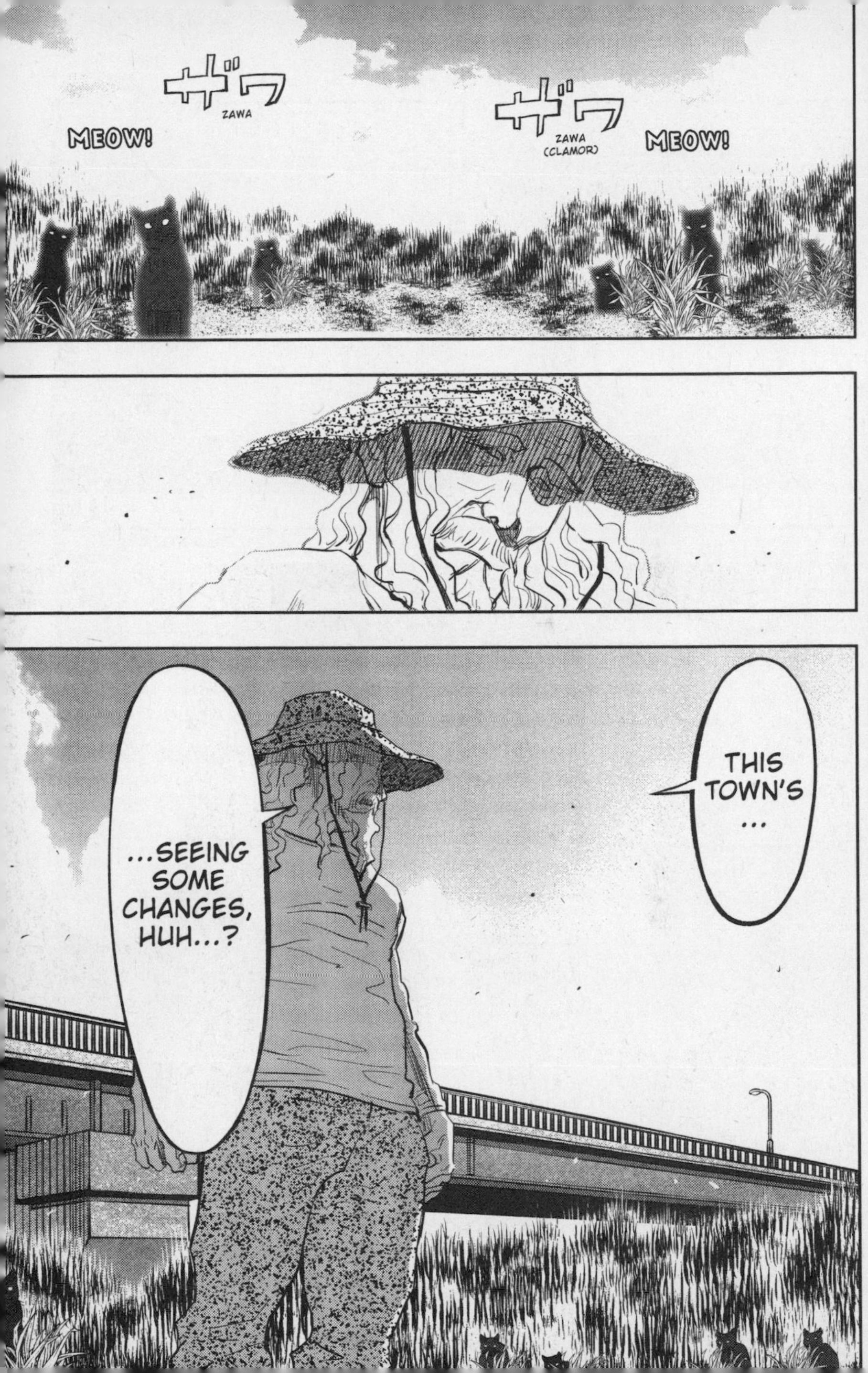
MEOW!
ザワ
ZAWA (CLAMOR)
ザワ
ZAWA
MEOW!
THIS TOWN'S...
...SEEING SOME CHANGES, HUH...?

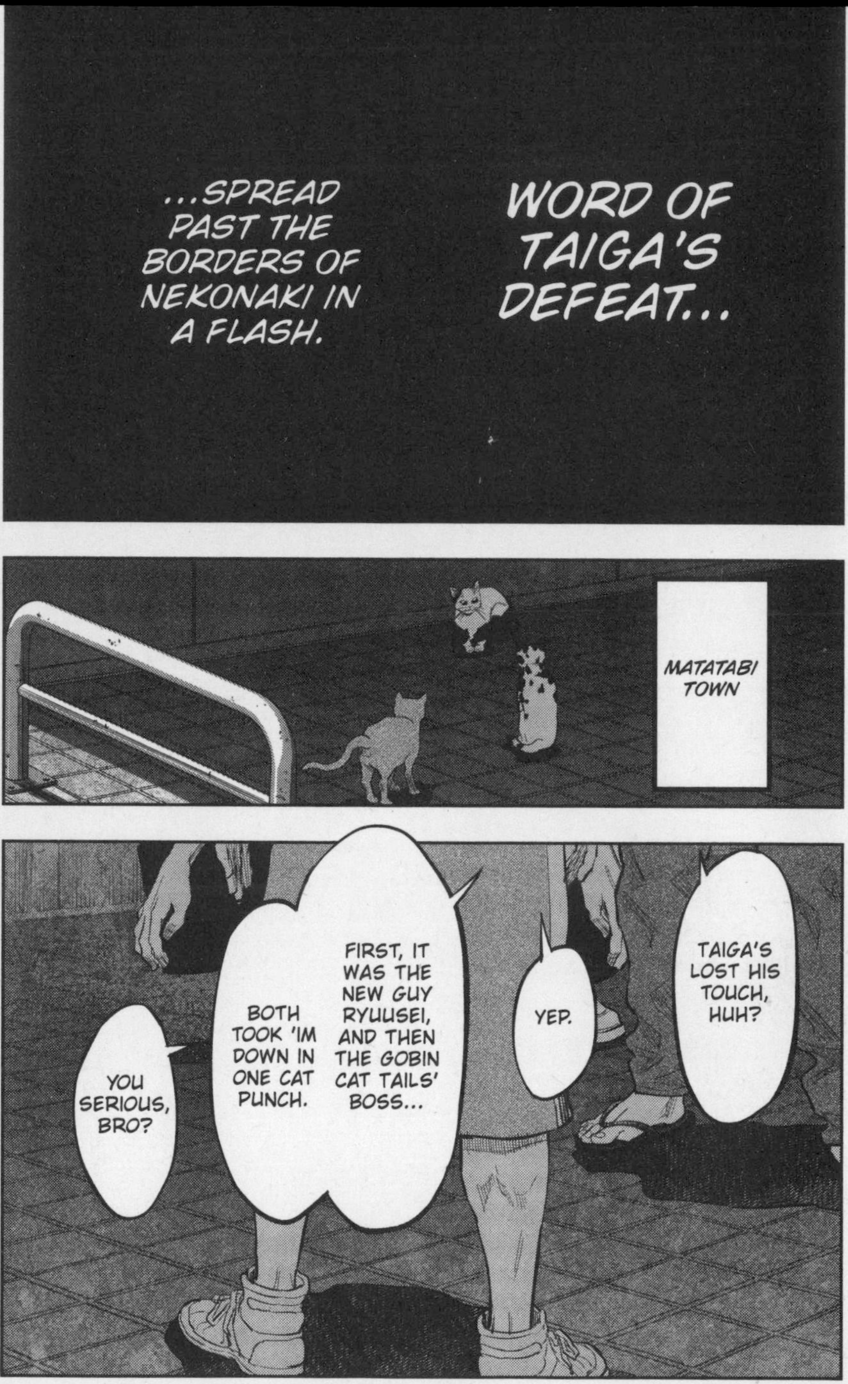
WORD OF TAIGA'S DEFEAT...
...SPREAD PAST THE BORDERS OF NEKONAKI IN A FLASH.
MATATABI TOWN
TAIGA'S LOST HIS TOUCH, HUH?
YEP.
FIRST, IT WAS THE NEW GUY RYUUSEI, AND THEN THE GOBIN CAT TAILS' BOSS...
BOTH TOOK 'IM DOWN IN ONE CAT PUNCH.
YOU SERIOUS, BRO?

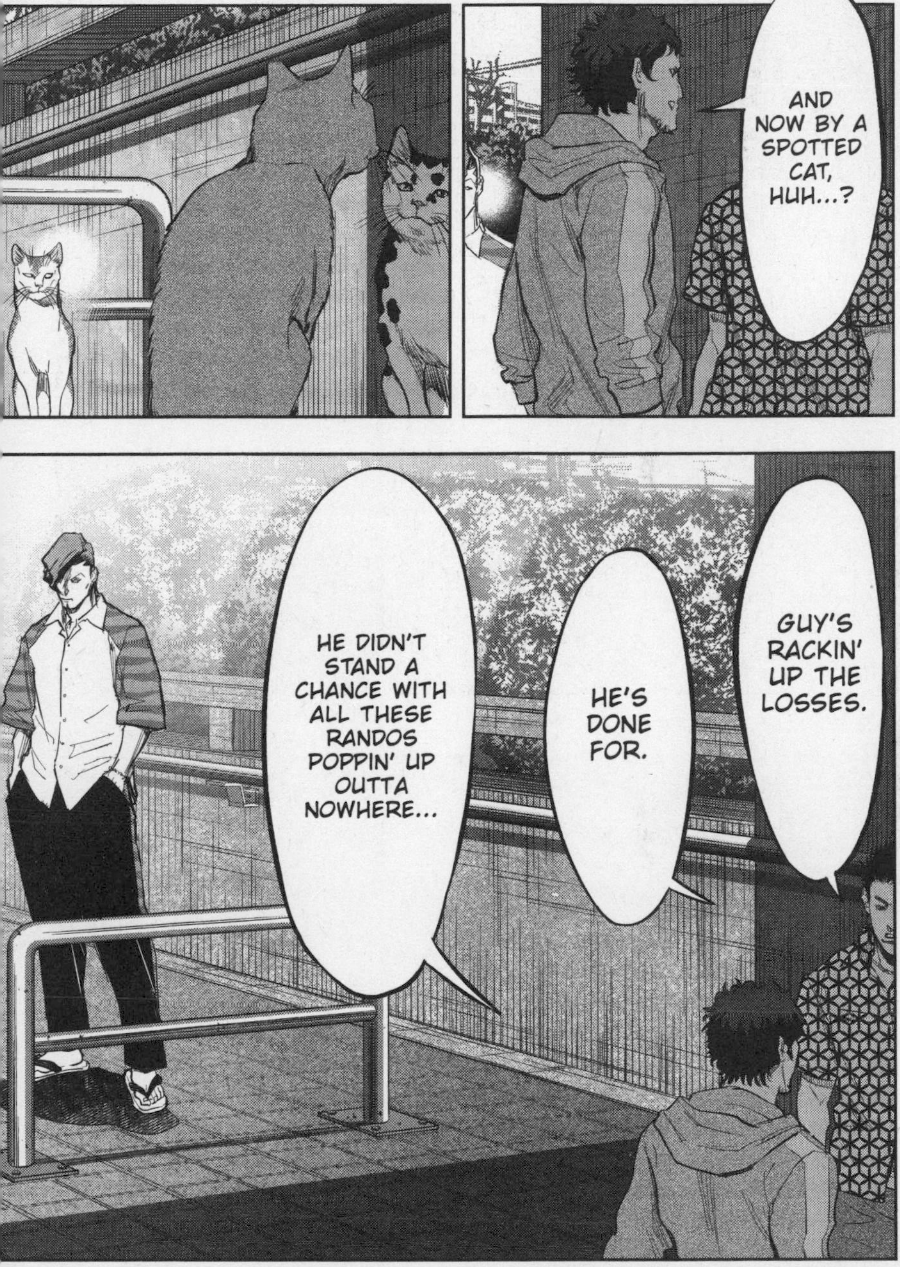
AND NOW BY A SPOTTED CAT, HUH...?
GUY'S RACKIN' UP THE LOSSES.
HE'S DONE FOR.
HE DIDN'T STAND A CHANCE WITH ALL THESE RANDOS POPPIN' UP OUTTA NOWHERE...

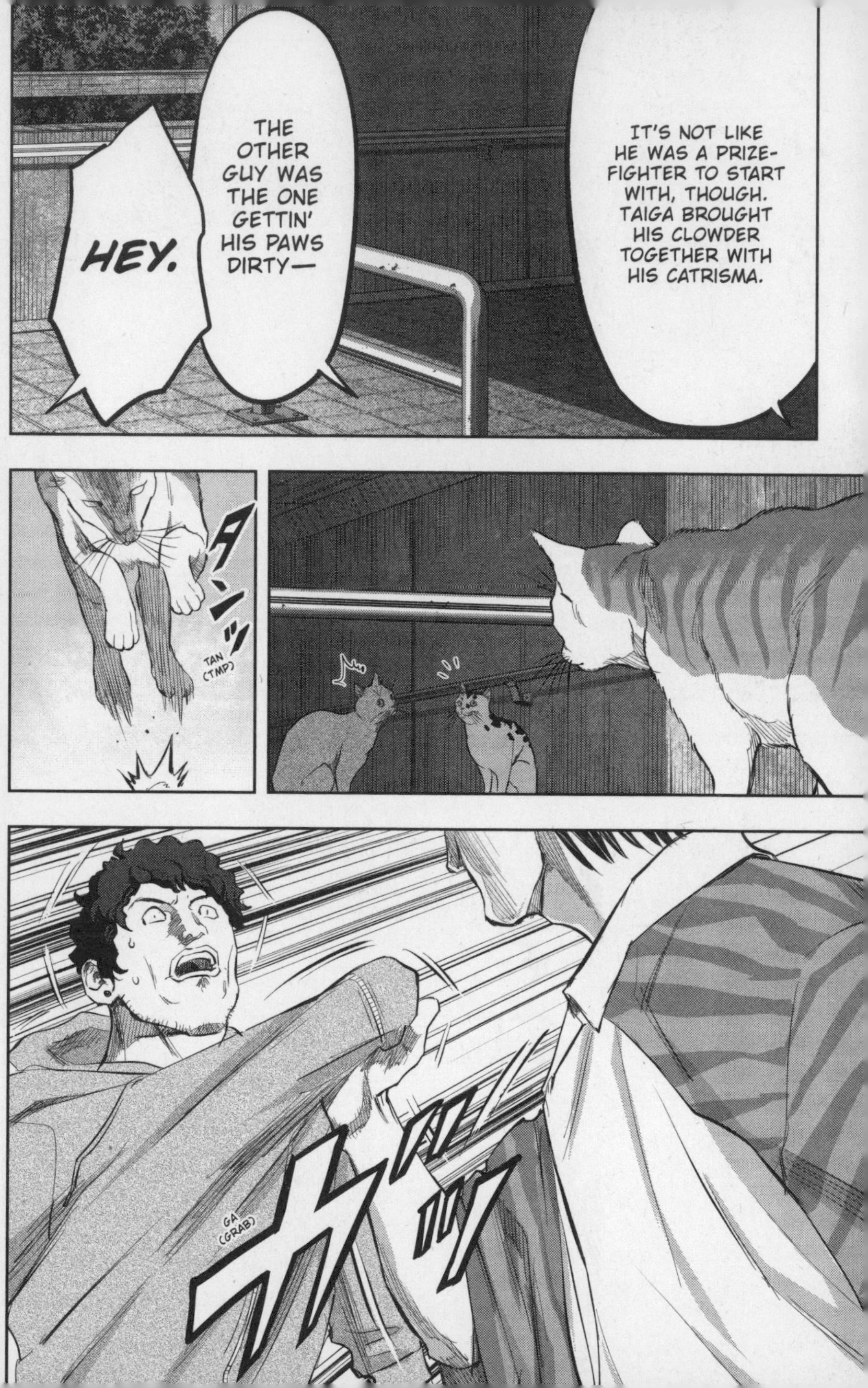
IT'S NOT LIKE HE WAS A PRIZE-FIGHTER TO START WITH, THOUGH. TAIGA BROUGHT HIS CLOWDER TOGETHER WITH HIS CATRISMA.
THE OTHER GUY WAS THE ONE GETTIN' HIS PAWS DIRTY—
HEY.
TAN (TMP)
GA (GRAB)

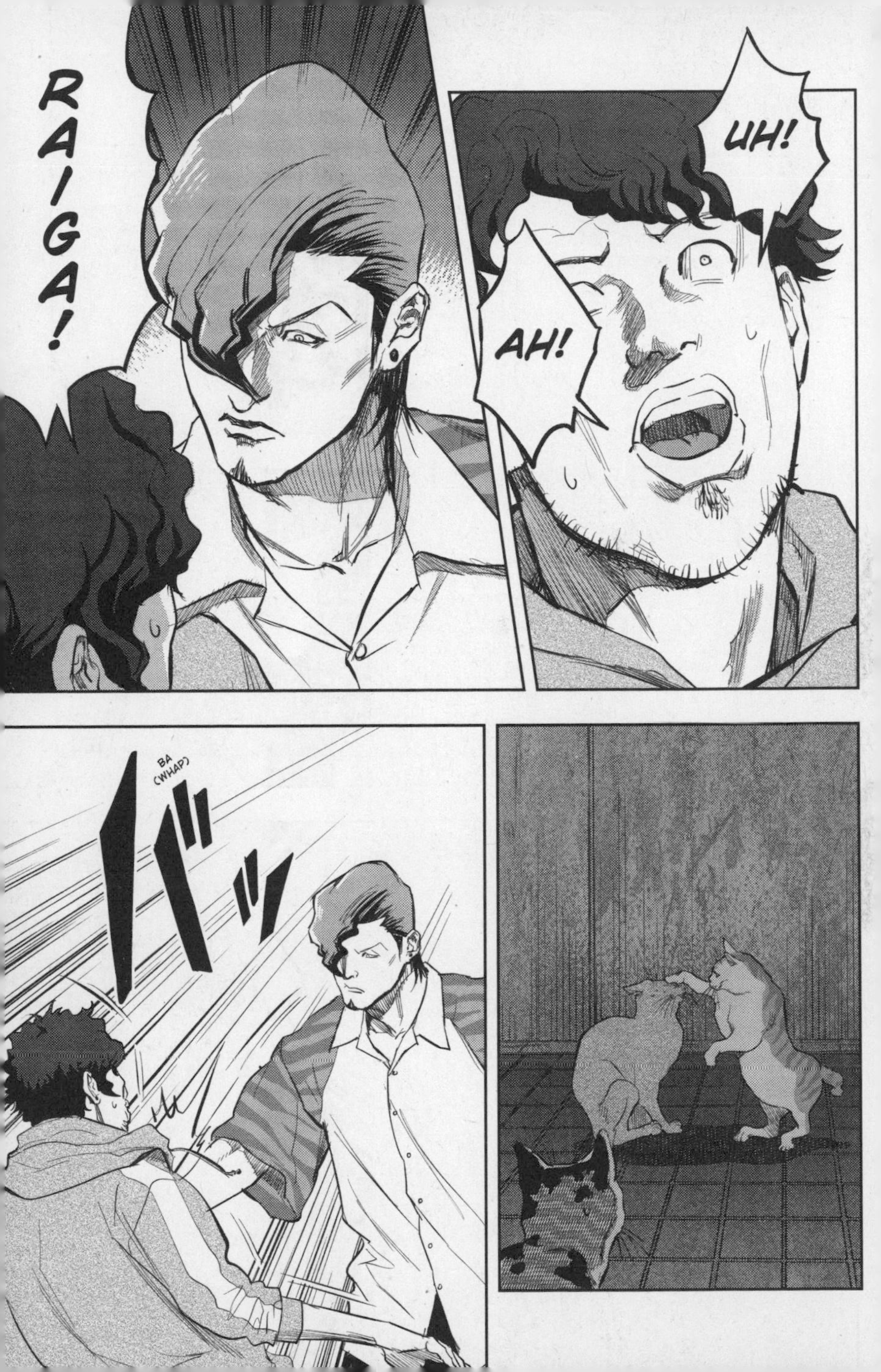
UH!
AH!
RAIGA!
BA
(WHAP)
バッ

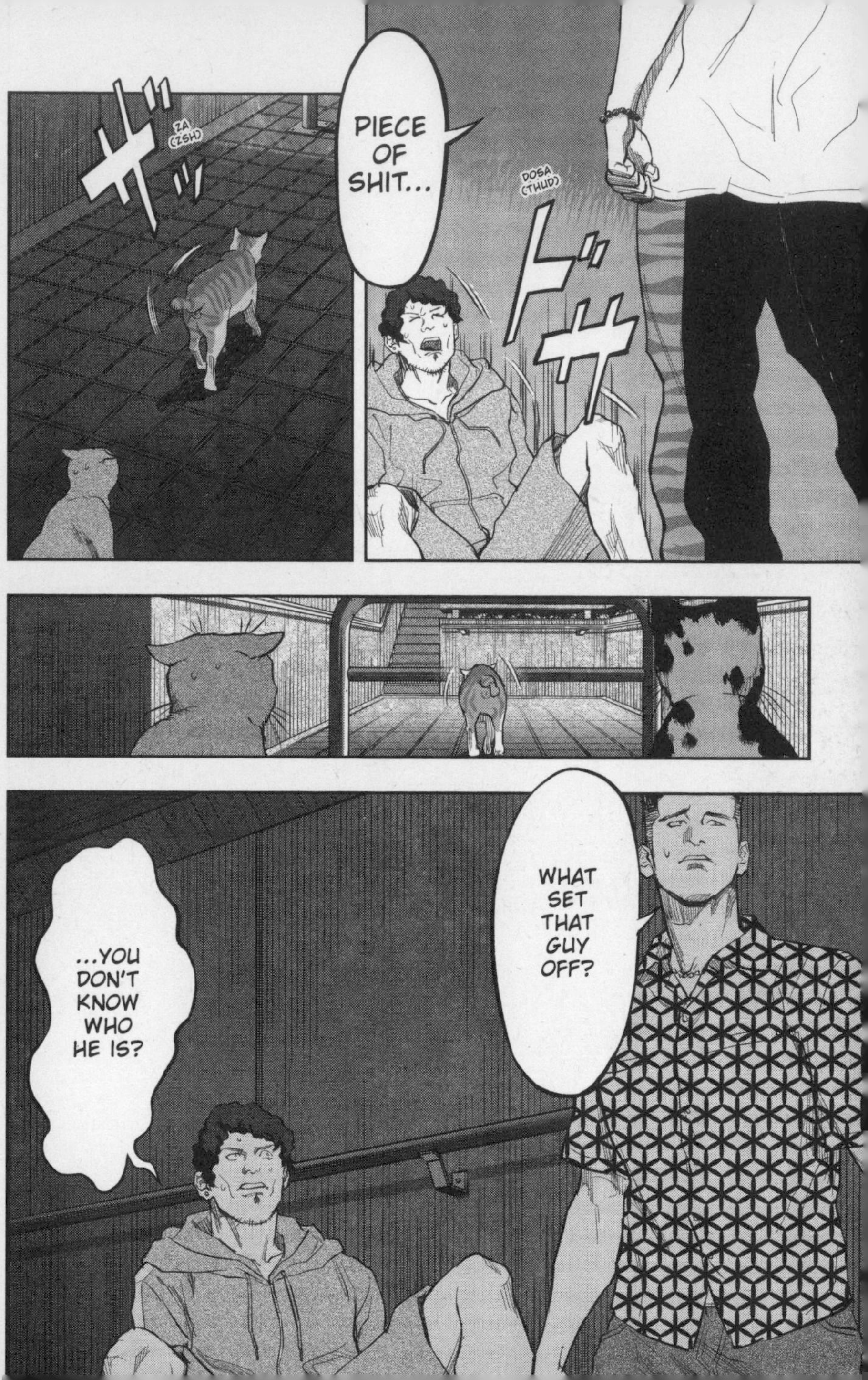
ドサ
DOSA (THUD)
PIECE OF SHIT...
ザッ
ZA (ZSH)
WHAT SET THAT GUY OFF?
...YOU DON'T KNOW WHO HE IS?

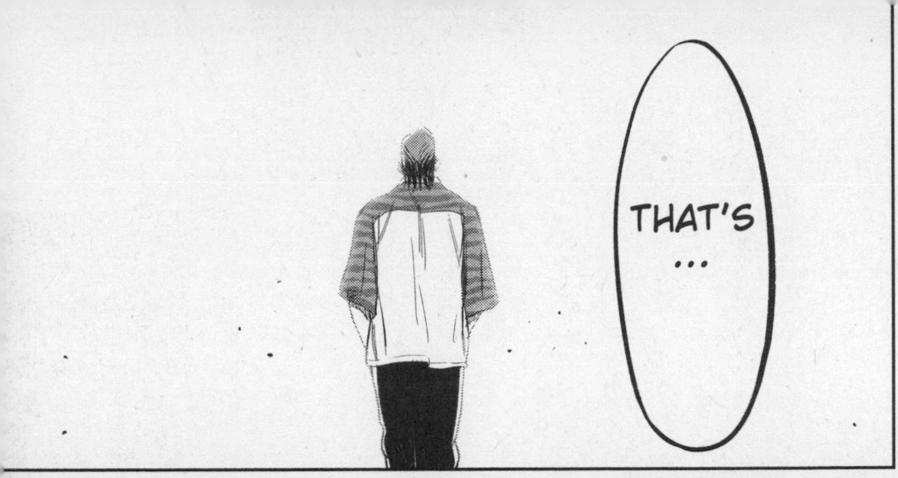
THAT'S ...
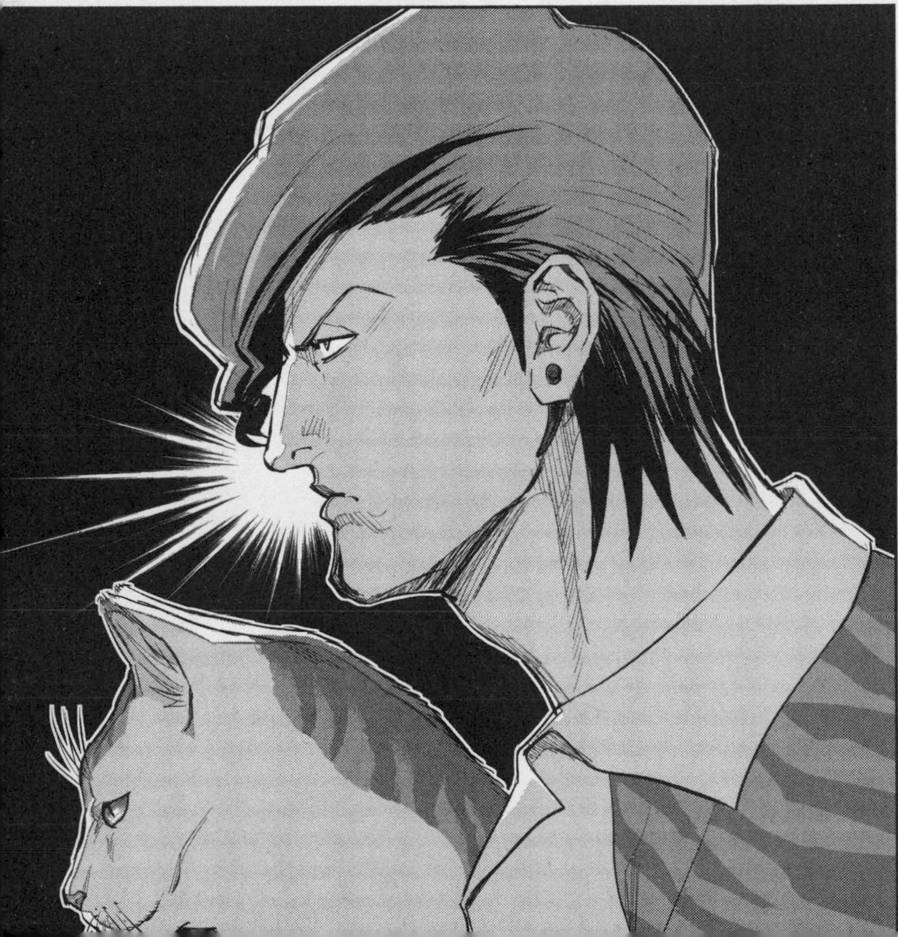

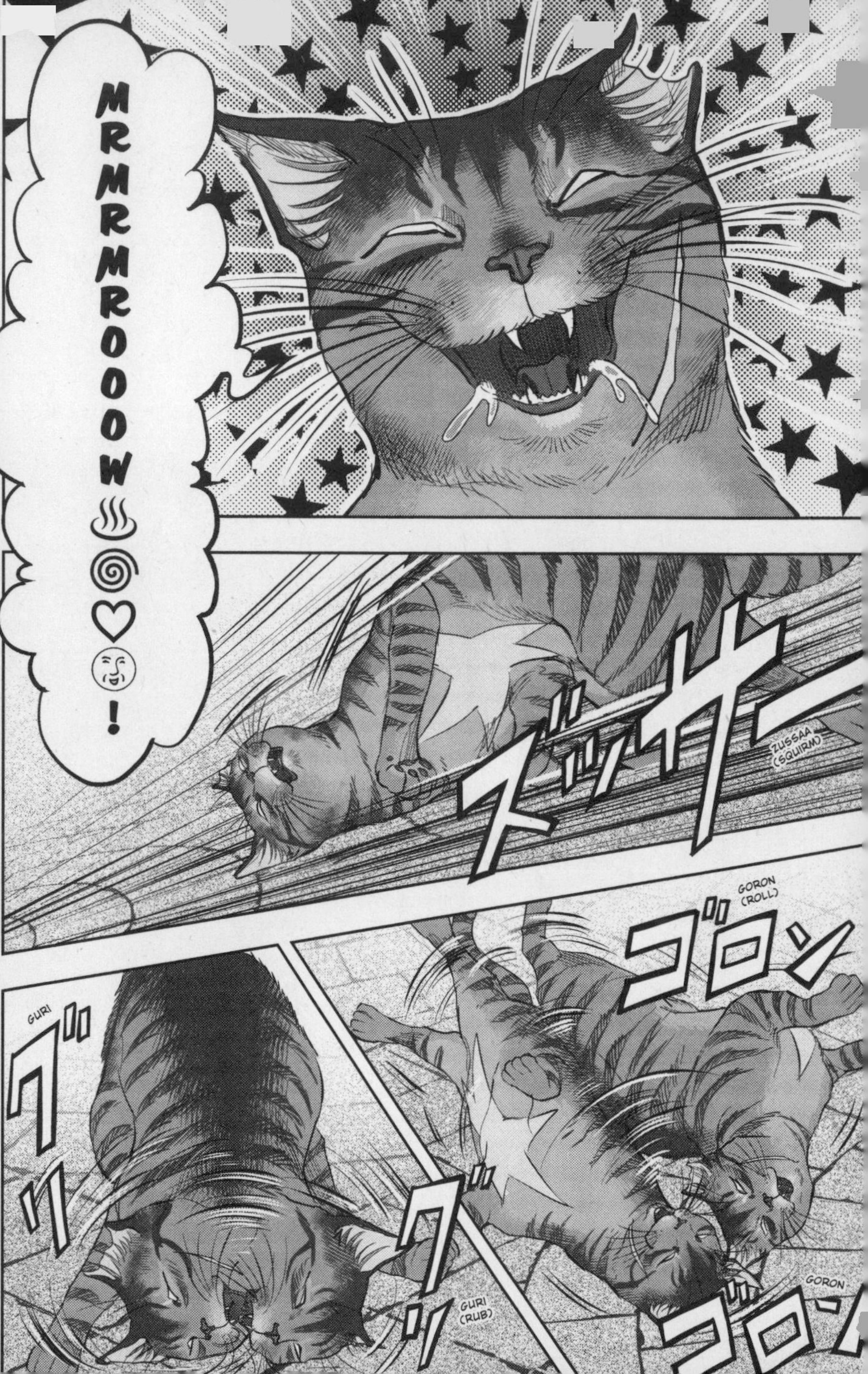

MRMRMROOOOW♨🌀♥☺!
ズッサー
ZUSSAA (SQUIRM)
ゴロン
GORON (ROLL)
グリ
GURI (RUB)
ゴロー
GORON
グリ
GURI

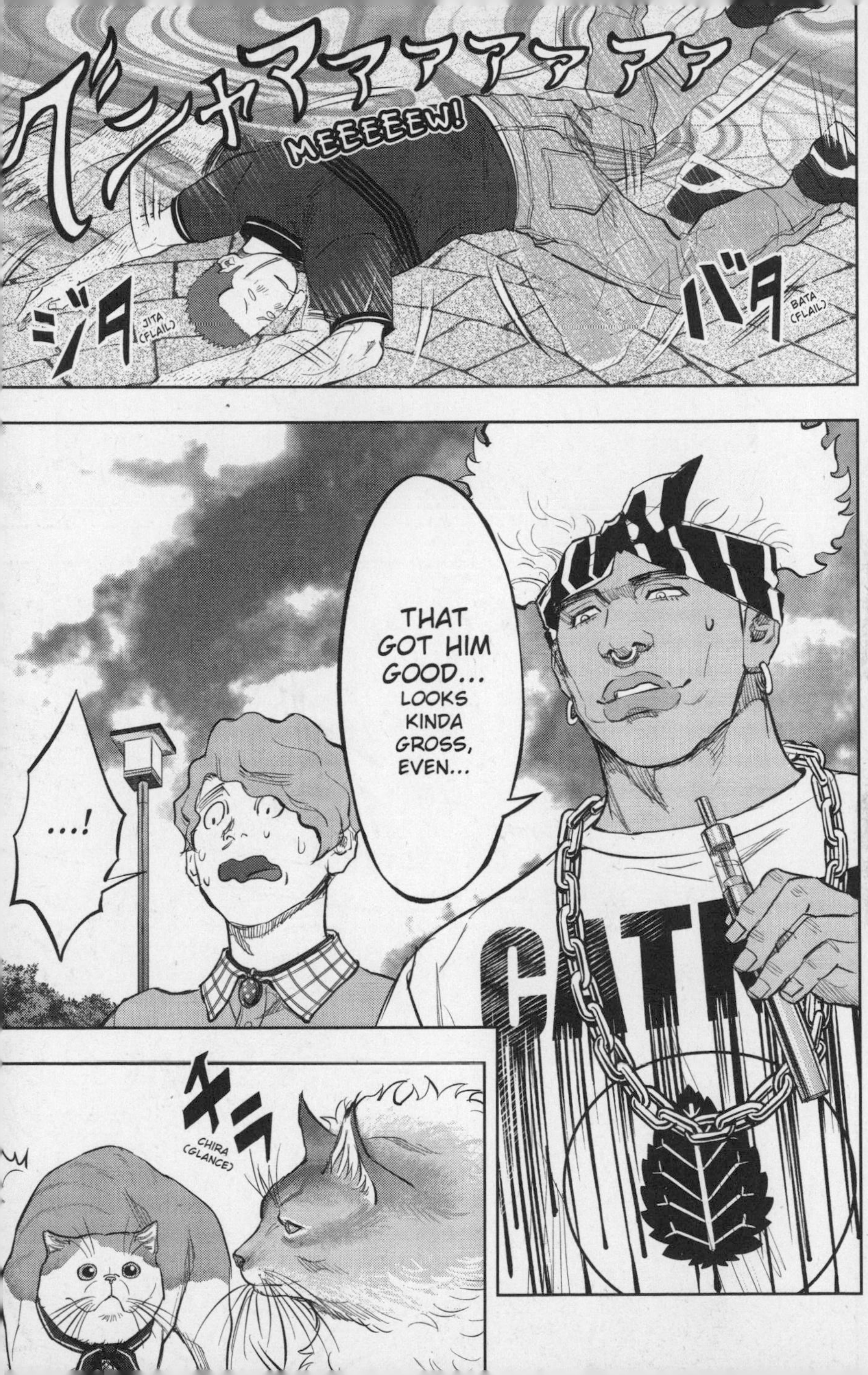
MEEEEEEW!
バタ
BATA (FLAIL)
ジタ
JITA (FLAIL)
THAT GOT HIM GOOD... LOOKS KINDA GROSS, EVEN...
...!
チラ
CHIRA (GLANCE)

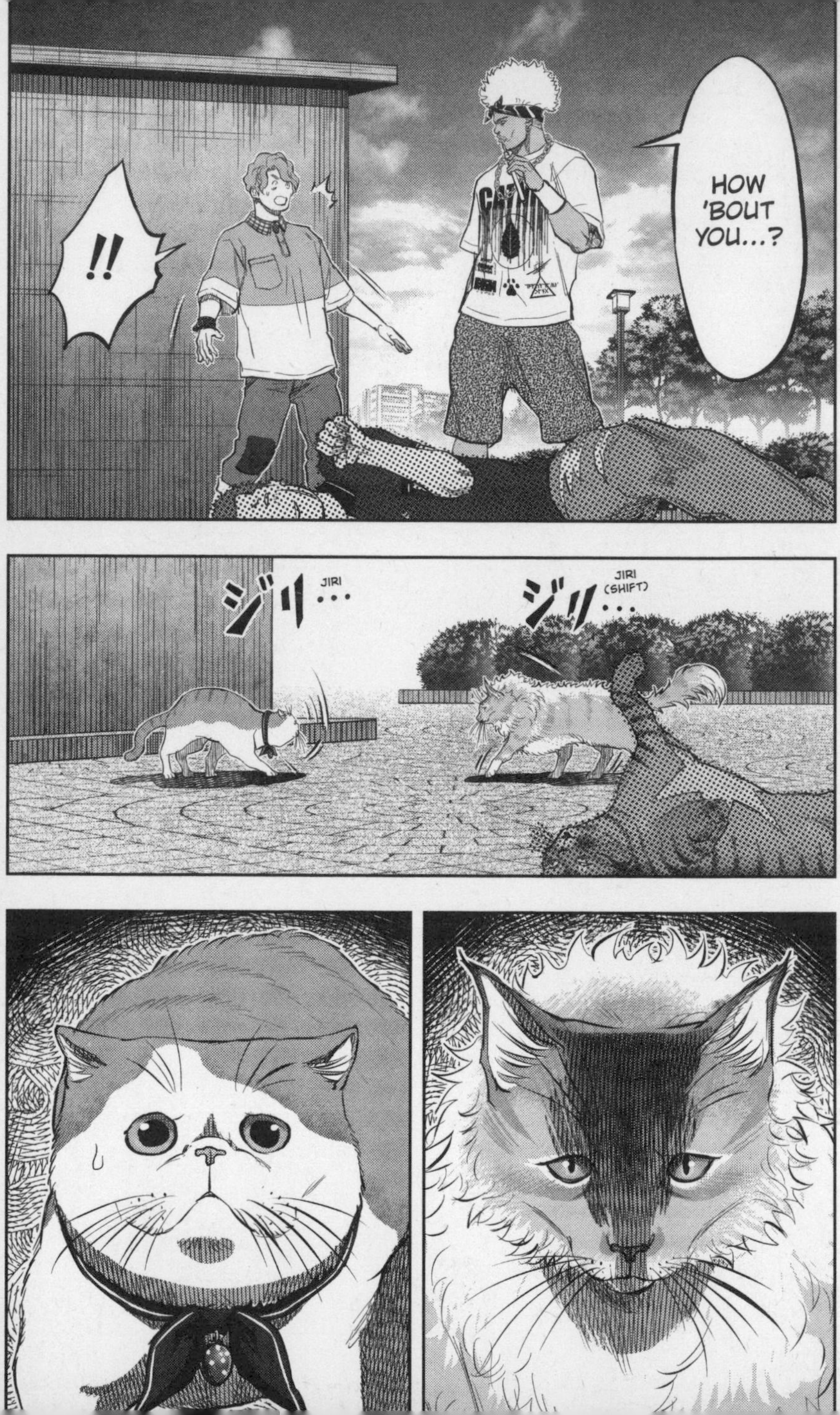
HOW 'BOUT YOU...?
!!
ジリ...
JIRI (SHIFT)
ジリ...
JIRI

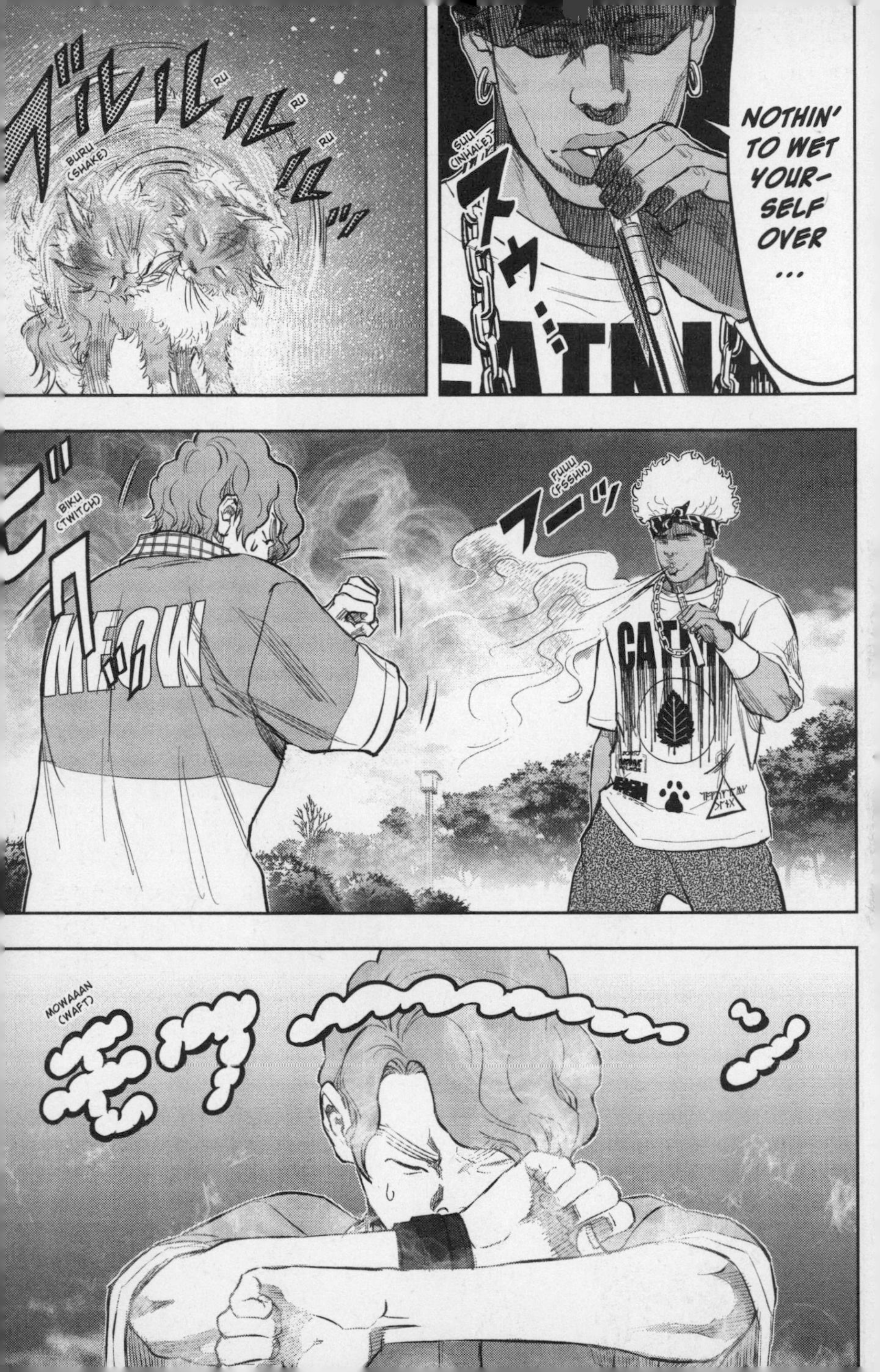
NOTHIN' TO WET YOURSELF OVER ...
SUU (INHALE)
BURU (SHAKE)
RU
RU
RU
FUUU (FSSHH)
BIKU (TWITCH)
MOWAAAN (WAFT)

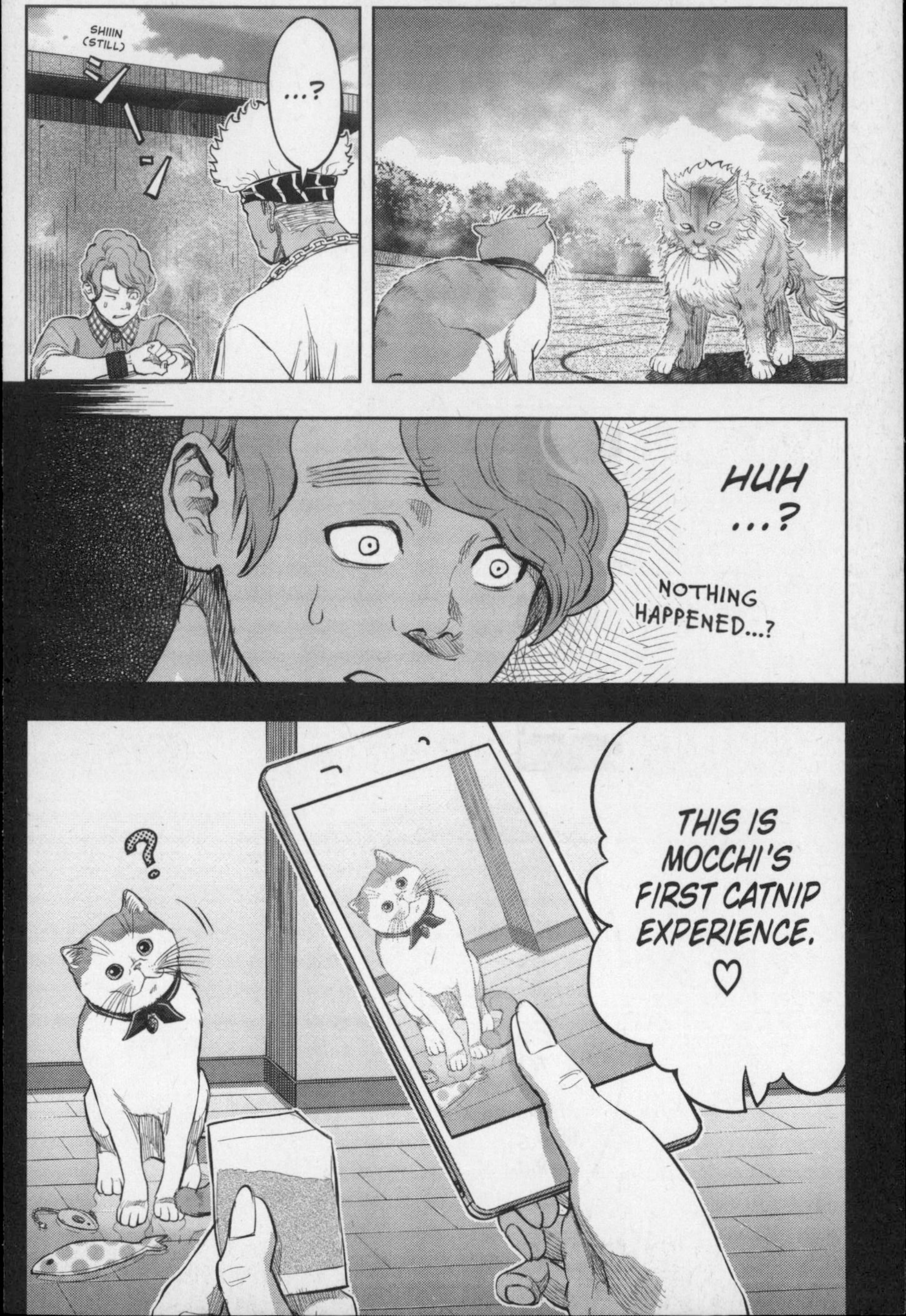
...?
SHIIIN (STILL)
HUH ...?
NOTHING HAPPENED...?
THIS IS MOCCHI'S FIRST CATNIP EXPERIENCE. ♡

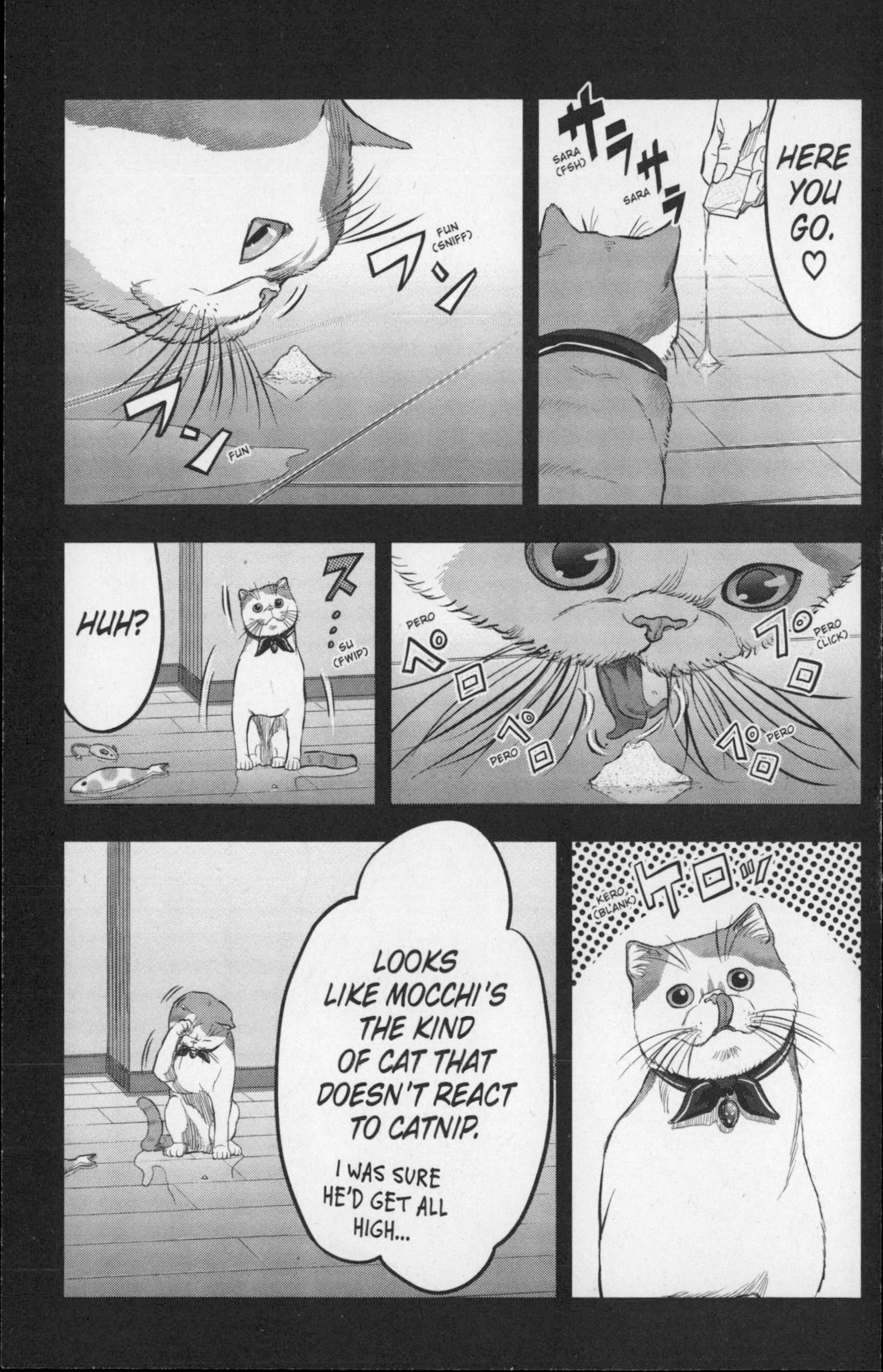
サラサラ
SARA (FSH)
SARA
HERE YOU GO. ♡
フン
FUN (SNIFF)
FUN
ペロ
PERO
ペロ
PERO (LICK)
ペロ
PERO
ペロ
PERO
ス
SU (FWIP)
HUH?
ケロ
KERO (BLANK)
LOOKS LIKE MOCCHI'S THE KIND OF CAT THAT DOESN'T REACT TO CATNIP.
I WAS SURE HE'D GET ALL HIGH...

IT'S THAT THING SATOMI-SAN GAVE ME BEFORE...

CHOI (SHWIP)
CHOI
チョイ

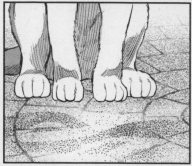

I KNEW IT...HIS SMOKE IS...

ﾍﾟﾛ PERO (LICKS)
ﾍﾟﾛ PERO
ﾍﾟﾛ PERO

96

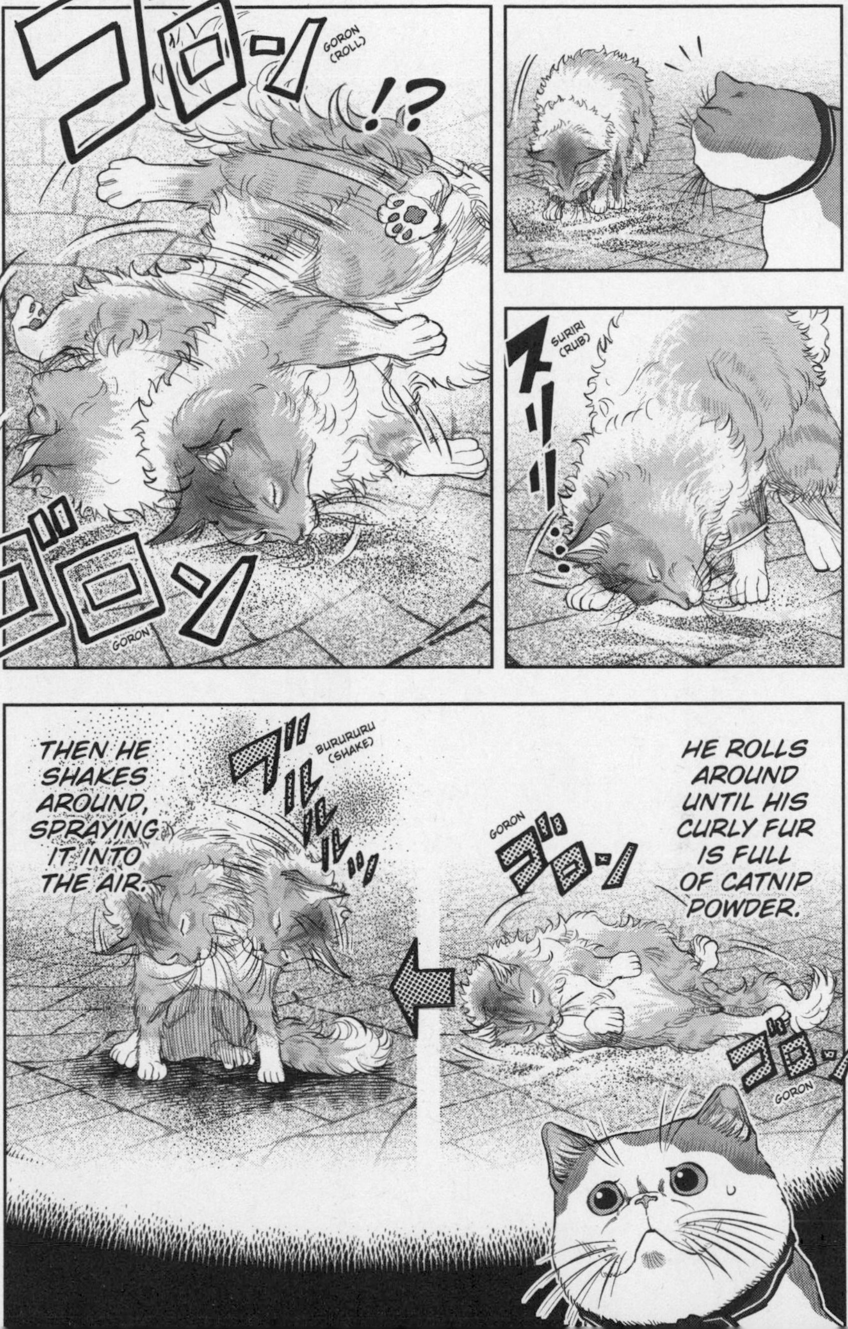
SURIRI (RUB)
GORON (ROLL)
!?
GORON
HE ROLLS AROUND UNTIL HIS CURLY FUR IS FULL OF CATNIP POWDER.
GORON
GORON
BURURURU (SHAKE)
THEN HE SHAKES AROUND, SPRAYING IT INTO THE AIR.

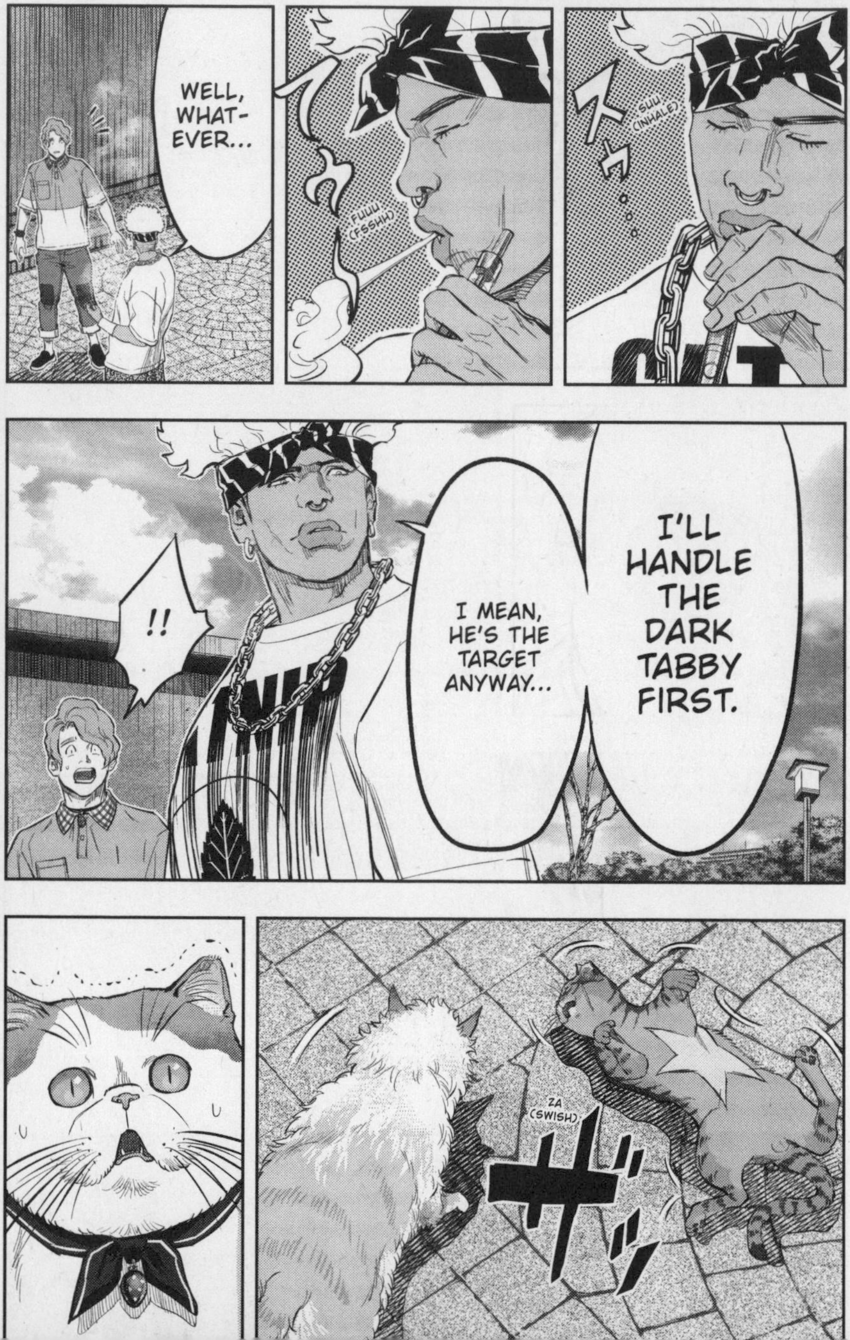
SUU (INHALE)
FUUU (FSSHH)
WELL, WHAT-EVER...
I'LL HANDLE THE DARK TABBY FIRST.
I MEAN, HE'S THE TARGET ANYWAY...
!!
ZA (SWISH)

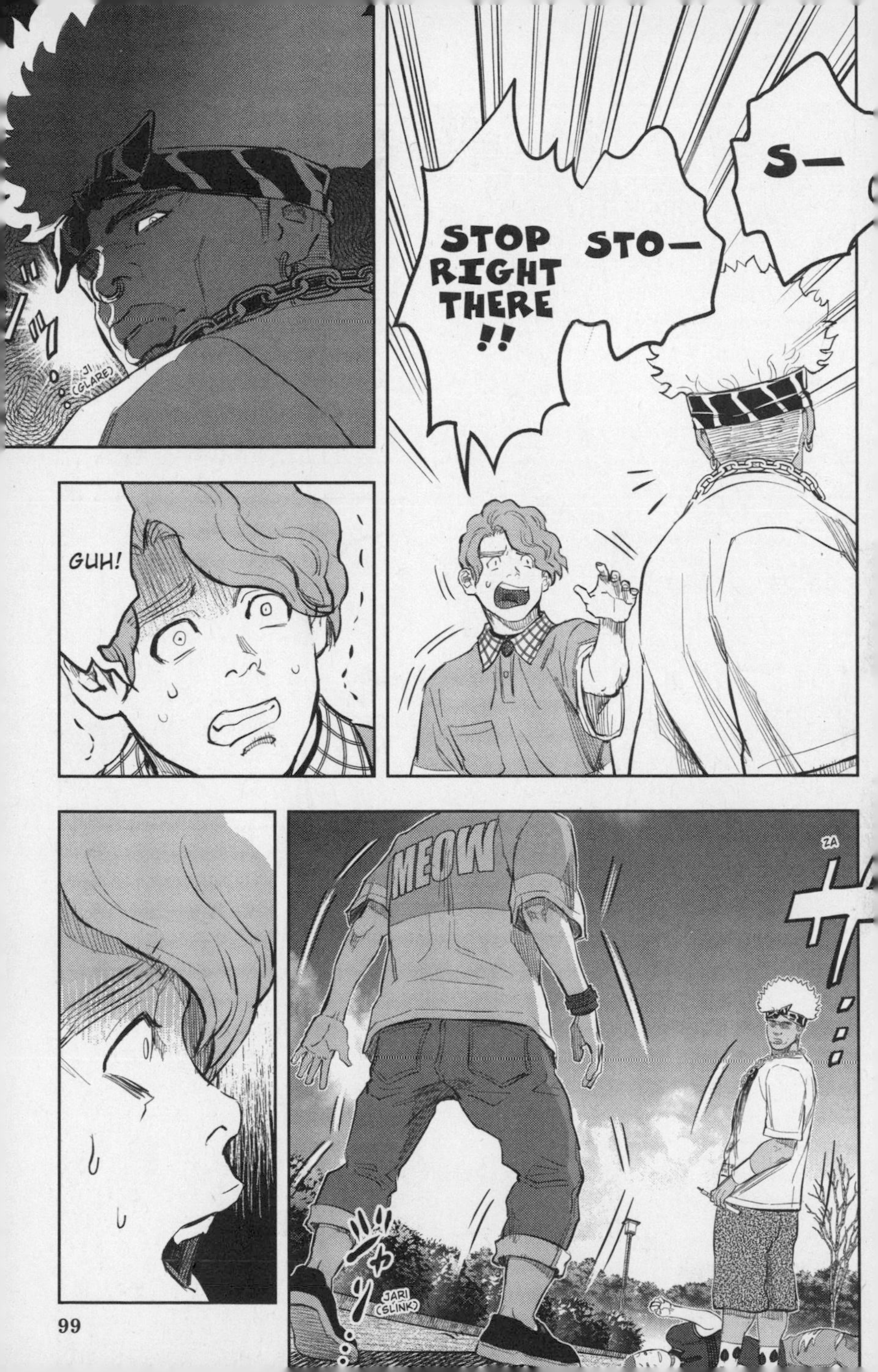
S—
STO—
STOP RIGHT THERE!!
JI (GLARE)
GUH!
ZA
JARI (SLINK)

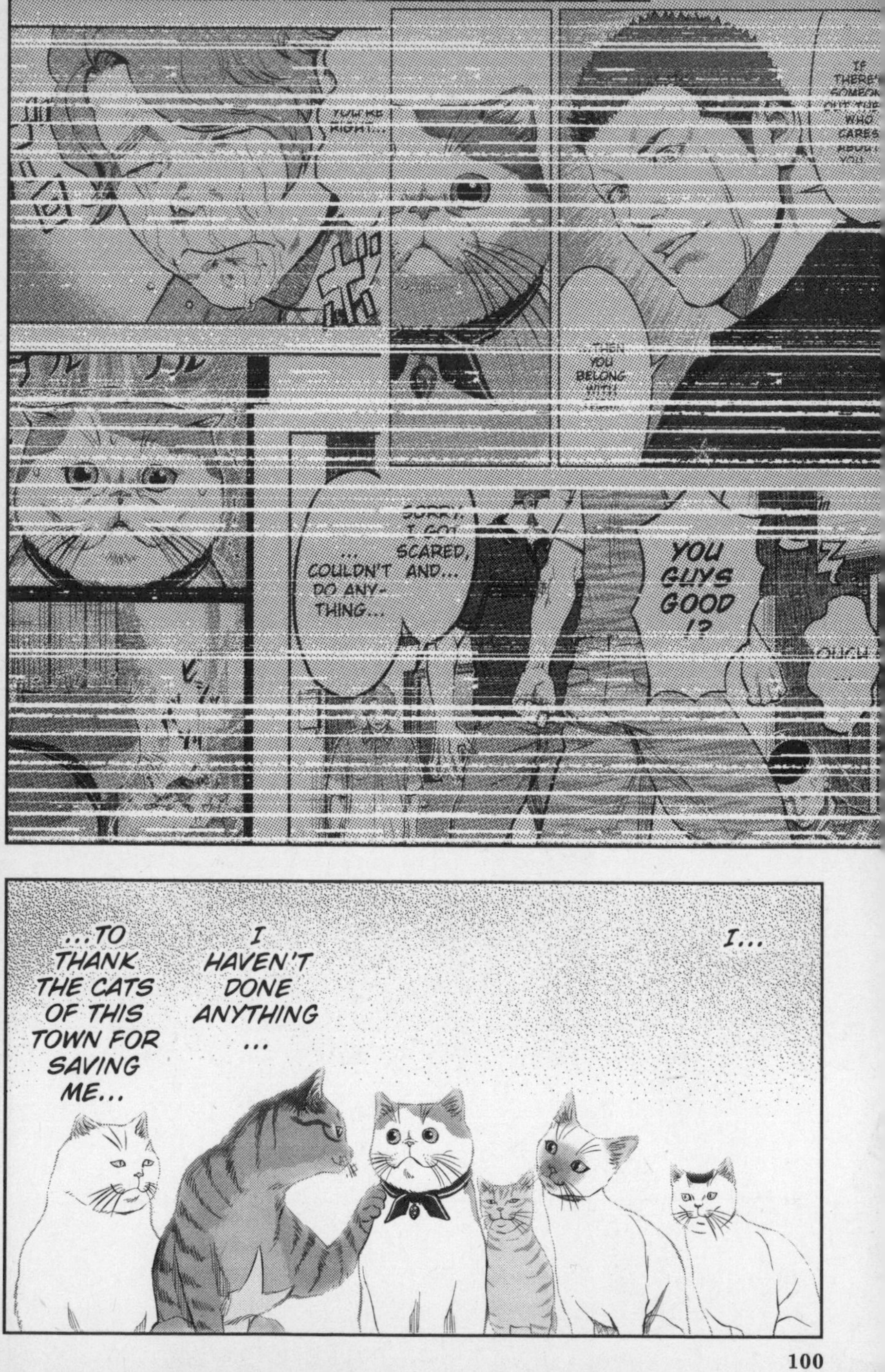
IF THERE'S ... WHO CARES ... YOU
...THEN YOU BELONG WITH
YOU'RE RIGHT...
YOU GUYS GOOD!?
OUCH...
SCARED, AND...
...COULDN'T DO ANY-THING...
I...
I HAVEN'T DONE ANYTHING...
...TO THANK THE CATS OF THIS TOWN FOR SAVING ME...

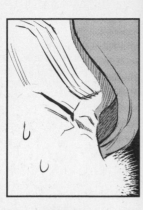

IF I TURN TAIL NOW...

...HOW AM I EVER GONNA REPAY THEM?

...THAT SMOKE...

IT'S REALLY JUST CATNIP POWDER, ISN'T IT?

ZUI
(FWIP)

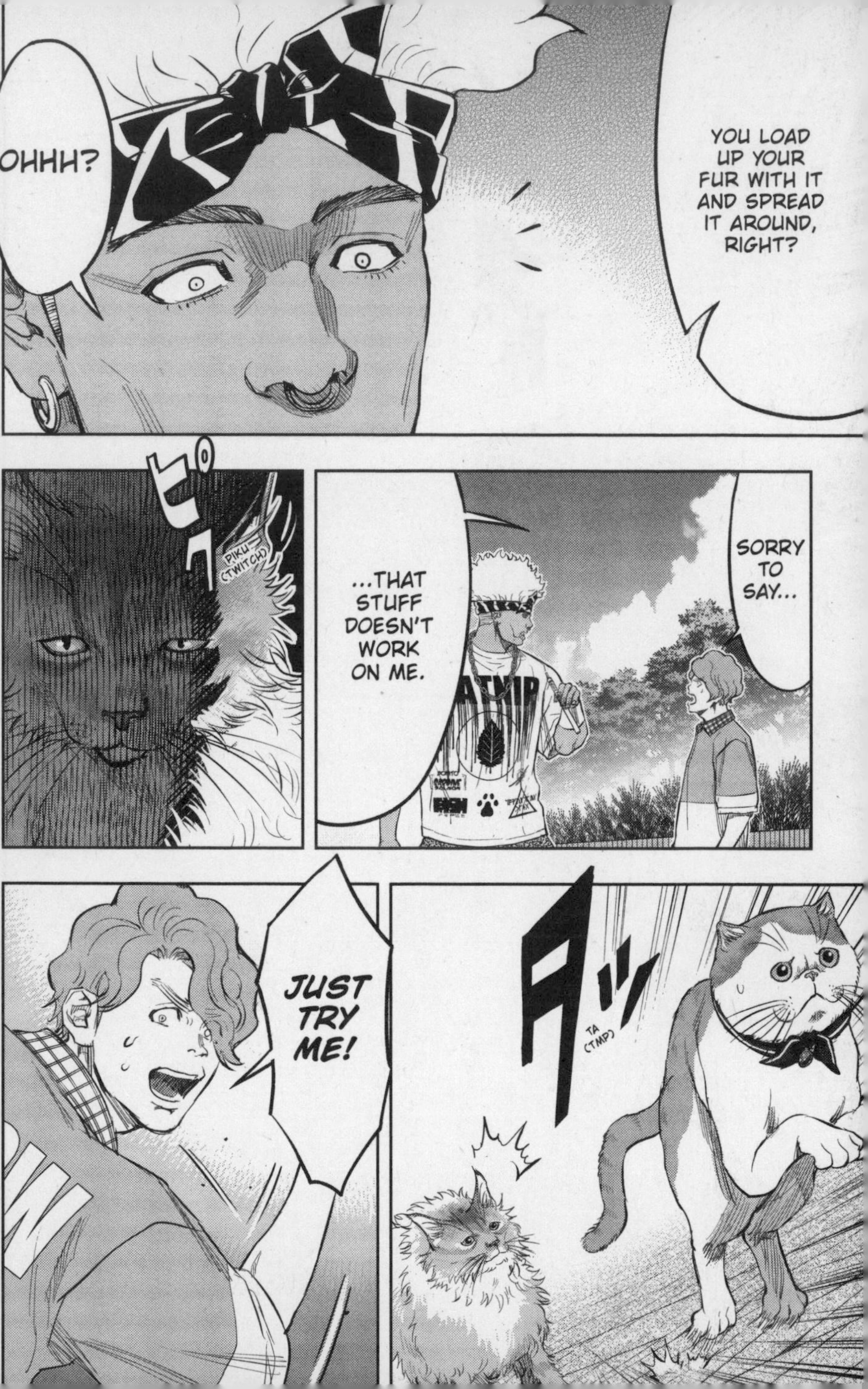
YOU LOAD UP YOUR FUR WITH IT AND SPREAD IT AROUND, RIGHT?
OHHH?
SORRY TO SAY...
...THAT STUFF DOESN'T WORK ON ME.
PIKU (TWITCH)
TA (TMP)
JUST TRY ME!

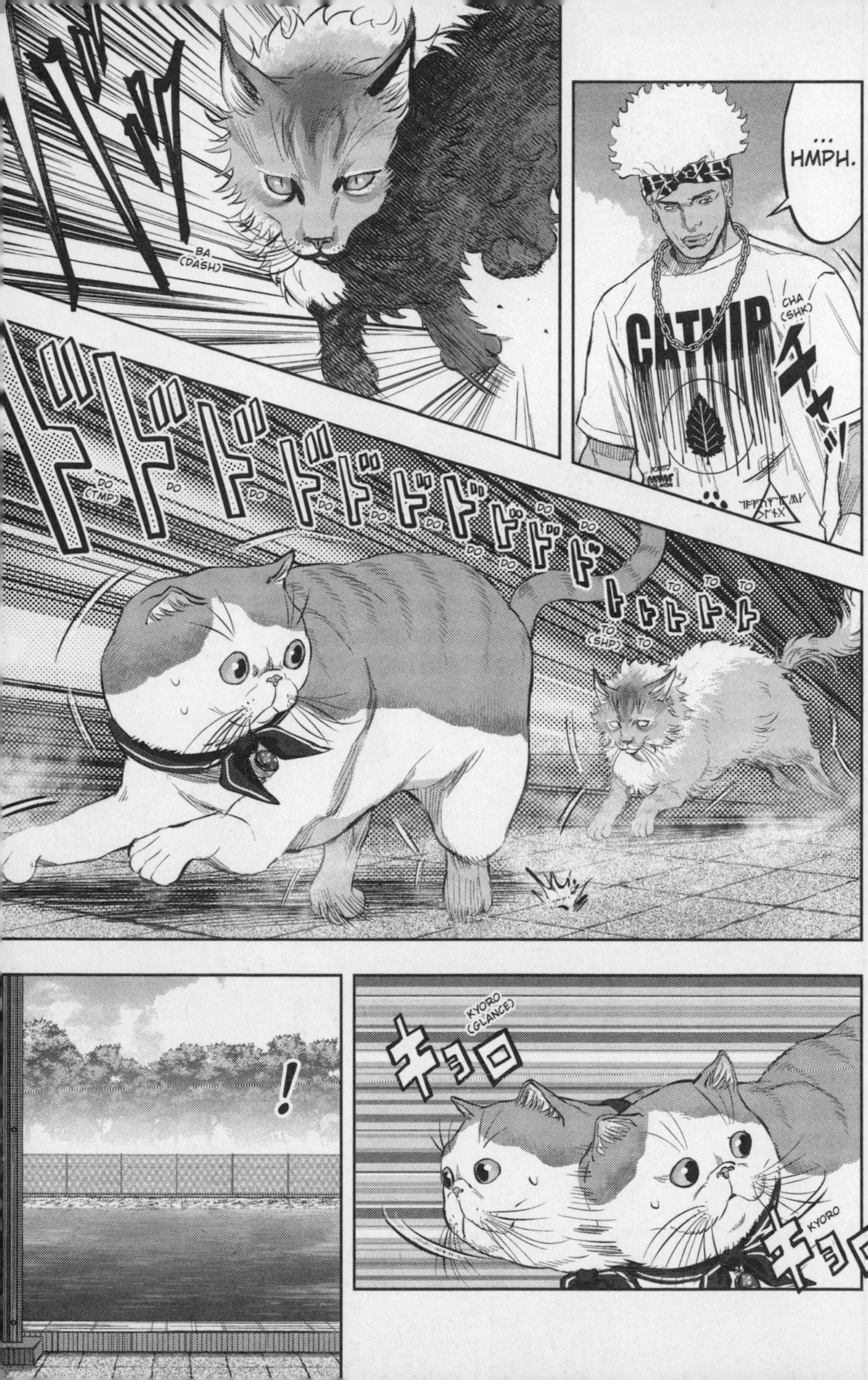
... HMPH.
CATNIP
CHA (SHK)
BA (DASH)
DO (TMP)
DO
DO
DO
DO
DO
DO
DO
DO
DO
TO (SHP)
TO
TO
TO
TO
KYORO (GLANCE)
KYORO
!

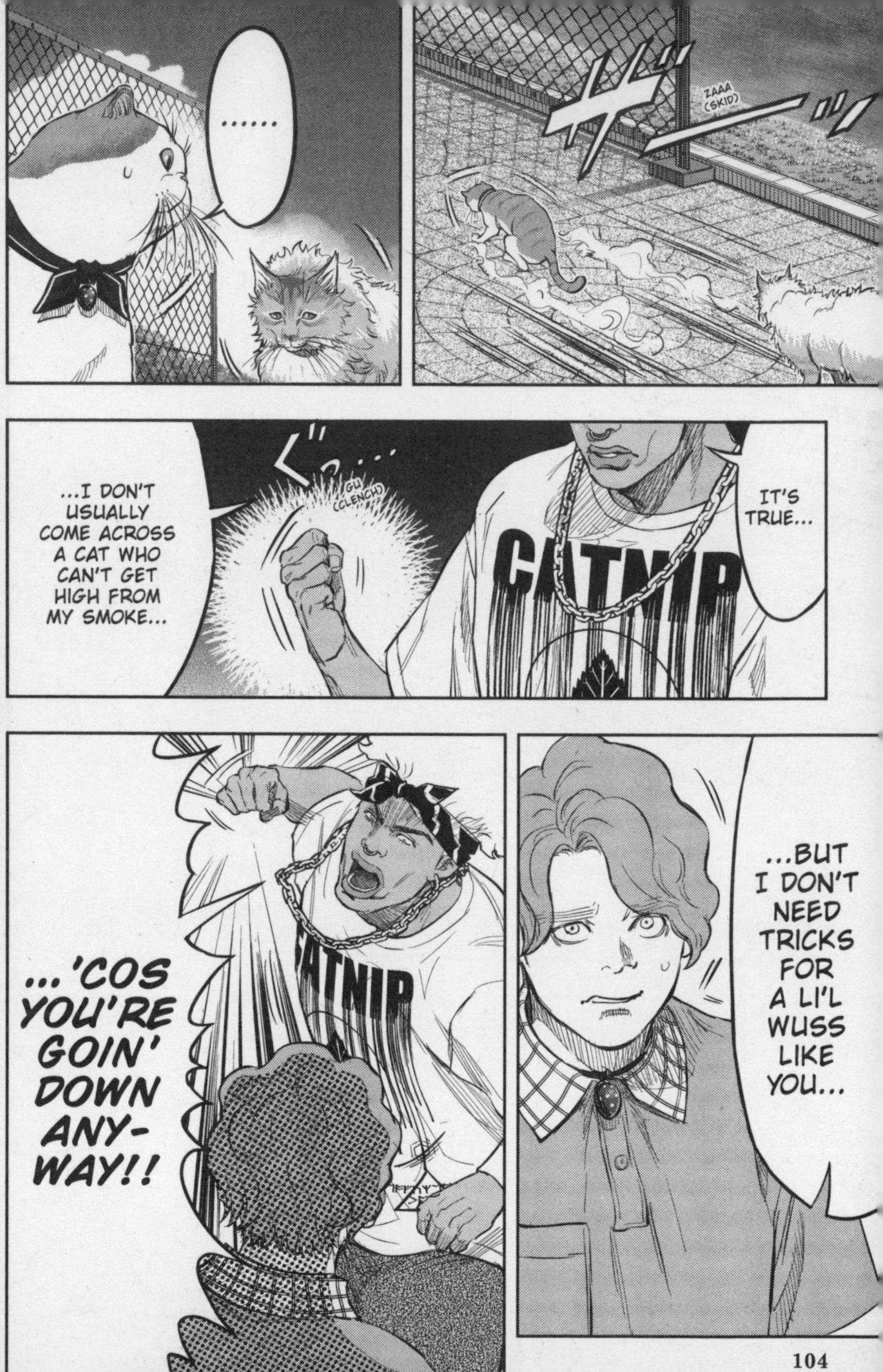
ZAAA (SKID)
......
IT'S TRUE...
GU (CLENCH)
...I DON'T USUALLY COME ACROSS A CAT WHO CAN'T GET HIGH FROM MY SMOKE...
...BUT I DON'T NEED TRICKS FOR A LI'L WUSS LIKE YOU...
...'COS YOU'RE GOIN' DOWN ANY-WAY!!

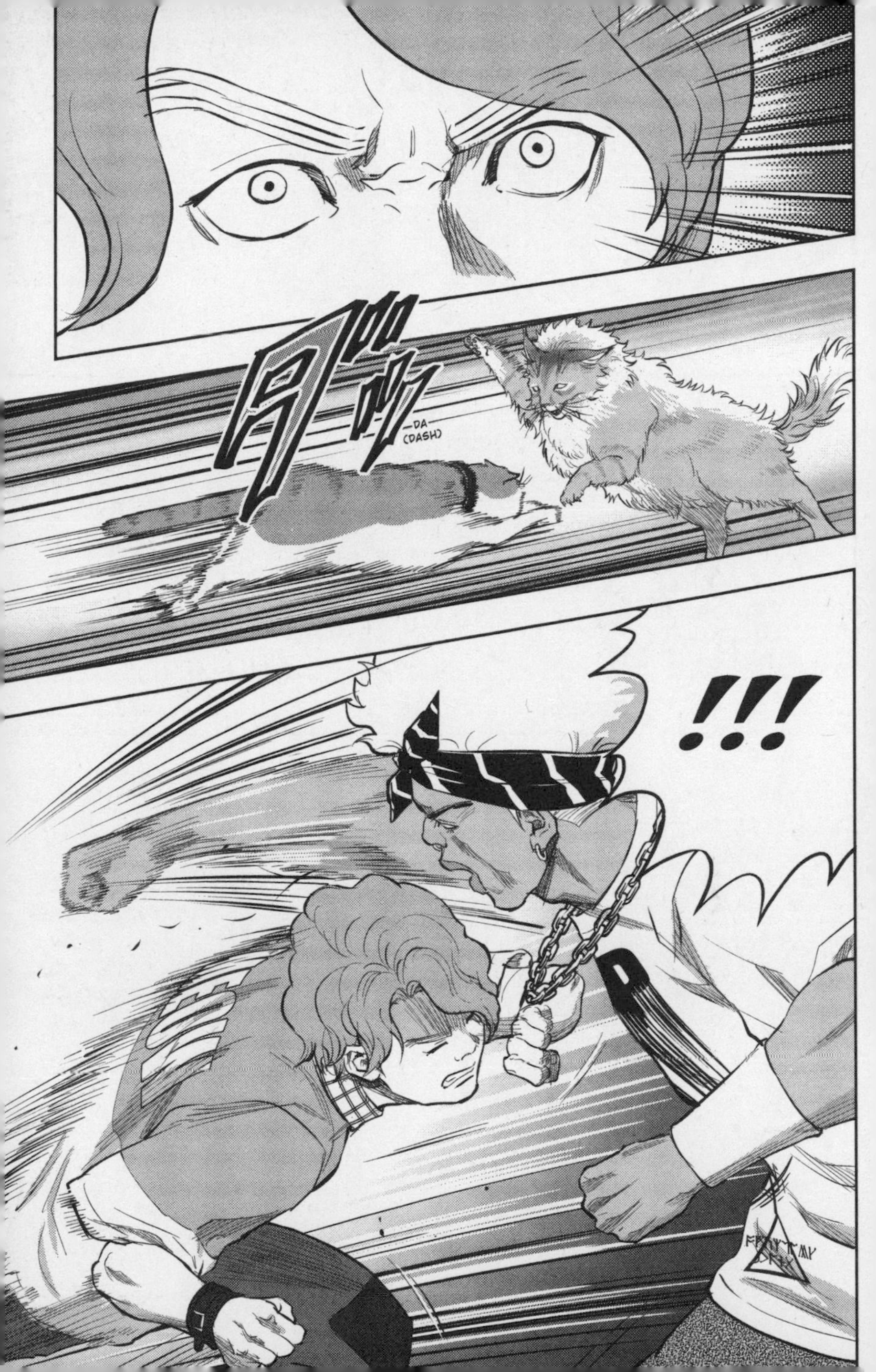
DA
(DASH)
!!!

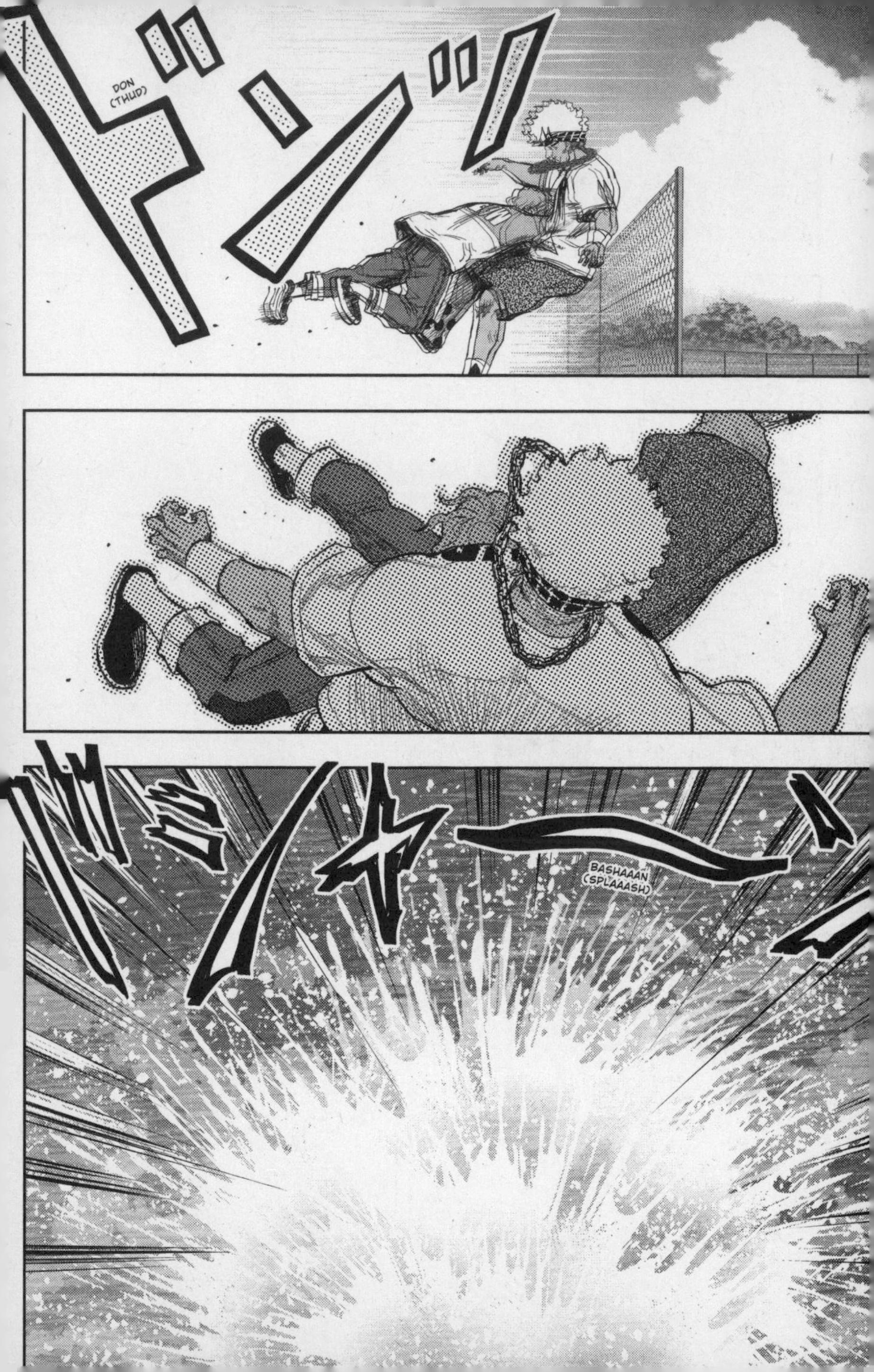
DON (THUD)
BASHAAAN (SPLAAASH)

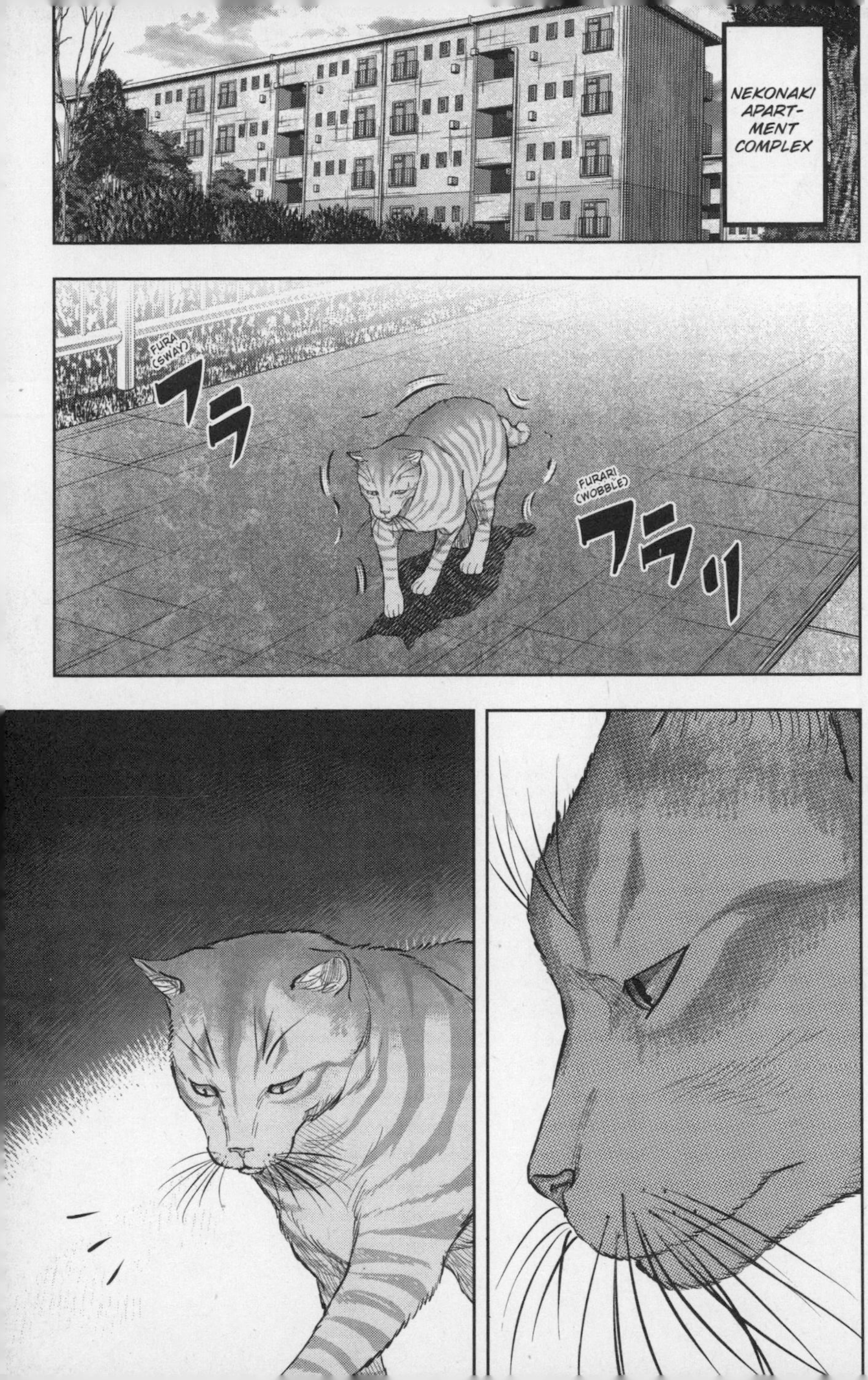
NEKONAKI APART-MENT COMPLEX
FURA (SWAY)
フラ
FURARI (WOBBLE)
フラリ

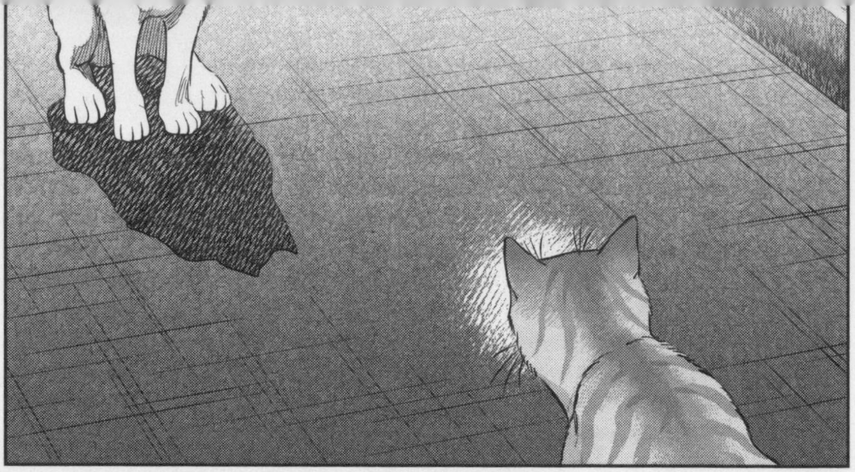

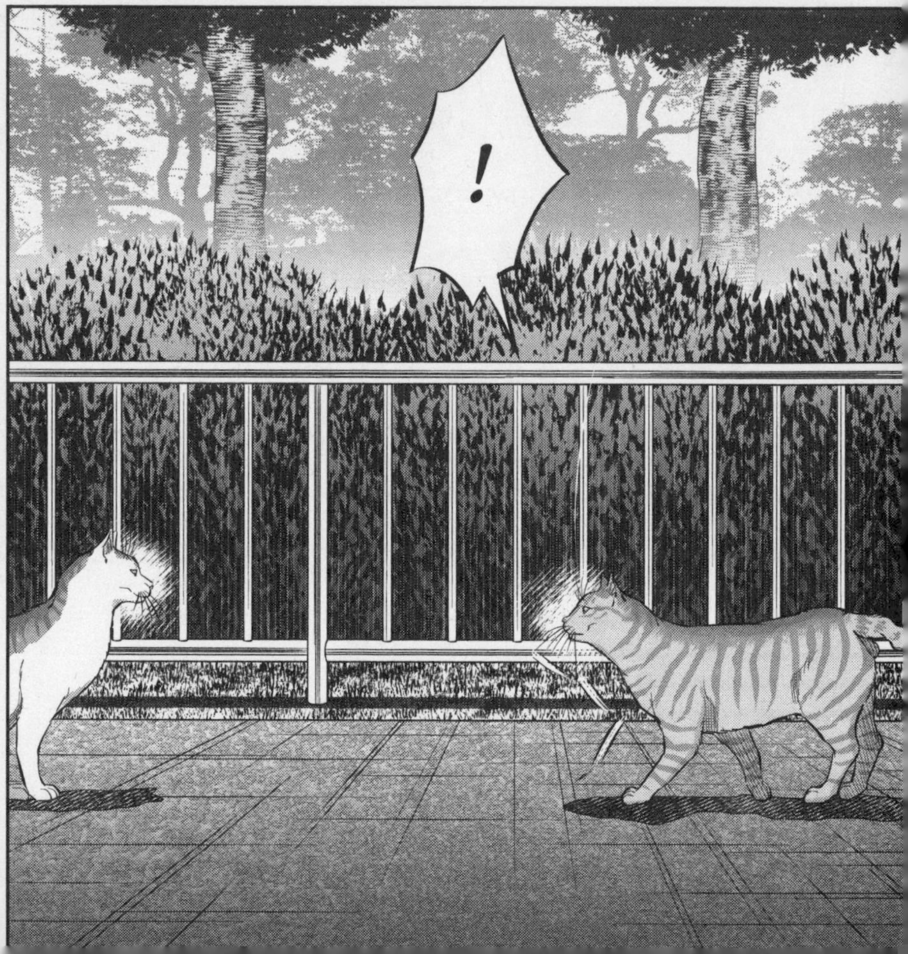
!

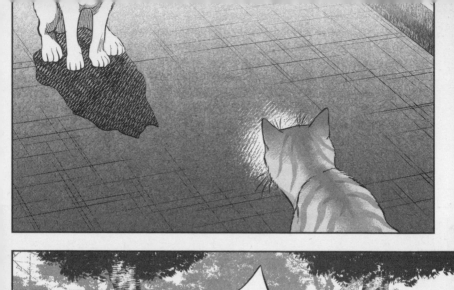

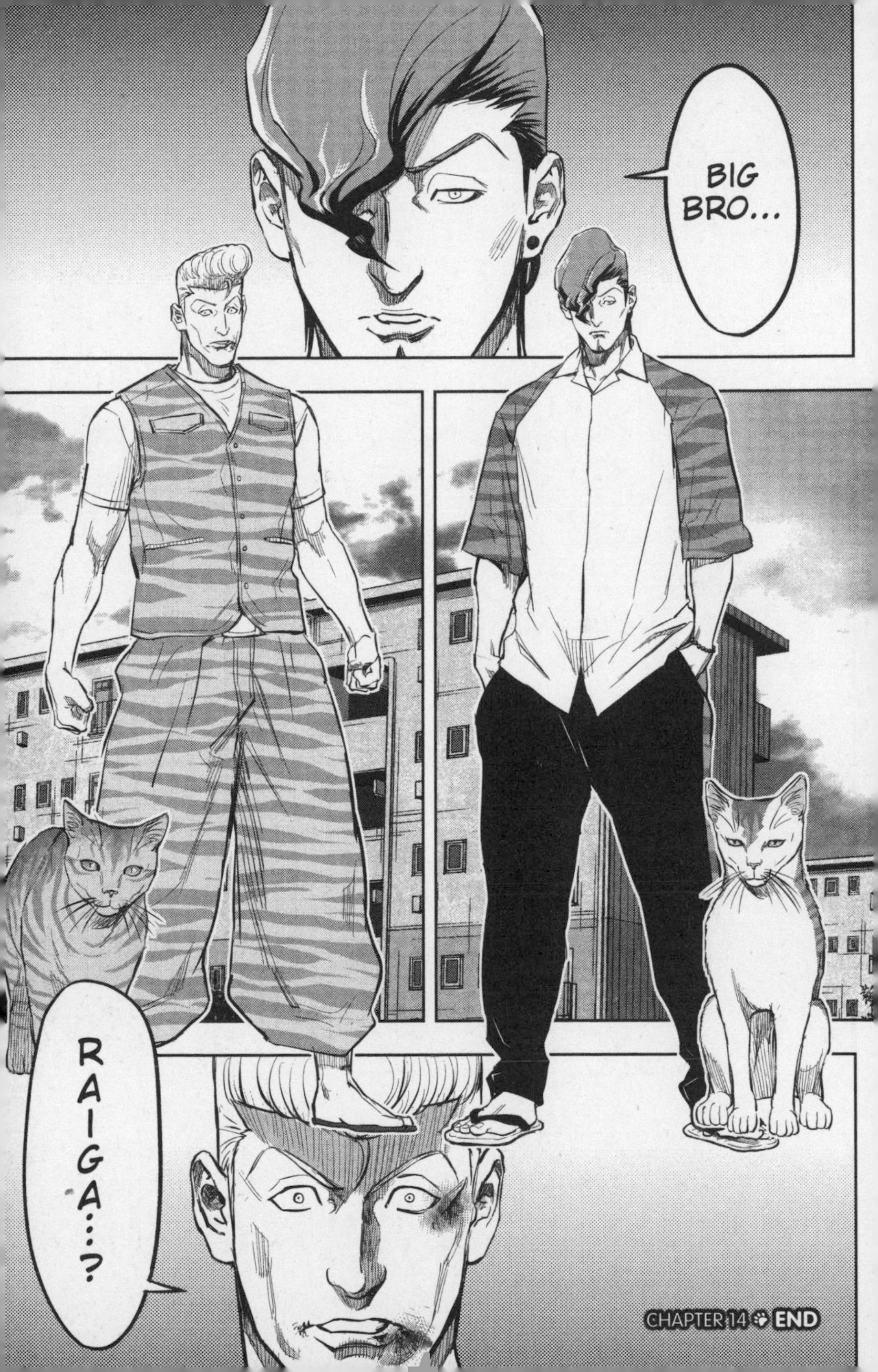
BIG BRO...
RAIGA...?
CHAPTER 14 END

NYANKEES

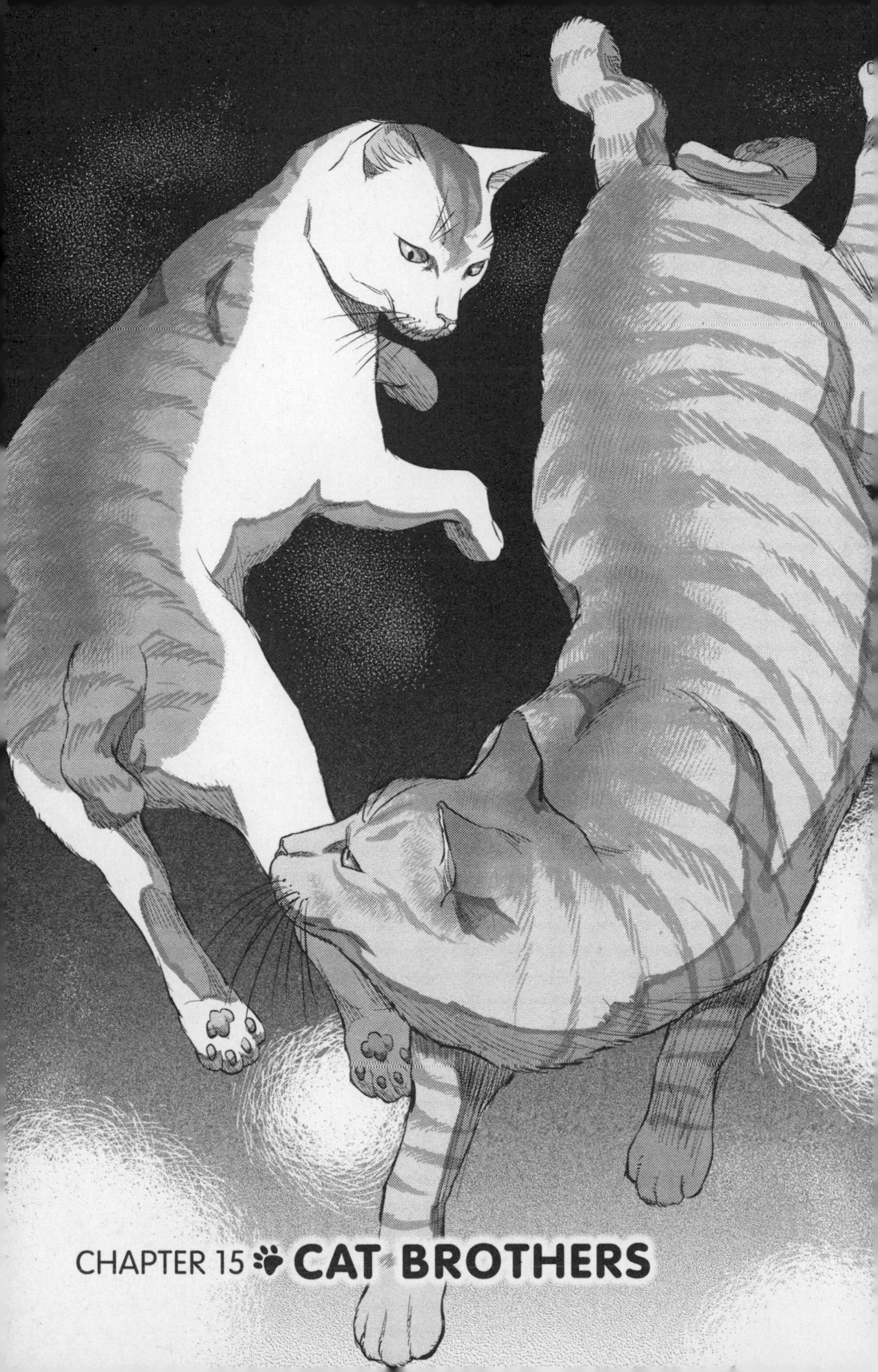

CHAPTER 15 CAT BROTHERS

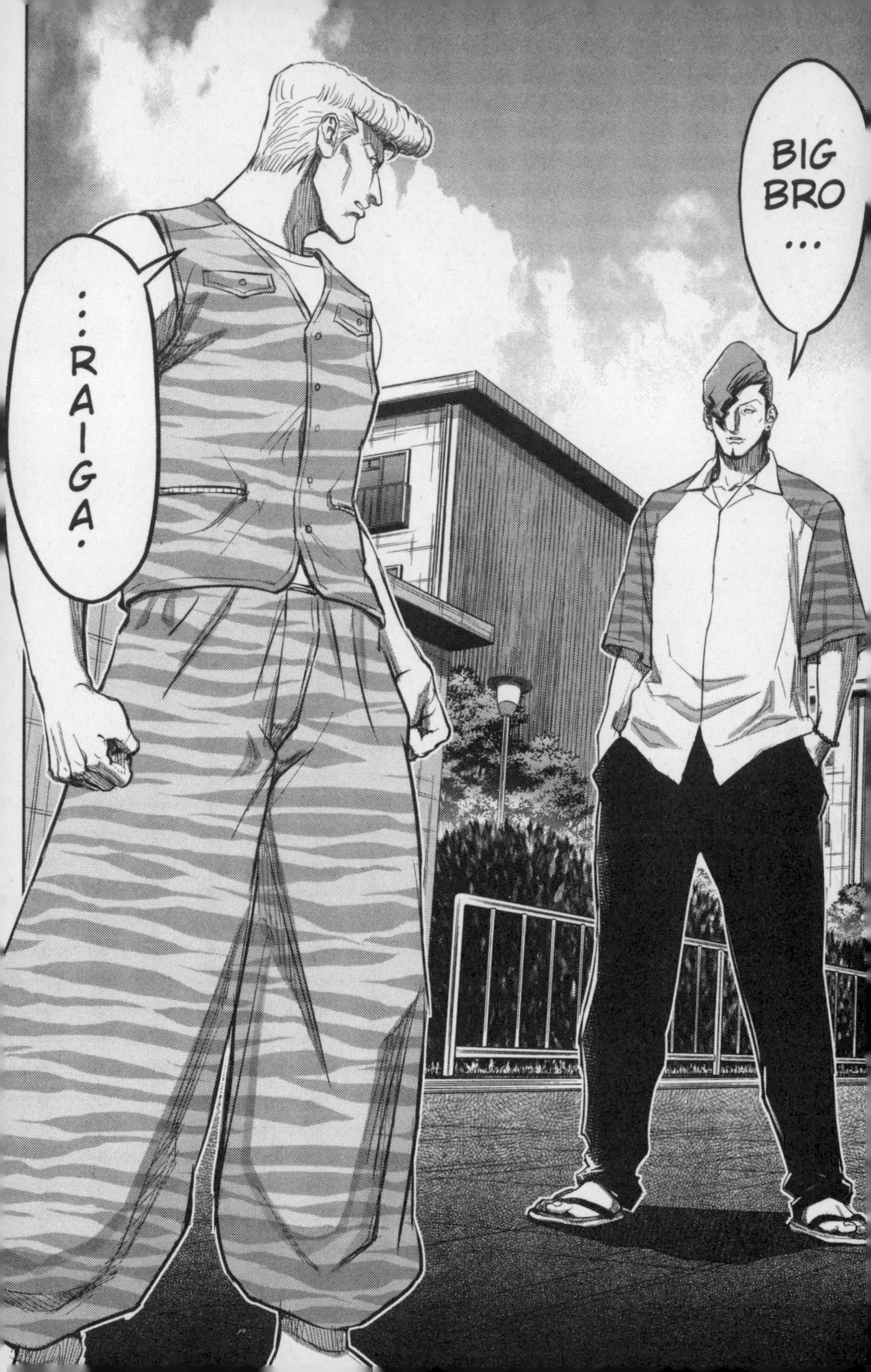
BIG BRO ...
...RAIGA.

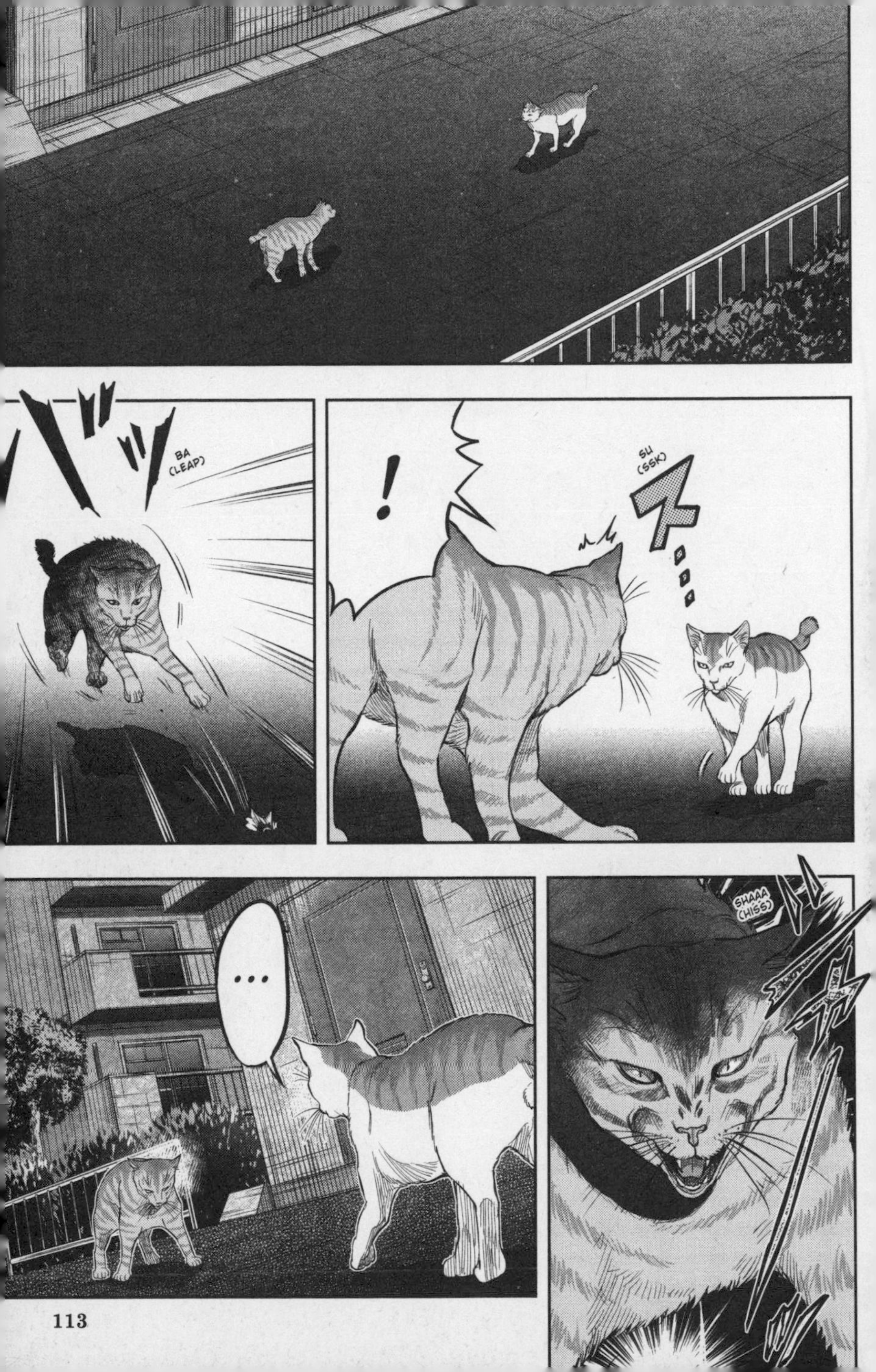

!
ス…
SU (SSK)
バッ
BA (LEAP)
SHAAA (HISS)
...

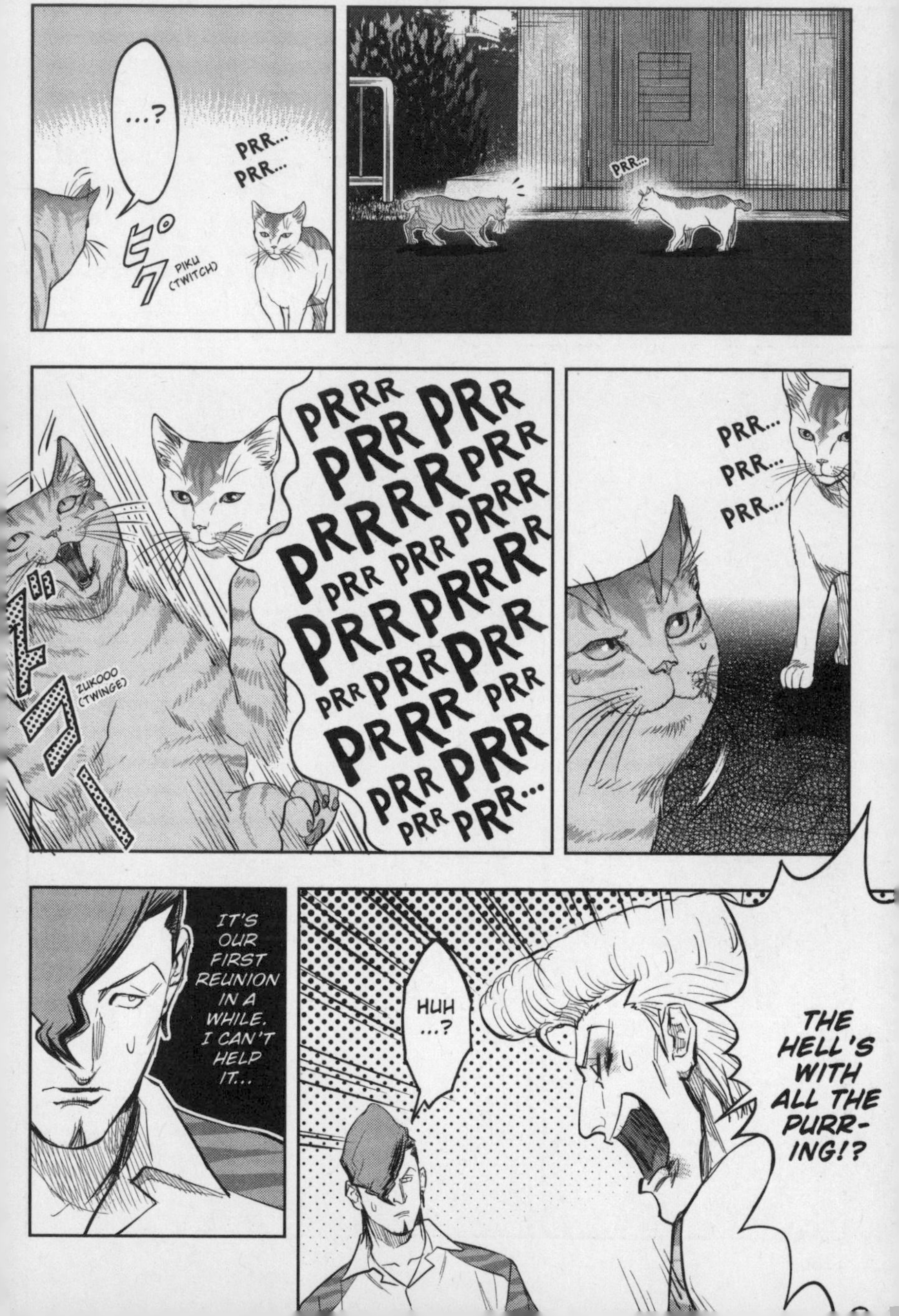
PRR...
...?
PRR...
PRR...
ピク
PIKU (TWITCH)
PRR...
PRR...
PRR...
PRRR PRR PRR PRRR PRRR PRRR PRRRR PRRR PRR PRR PRRR PRRR PRRR PRR PRRR PRR PRRR PRR PRR PRR PRR PRR...
ZUKOOO (TWINGE)
HUH ...?
THE HELL'S WITH ALL THE PURR-ING!?
IT'S OUR FIRST REUNION IN A WHILE. I CAN'T HELP IT...

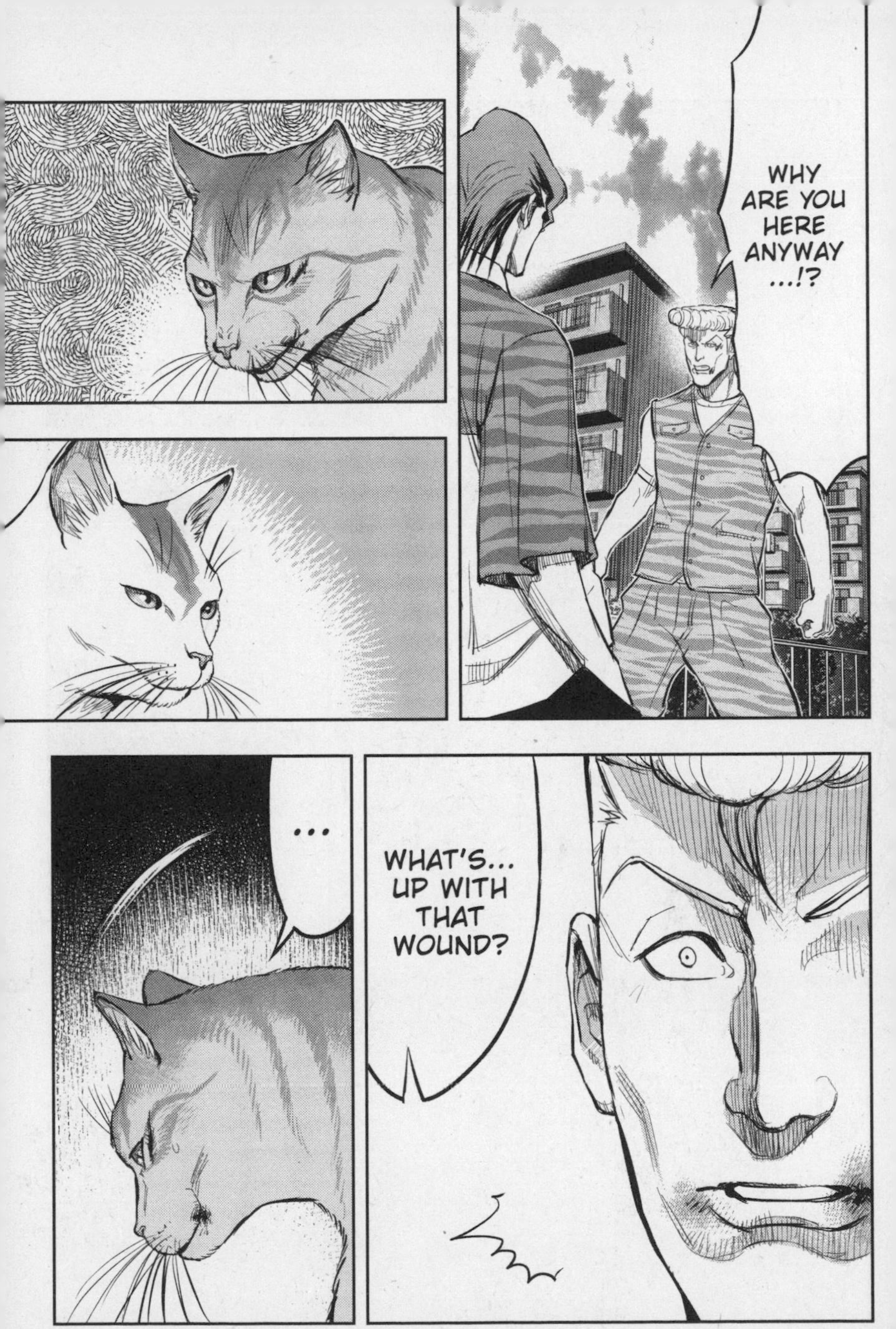
WHY ARE YOU HERE ANYWAY ...!?
WHAT'S... UP WITH THAT WOUND?
...

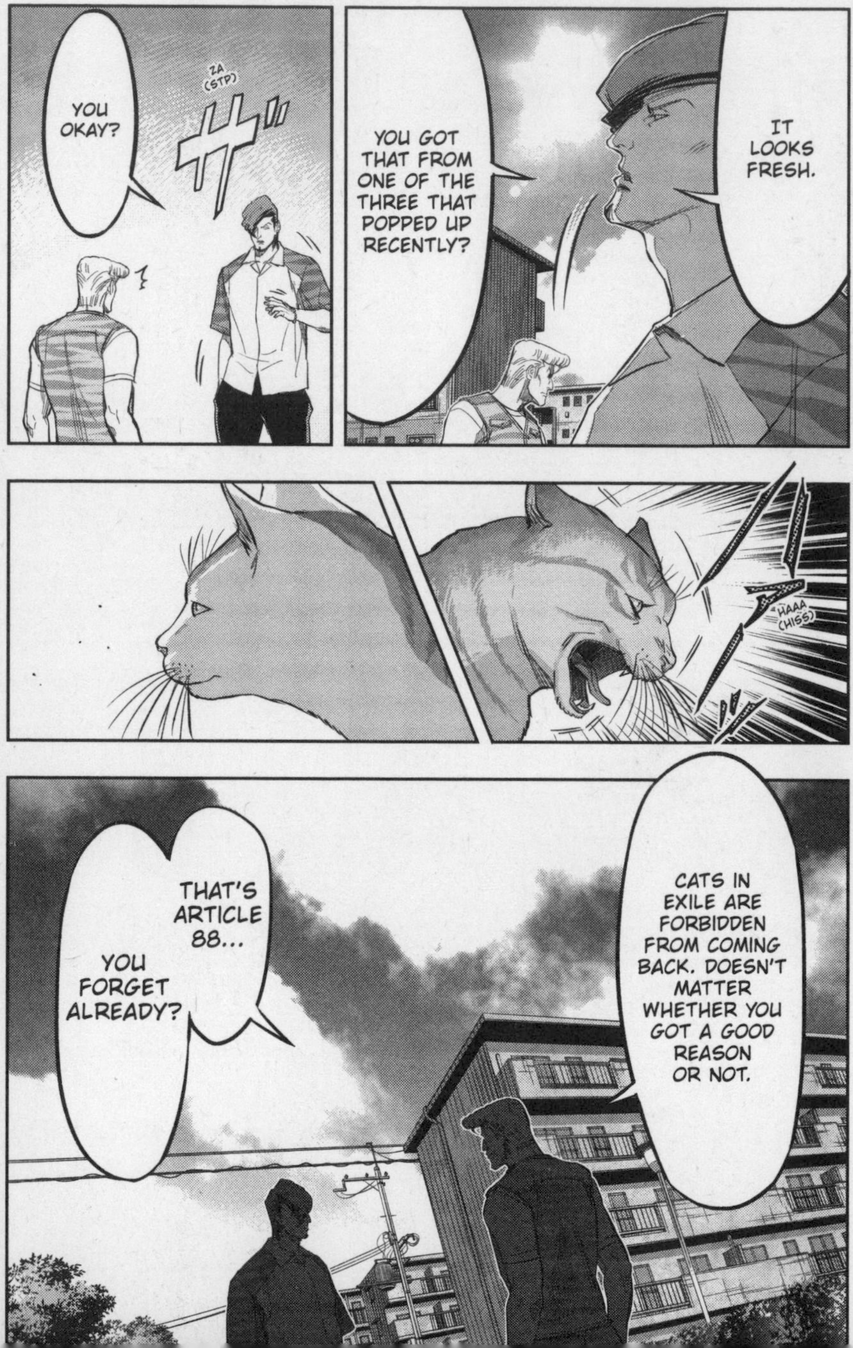
IT LOOKS FRESH.
YOU GOT THAT FROM ONE OF THE THREE THAT POPPED UP RECENTLY?
ZA (STP)
YOU OKAY?
HAAA (HISS)
CATS IN EXILE ARE FORBIDDEN FROM COMING BACK. DOESN'T MATTER WHETHER YOU GOT A GOOD REASON OR NOT.
THAT'S ARTICLE 88...
YOU FORGET ALREADY?

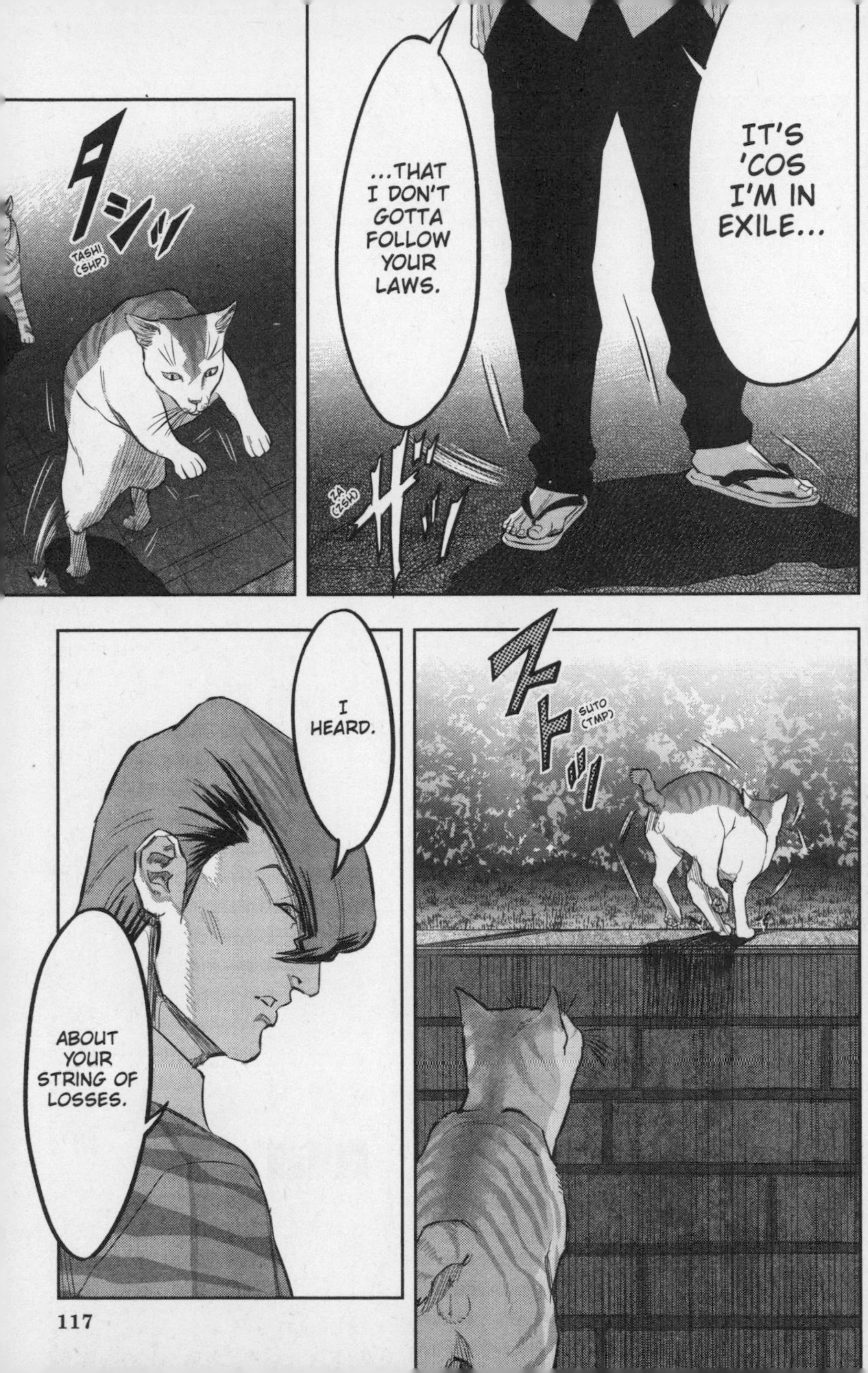
IT'S 'COS I'M IN EXILE...
...THAT I DON'T GOTTA FOLLOW YOUR LAWS.
ZA (ZSH)
TASHI (SHP)
SUTO (TMP)
I HEARD.
ABOUT YOUR STRING OF LOSSES.

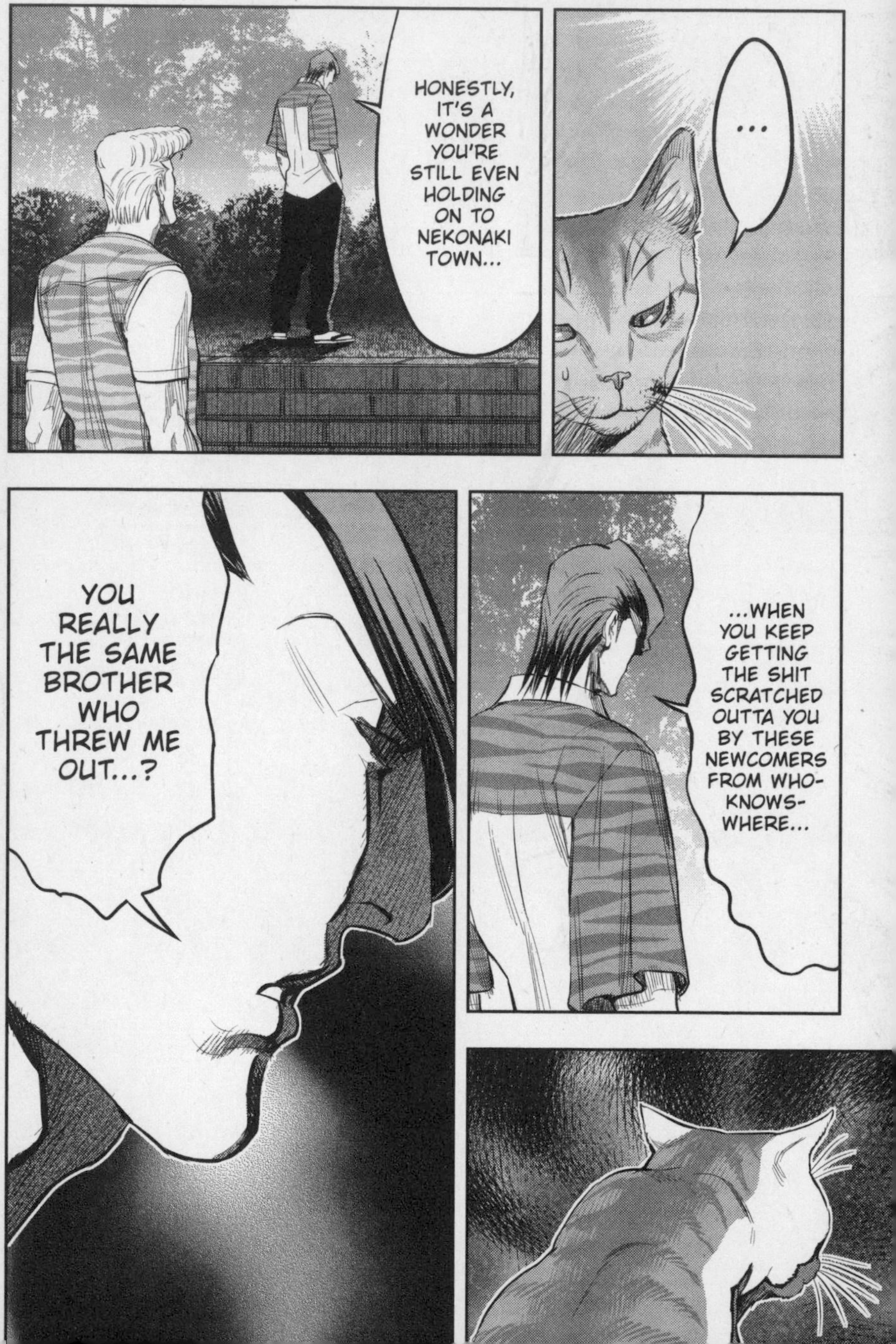
...
HONESTLY, IT'S A WONDER YOU'RE STILL EVEN HOLDING ON TO NEKONAKI TOWN...
...WHEN YOU KEEP GETTING THE SHIT SCRATCHED OUTTA YOU BY THESE NEWCOMERS FROM WHO-KNOWS-WHERE...
YOU REALLY THE SAME BROTHER WHO THREW ME OUT...?

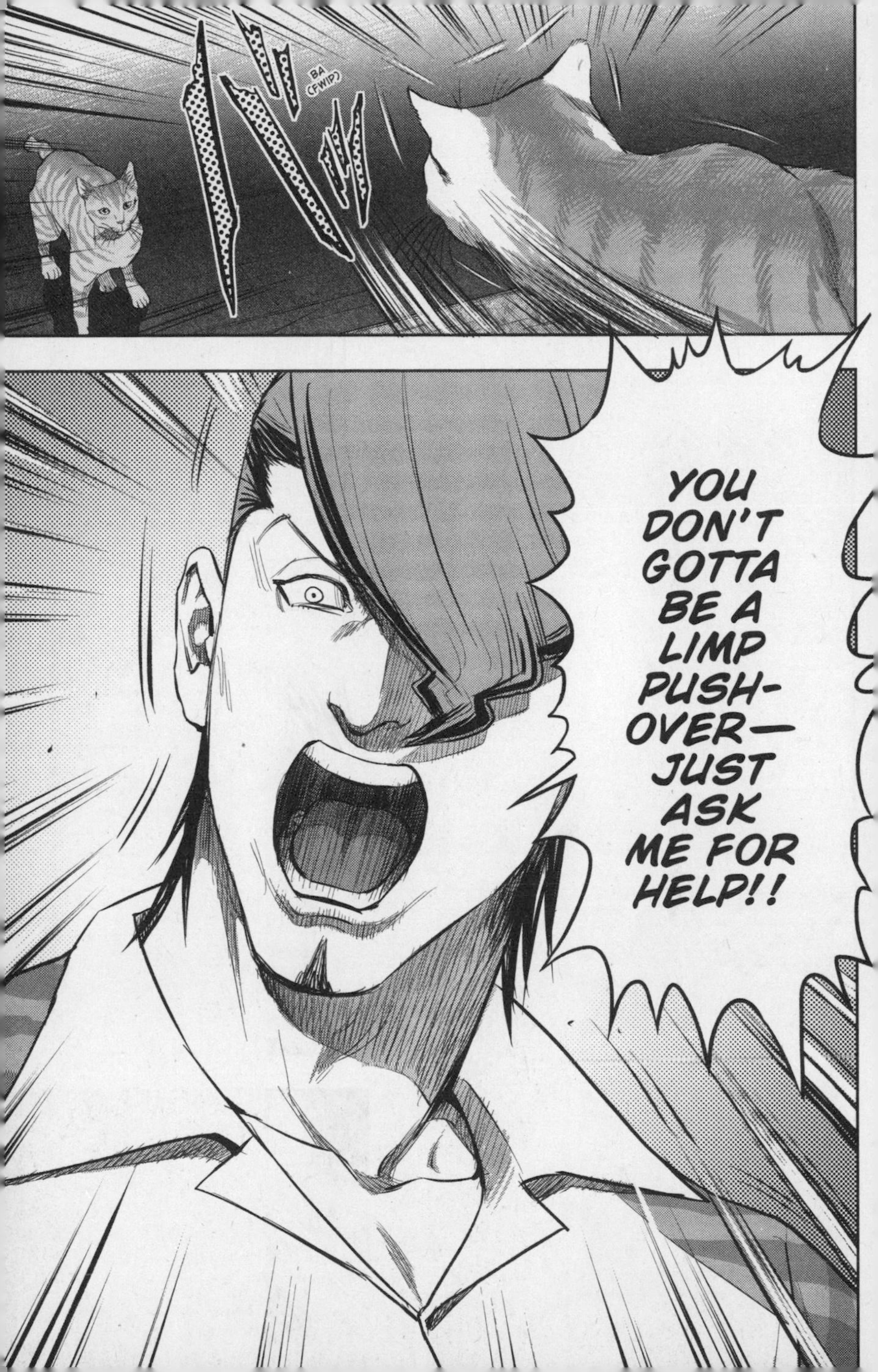
BA (FWIP)
YOU DON'T GOTTA BE A LIMP PUSH-OVER—JUST ASK ME FOR HELP!!

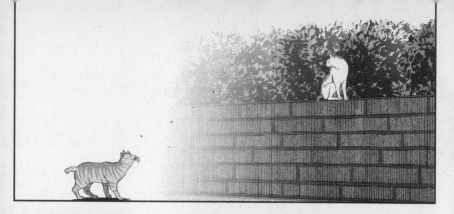

...I'VE SAID IT BEFORE.

TO (TMP)

YOUR CATRISMA IS ONE OF A KIND.

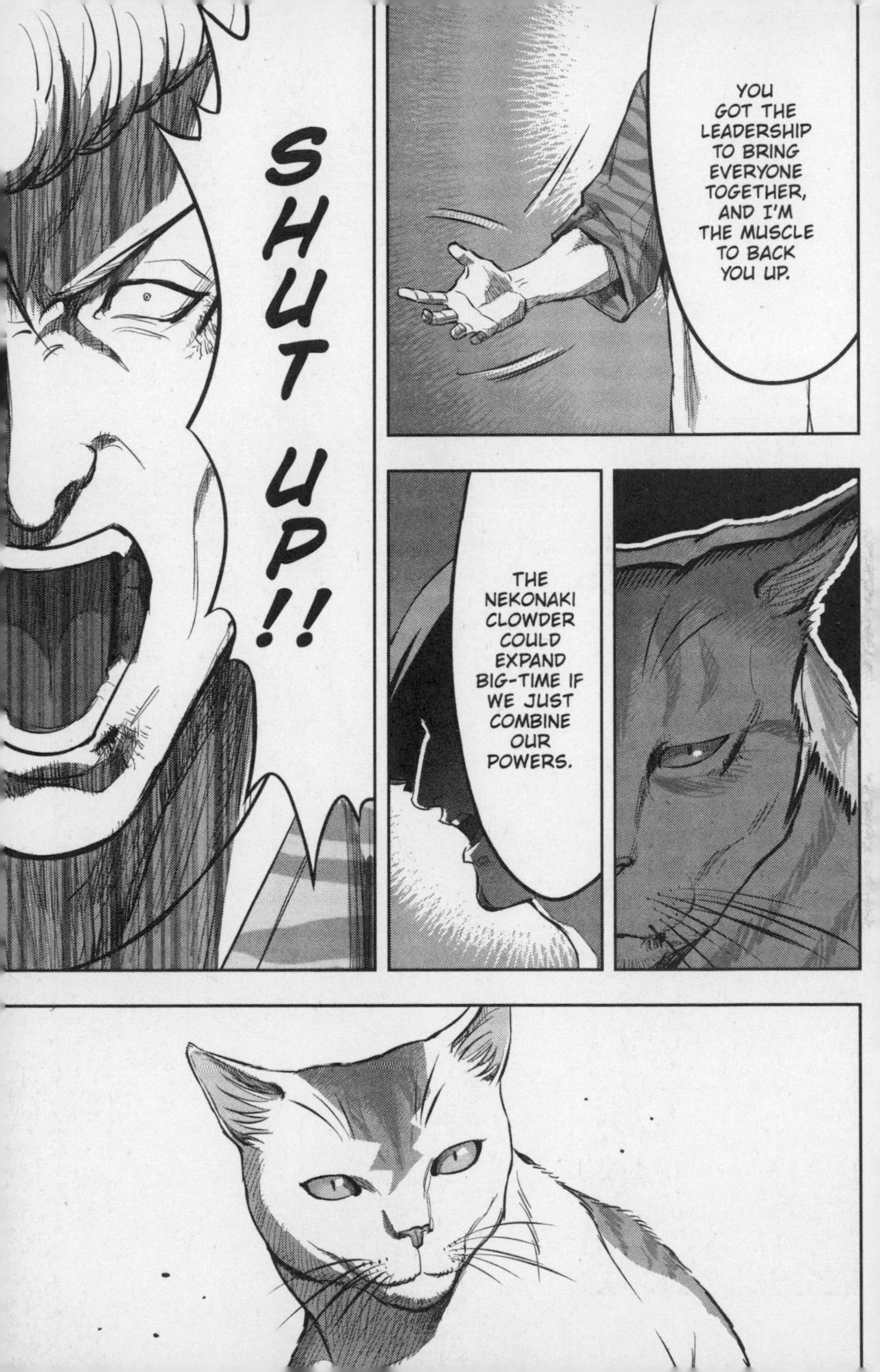
YOU GOT THE LEADERSHIP TO BRING EVERYONE TOGETHER, AND I'M THE MUSCLE TO BACK YOU UP.
THE NEKONAKI CLOWDER COULD EXPAND BIG-TIME IF WE JUST COMBINE OUR POWERS.
SHUT UP!!

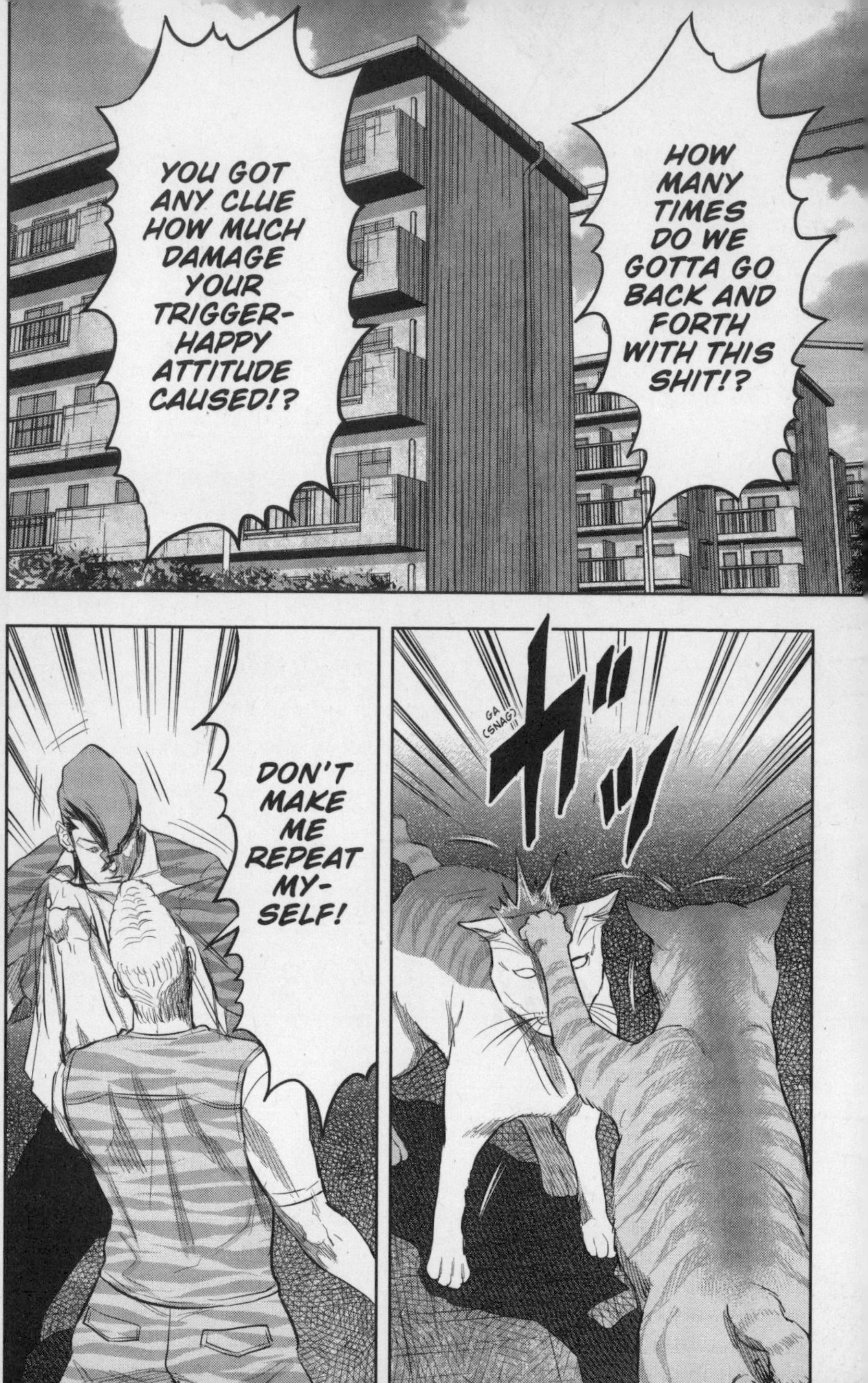
HOW MANY TIMES DO WE GOTTA GO BACK AND FORTH WITH THIS SHIT!?
YOU GOT ANY CLUE HOW MUCH DAMAGE YOUR TRIGGER-HAPPY ATTITUDE CAUSED!?
GA (SNAG)
DON'T MAKE ME REPEAT MY-SELF!

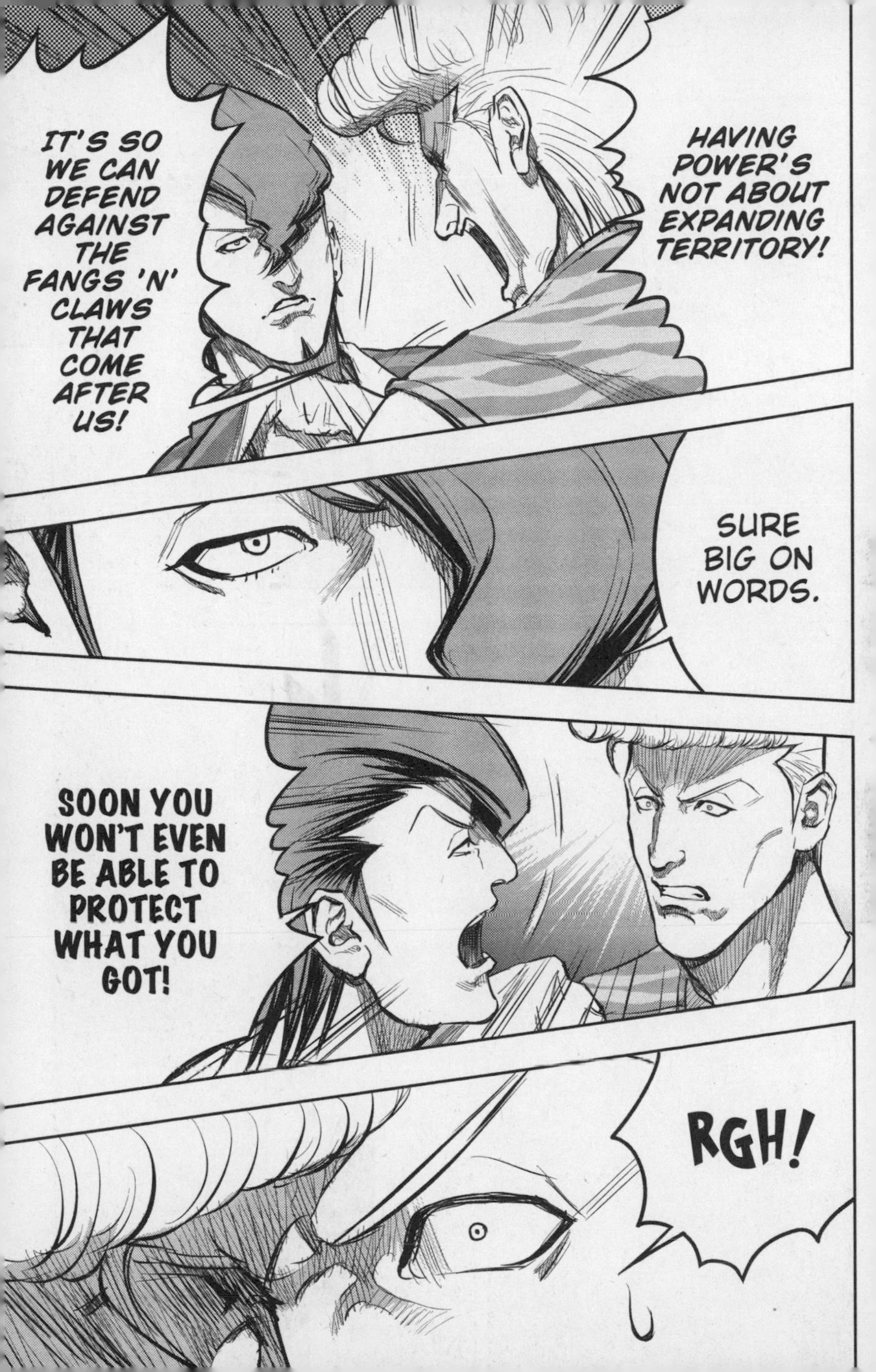
HAVING POWER'S NOT ABOUT EXPANDING TERRITORY!
IT'S SO WE CAN DEFEND AGAINST THE FANGS 'N' CLAWS THAT COME AFTER US!
SURE BIG ON WORDS.
SOON YOU WON'T EVEN BE ABLE TO PROTECT WHAT YOU GOT!
RGH!

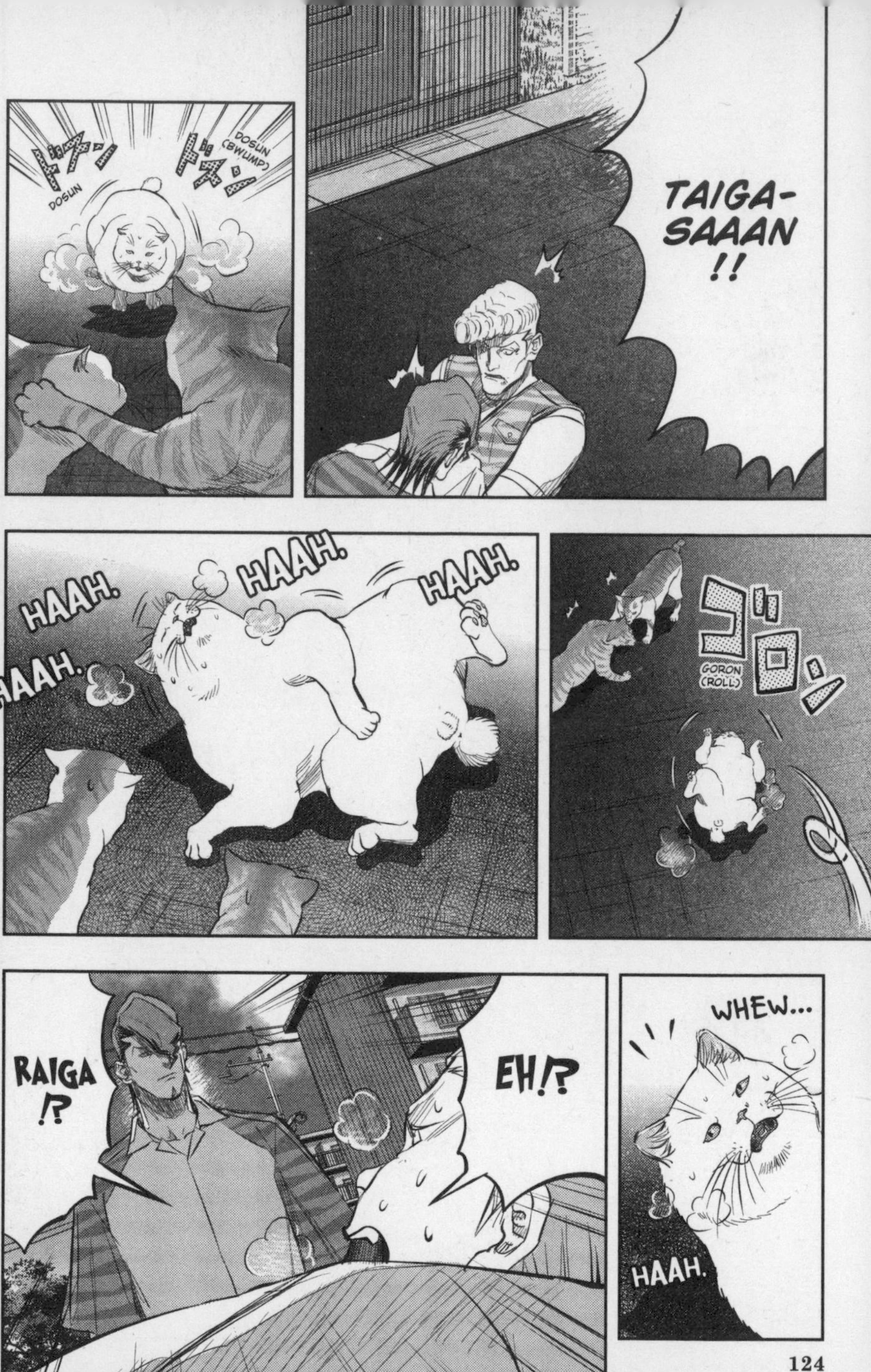
TAIGA-SAAAN!!
ドスン
DOSUN (BWUMP)
ドスン
DOSUN
ゴロン
GORON (ROLL)
HAAAH.
HAAAH.
HAAAH.
HAAAH.
WHEW...
HAAH.
EH!?
RAIGA!?

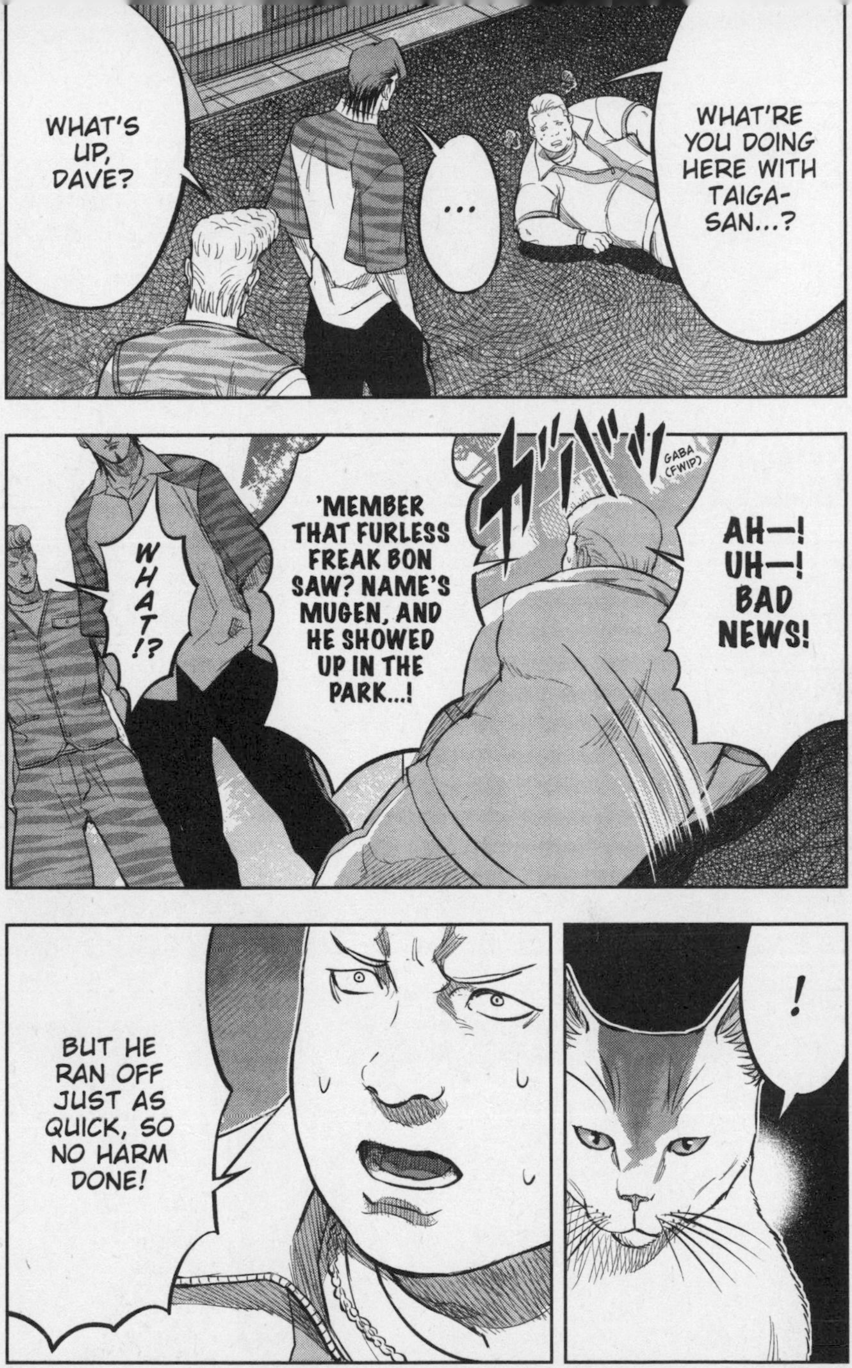
WHAT'RE YOU DOING HERE WITH TAIGA-SAN...?
...
WHAT'S UP, DAVE?
ガバッ
GABA (FWIP)
AH—! UH—! BAD NEWS!
'MEMBER THAT FURLESS FREAK BON SAW? NAME'S MUGEN, AND HE SHOWED UP IN THE PARK...!
WHAT!?
!
BUT HE RAN OFF JUST AS QUICK, SO NO HARM DONE!

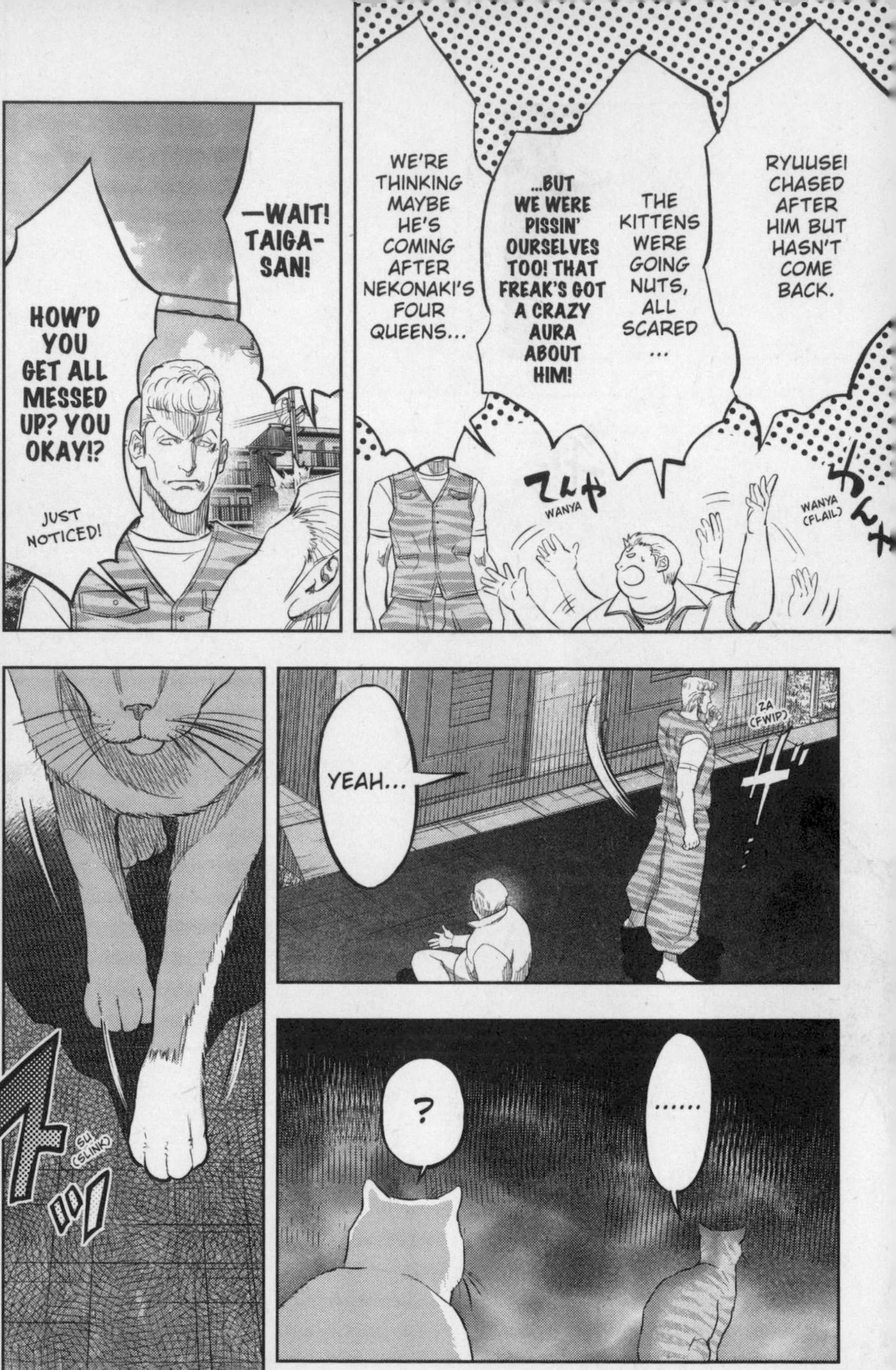
RYUUSEI CHASED AFTER HIM BUT HASN'T COME BACK.
THE KITTENS WERE GOING NUTS, ALL SCARED …
...BUT WE WERE PISSIN' OURSELVES TOO! THAT FREAK'S GOT A CRAZY AURA ABOUT HIM!
WE'RE THINKING MAYBE HE'S COMING AFTER NEKONAKI'S FOUR QUEENS...
WANYA (FLAIL)
WANYA
—WAIT! TAIGA-SAN!
HOW'D YOU GET ALL MESSED UP? YOU OKAY!?
JUST NOTICED!
ZA (FWIP)
YEAH...
......
?
SU (SLINK)

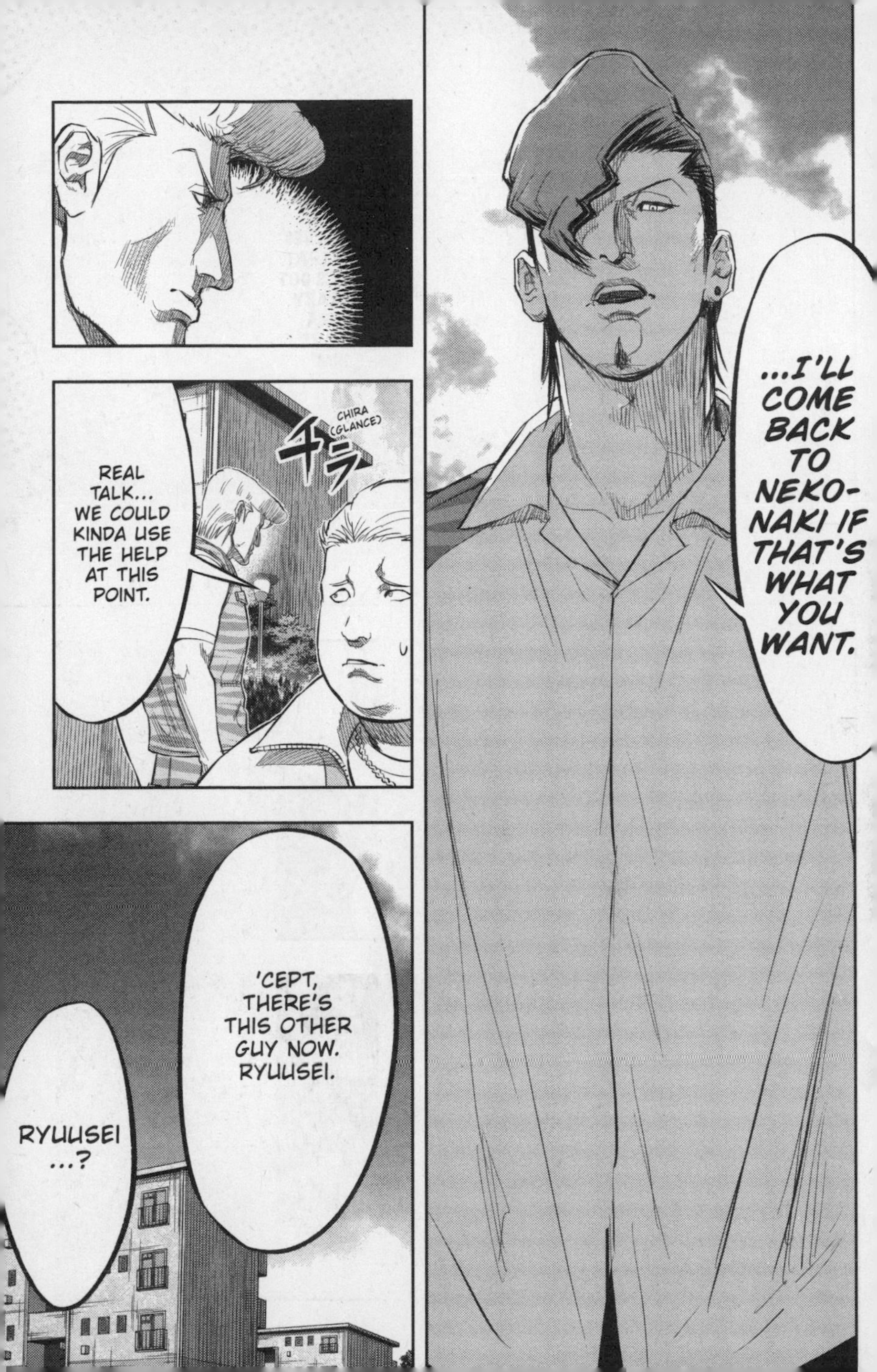
...I'LL COME BACK TO NEKO-NAKI IF THAT'S WHAT YOU WANT.
CHIRA (GLANCE)
チラ
REAL TALK... WE COULD KINDA USE THE HELP AT THIS POINT.
'CEPT, THERE'S THIS OTHER GUY NOW. RYUUSEI.
RYUUSEI ...?

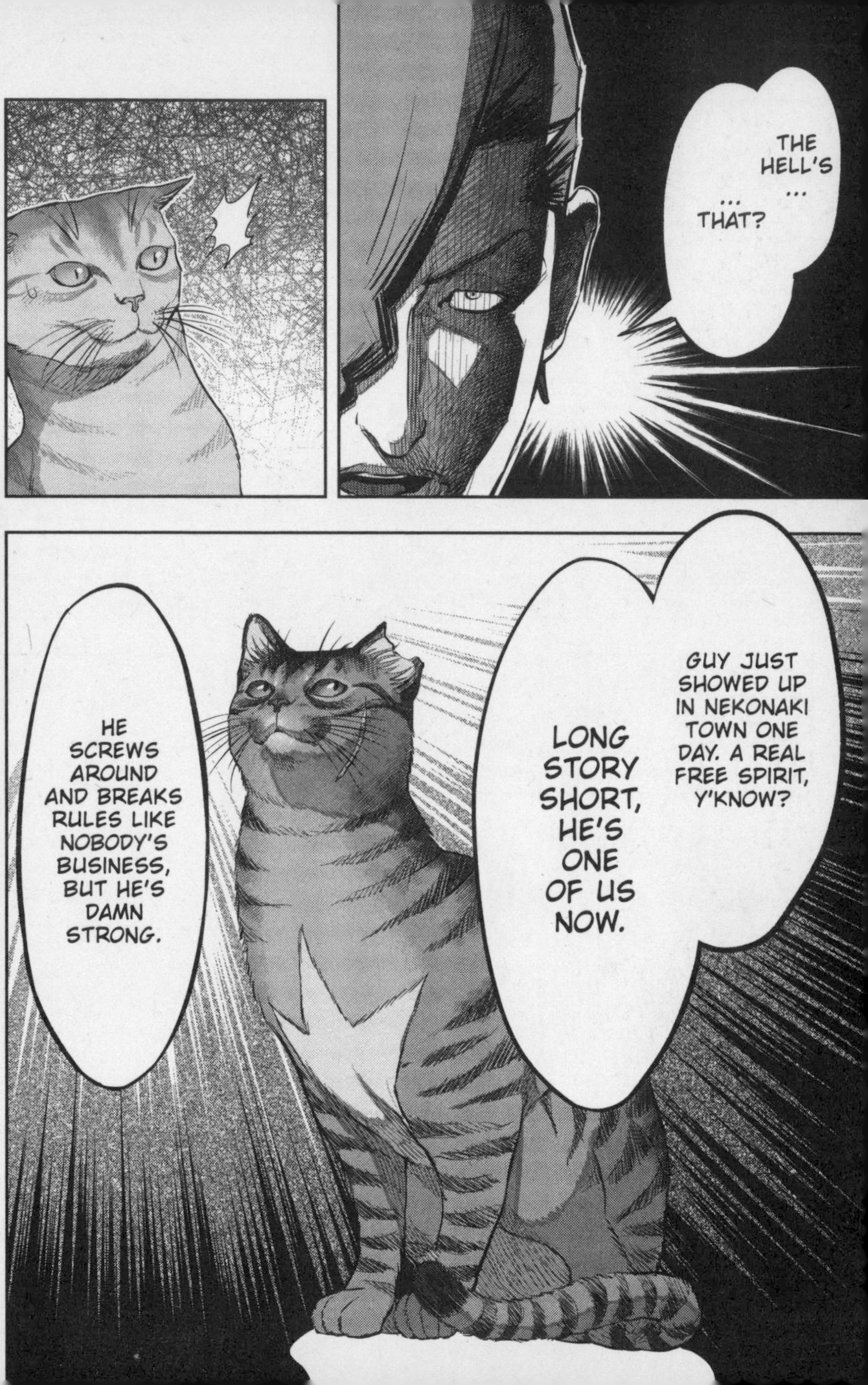
THE HELL'S ... ... THAT?
GUY JUST SHOWED UP IN NEKONAKI TOWN ONE DAY. A REAL FREE SPIRIT, Y'KNOW?
LONG STORY SHORT, HE'S ONE OF US NOW.
HE SCREWS AROUND AND BREAKS RULES LIKE NOBODY'S BUSINESS, BUT HE'S DAMN STRONG.

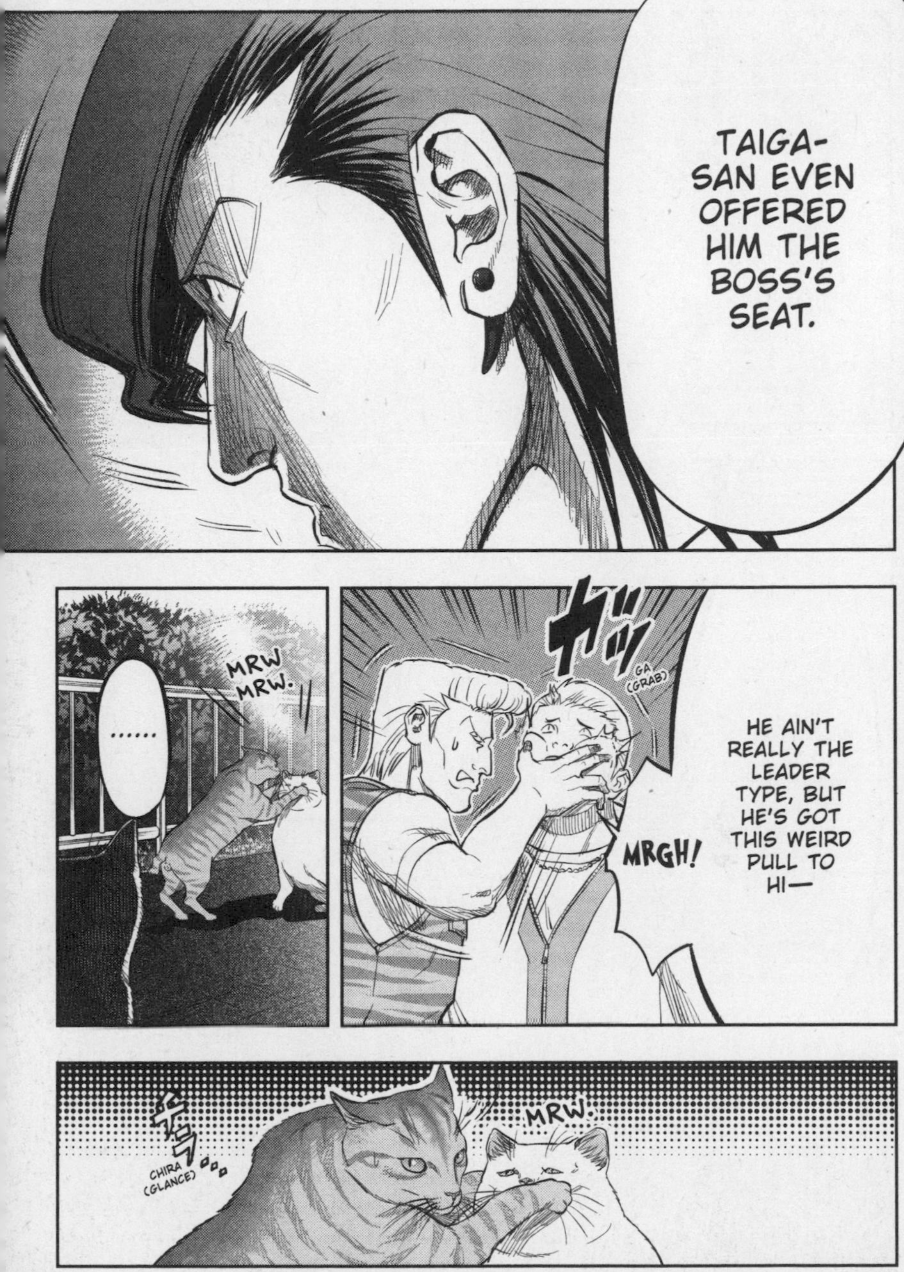
TAIGA-SAN EVEN OFFERED HIM THE BOSS'S SEAT.
ガッ
GA (GRAB)
HE AIN'T REALLY THE LEADER TYPE, BUT HE'S GOT THIS WEIRD PULL TO HI—
MRGH!
MRW MRW.
......
MRW.
チラ
CHIRA (GLANCE)

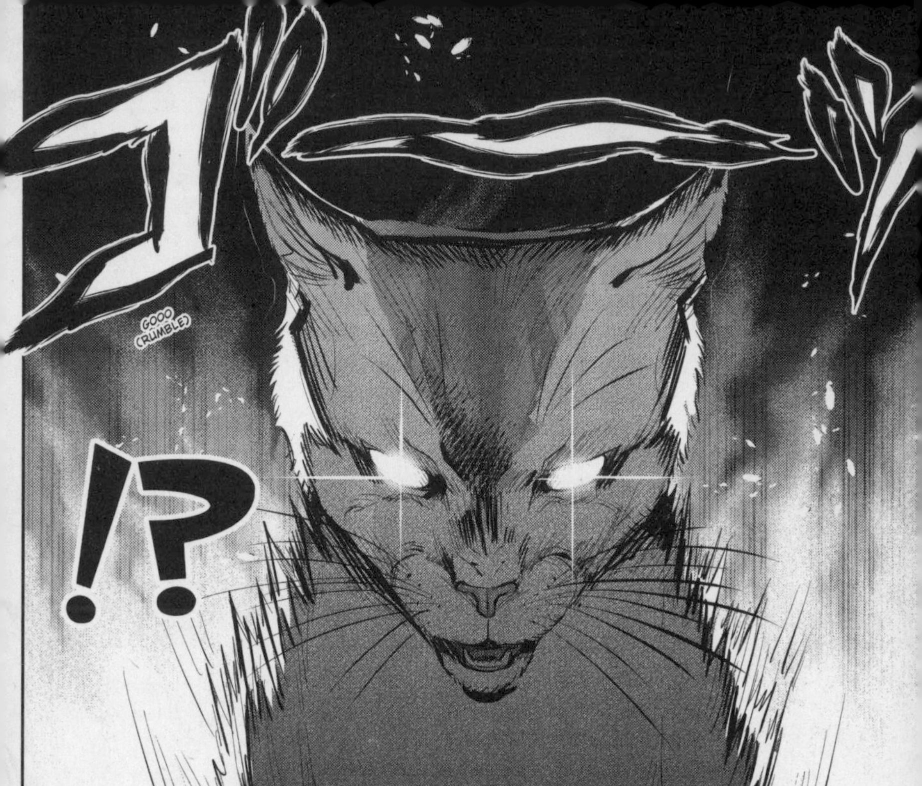
GOOO (RUMBLE)
!?

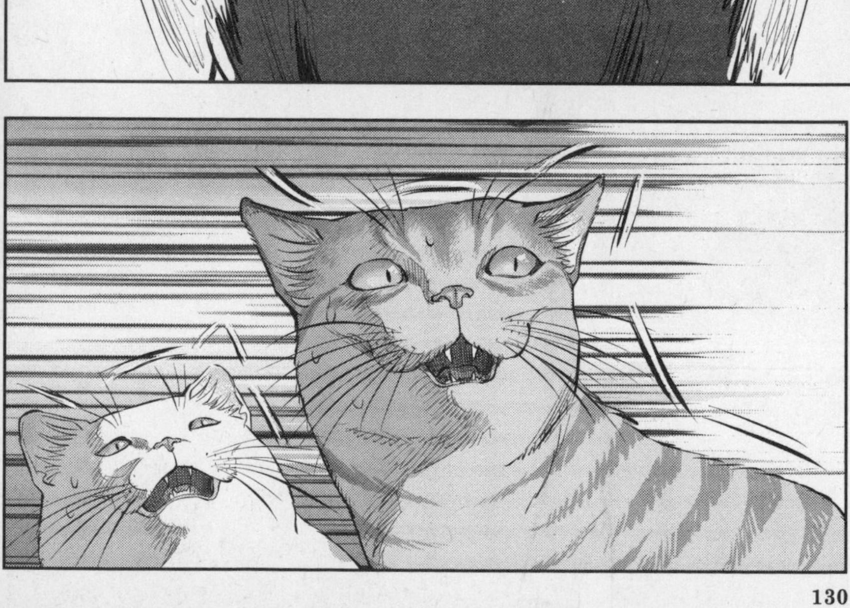

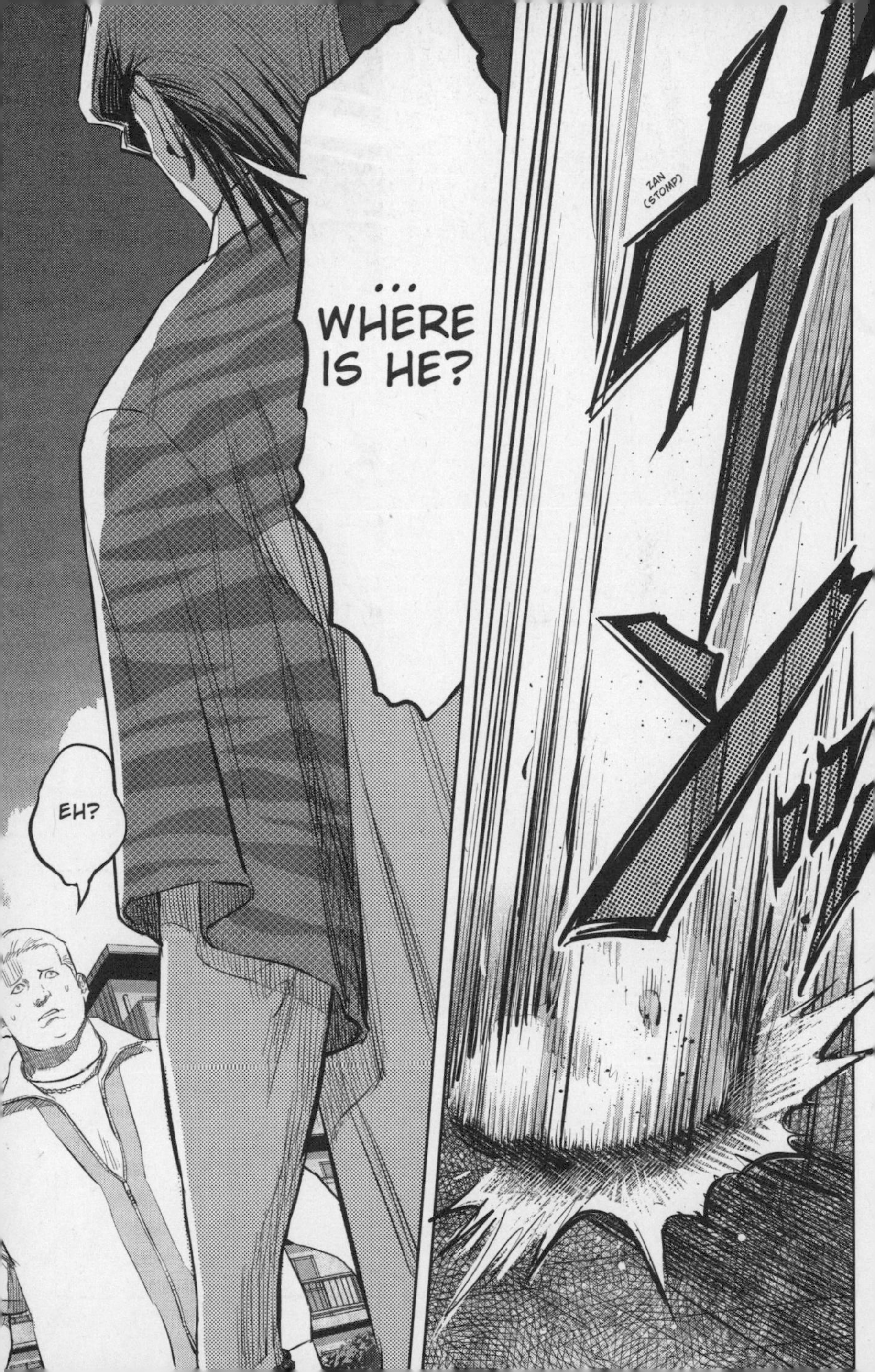
ZAN (STOMP)
... WHERE IS HE?
EH?

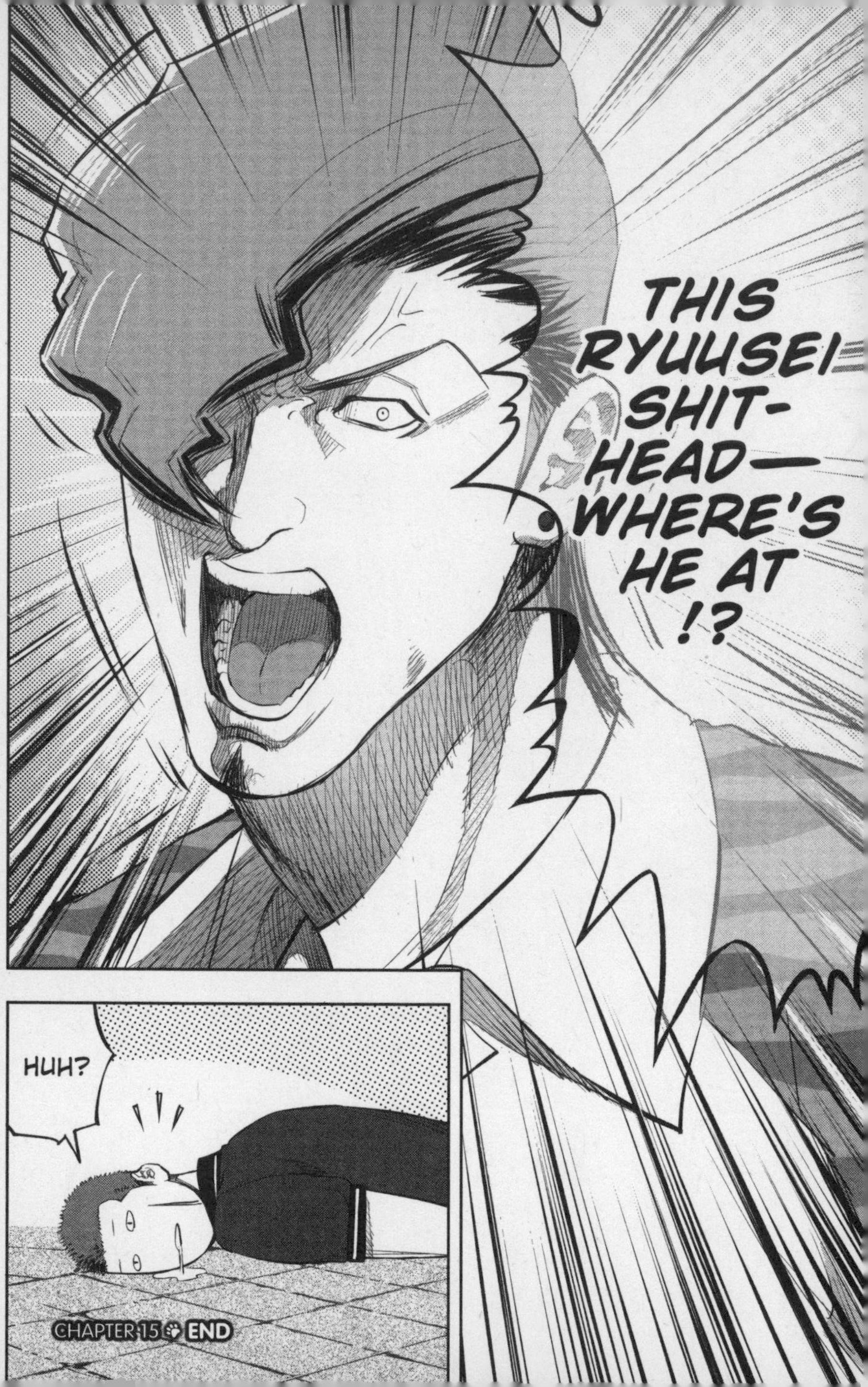
THIS RYUUSEI SHIT-HEAD— WHERE'S HE AT !?
HUH?
CHAPTER 15 END

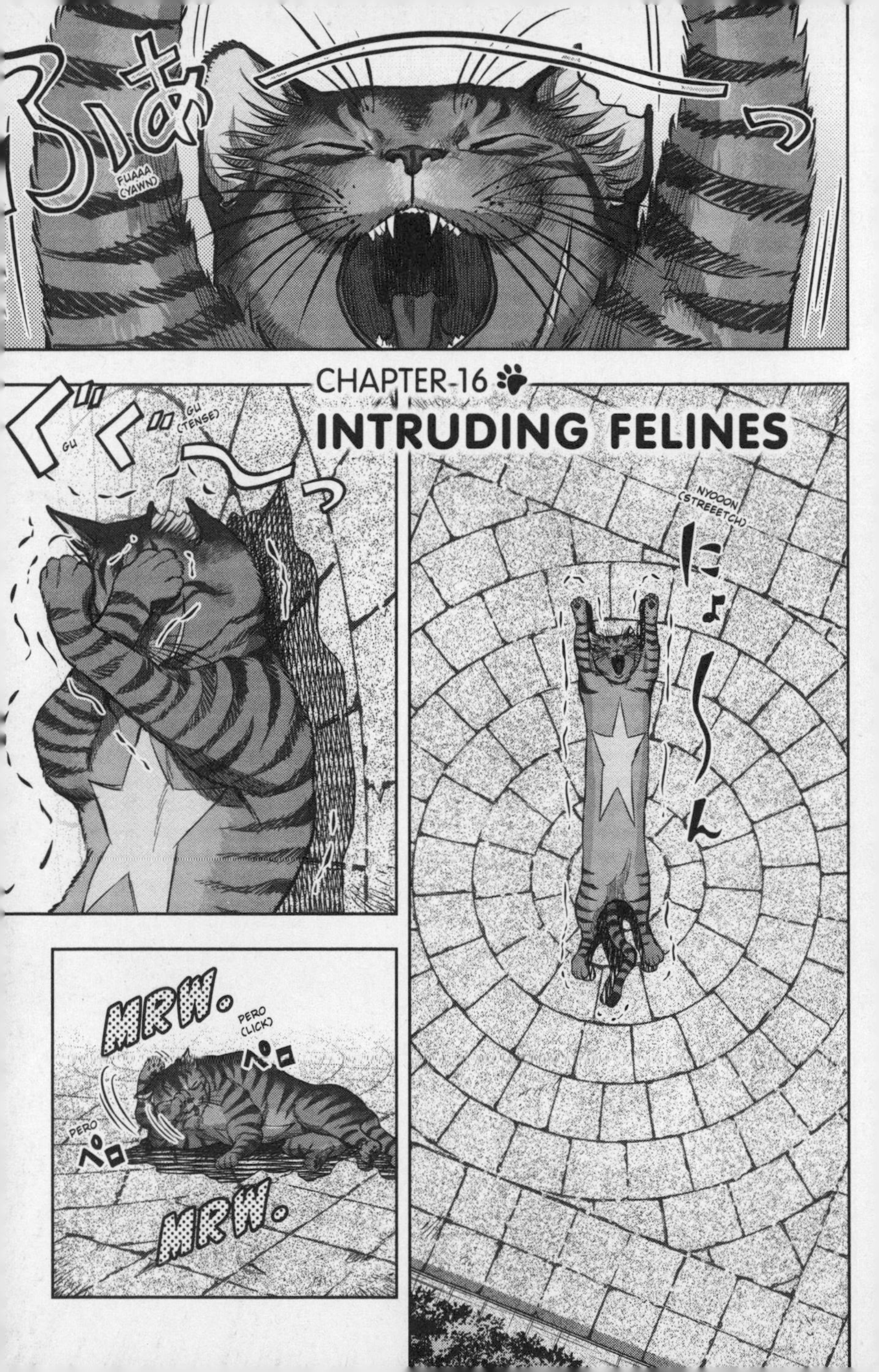

ふぁーっ
FUAAA (YAWN)
CHAPTER-16
INTRUDING FELINES
にょーーん
NYOOON (STREEETCH)
ぐ
GU
ぐ～っ
GU (TENSE)
MRW.
PERO (LICK)
ぺろ
PERO
ぺろ
MRW.

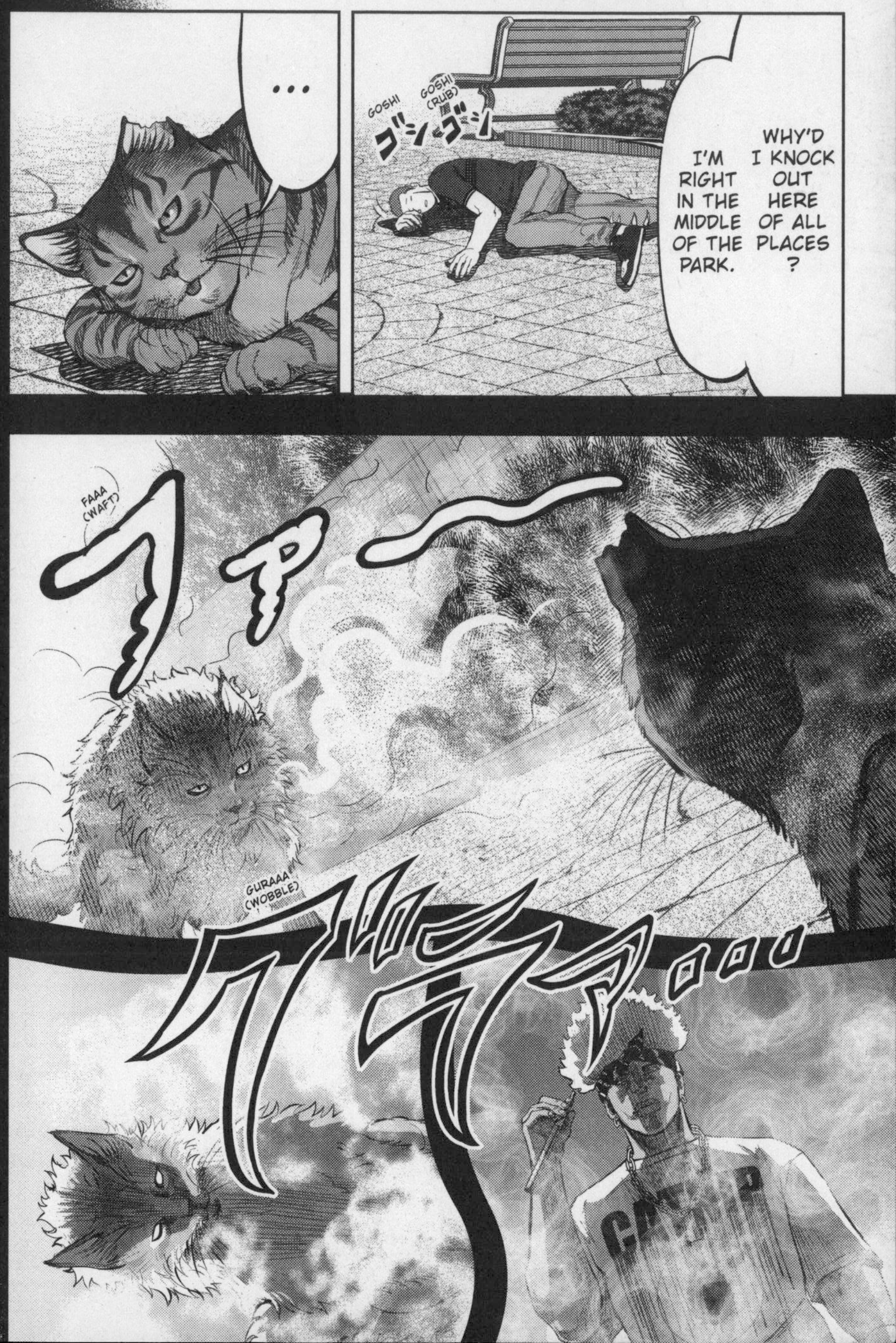
WHY'D I KNOCK OUT HERE OF ALL PLACES?
I'M RIGHT IN THE MIDDLE OF THE PARK.
GOSHI GOSHI (RUB)
...
FAAA (WAFT)
GURAAA (WOBBLE)

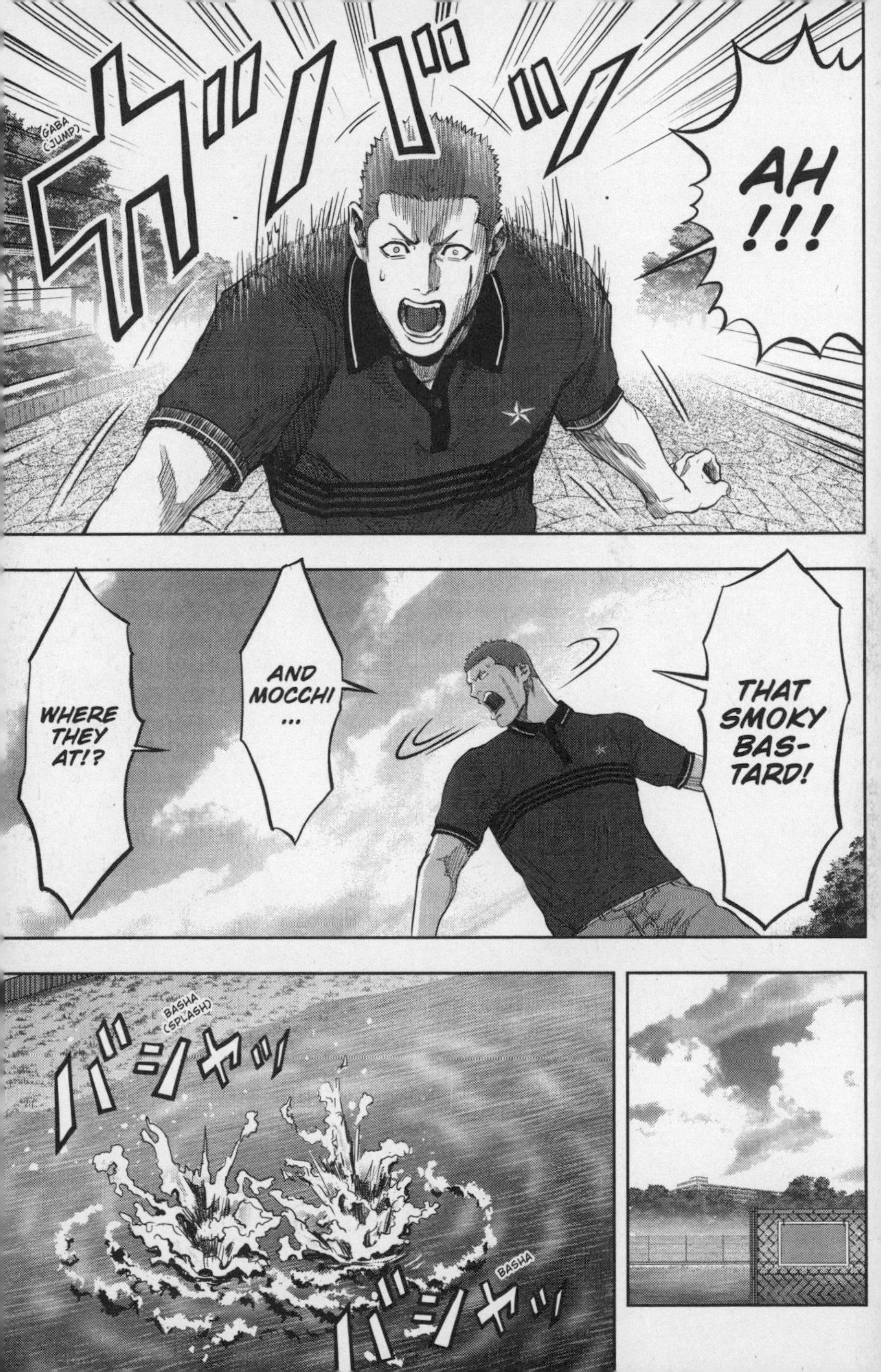
AH!!!
ガバッ
GABA (JUMP)
THAT SMOKY BAS- TARD!
AND MOCCHI ...
WHERE THEY AT!?
バシャッ
BASHA (SPLASH)
バシャッ
BASHA

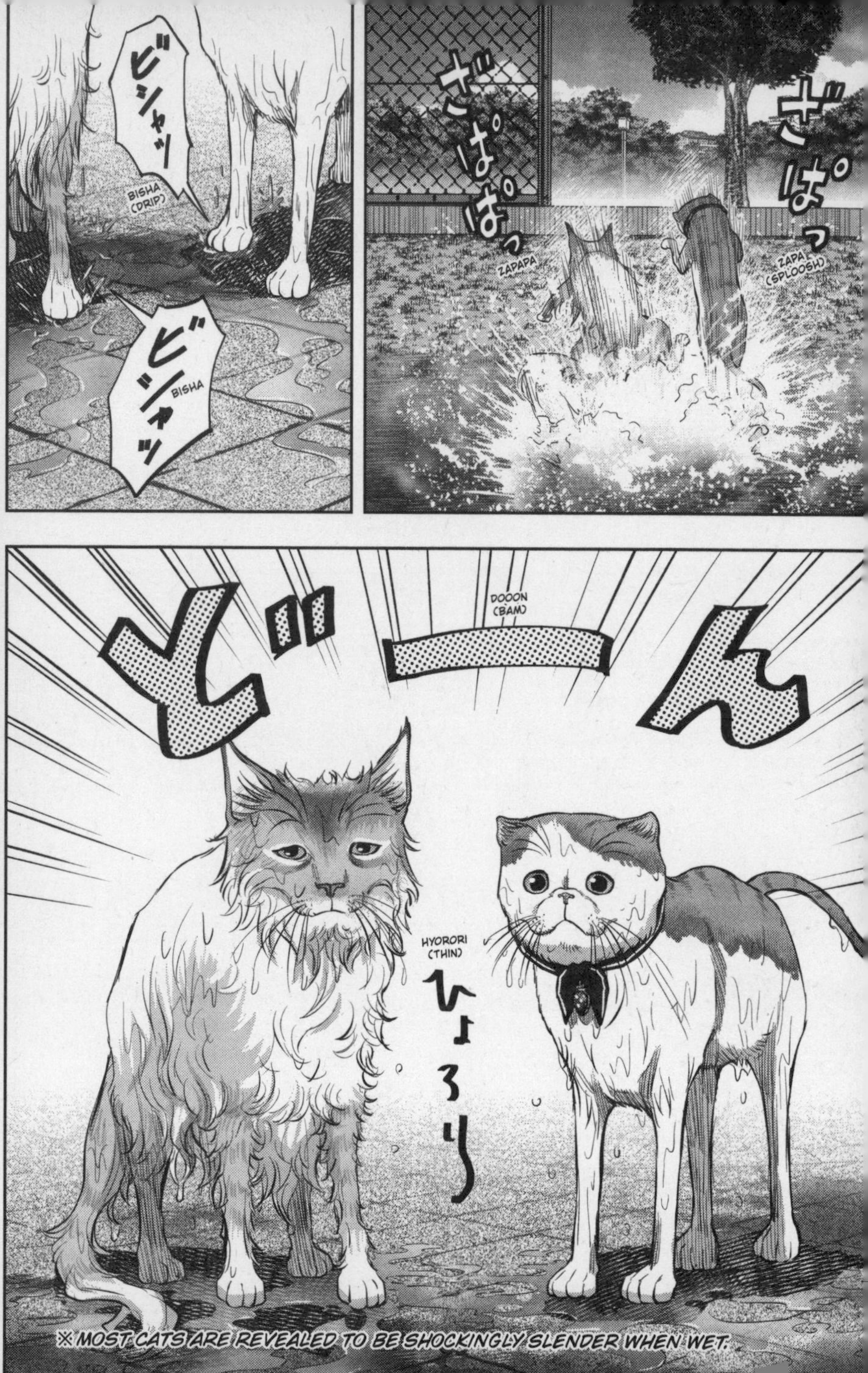
ざぱっ
ZAPA (SPLOOSH)
ざぱぱっ
ZAPAPA
ビシャッ
BISHA (DRIP)
ビシャッ
BISHA
ドーん
DOOON (BAM)
ひょろり
HYORORI (THIN)
※ MOST CATS ARE REVEALED TO BE SHOCKINGLY SLENDER WHEN WET.

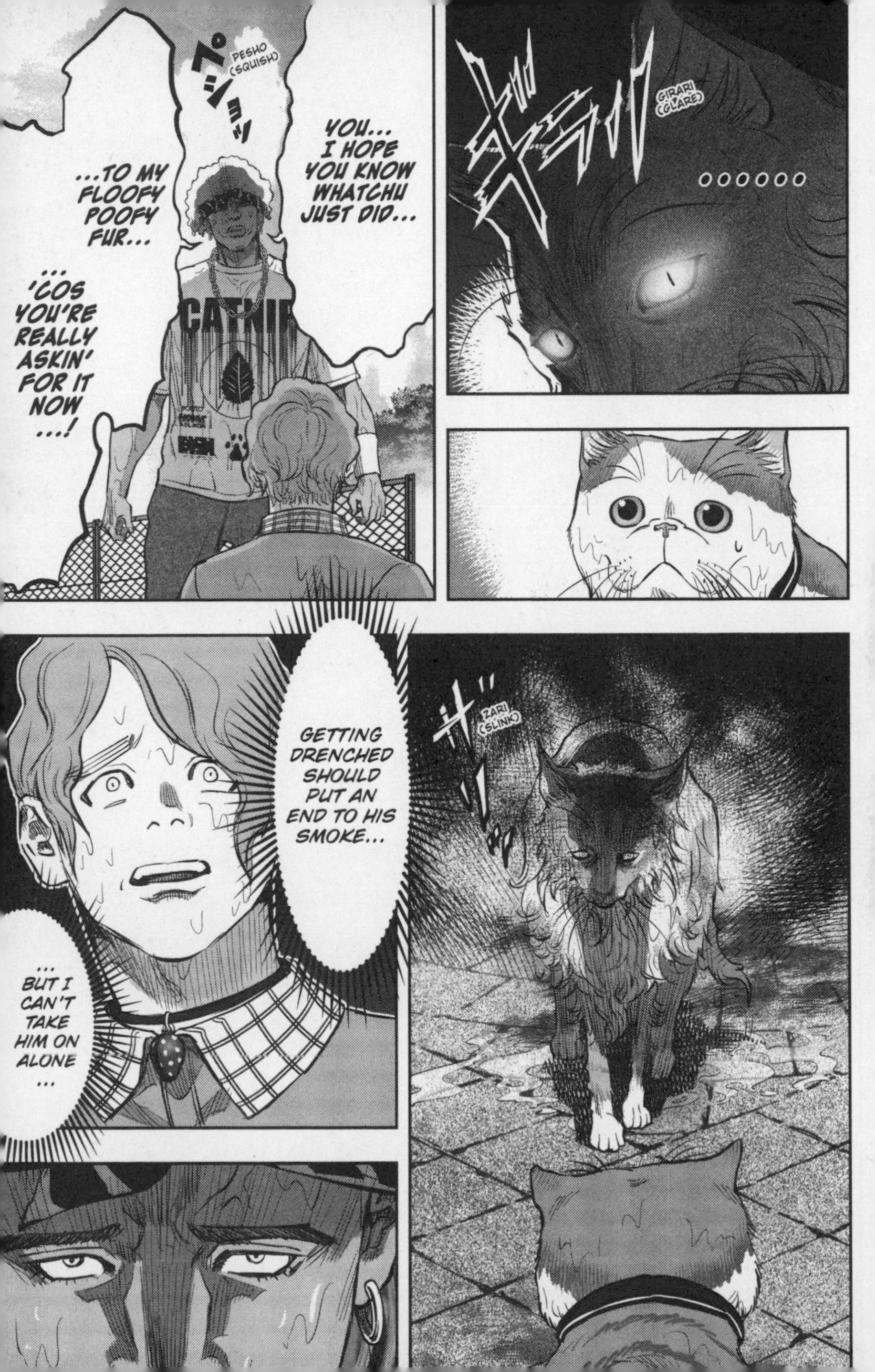
GIRARI (GLARE)
OOOOOOO
PESHO (SQUISH)
YOU... I HOPE YOU KNOW WHATCHU JUST DID...
...TO MY FLOOFY POOFY FUR...
...'COS YOU'RE REALLY ASKIN' FOR IT NOW...!
ZARI (SLINK)
GETTING DRENCHED SHOULD PUT AN END TO HIS SMOKE...
...BUT I CAN'T TAKE HIM ON ALONE...

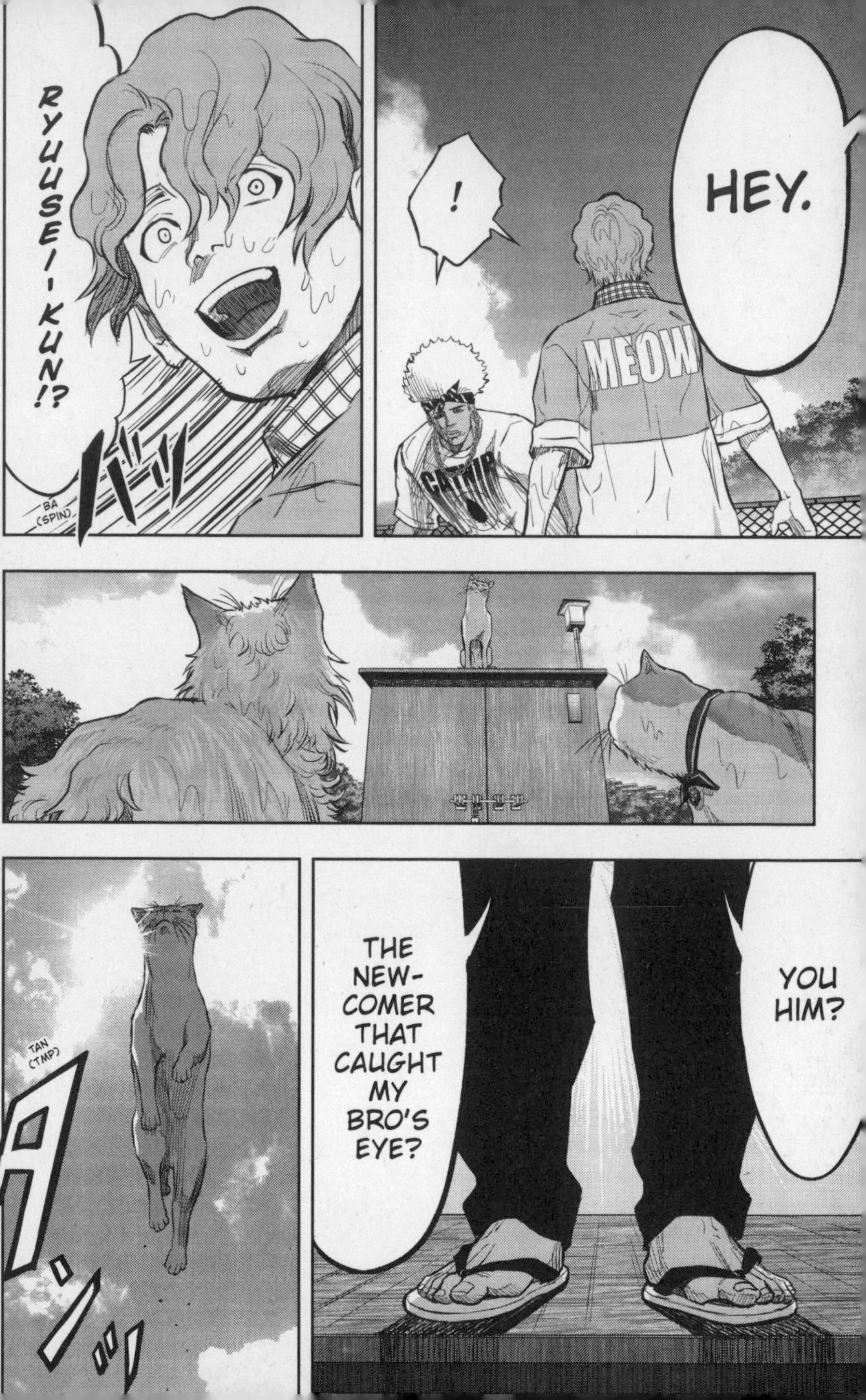
HEY.
!
RYUUSEI-I-KUN!?
BA (SPIN)
YOU HIM?
THE NEW-COMER THAT CAUGHT MY BRO'S EYE?
TAN (TMP)

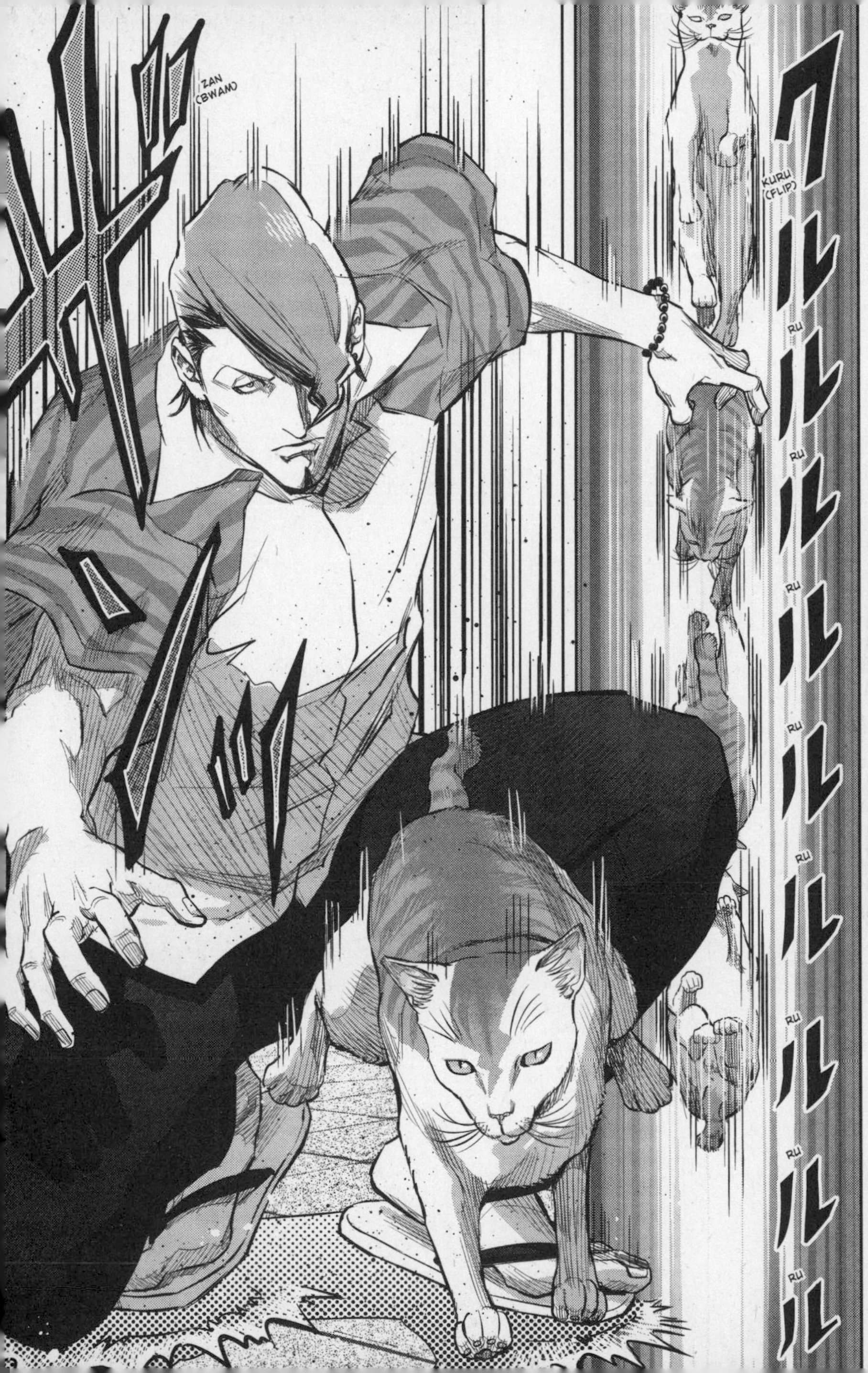
KURU (FLIP)
RU
RU
RU
RU
RU
RU
RU
RU
ZAN (BWAM)

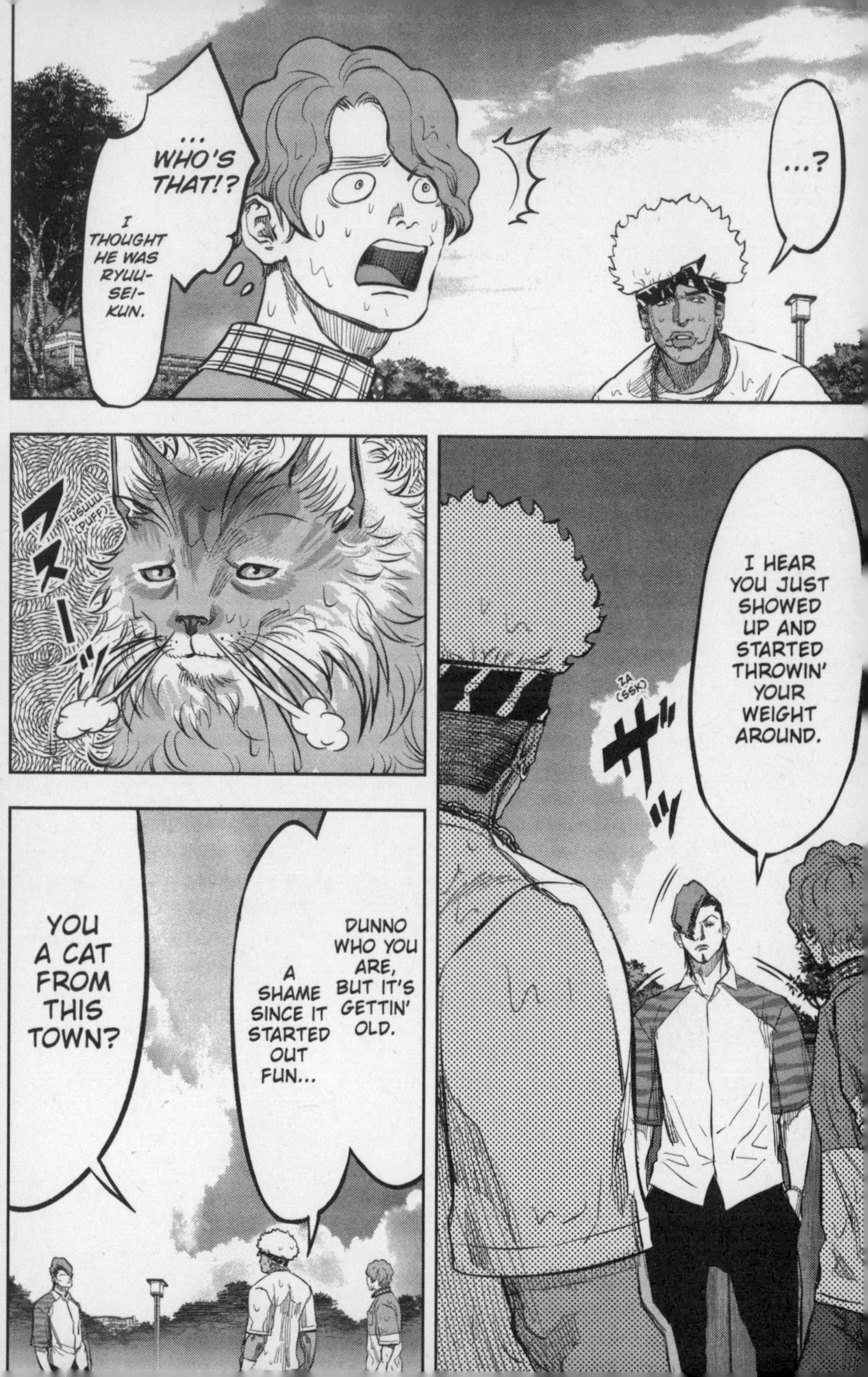
...?
... WHO'S THAT!?
I THOUGHT HE WAS RYUU-SEI-KUN.
ZA (SSK)
I HEAR YOU JUST SHOWED UP AND STARTED THROWIN' YOUR WEIGHT AROUND.
FUSUUU (PUFF)
DUNNO WHO YOU ARE, BUT IT'S GETTIN' OLD.
A SHAME SINCE IT STARTED OUT FUN...
YOU A CAT FROM THIS TOWN?

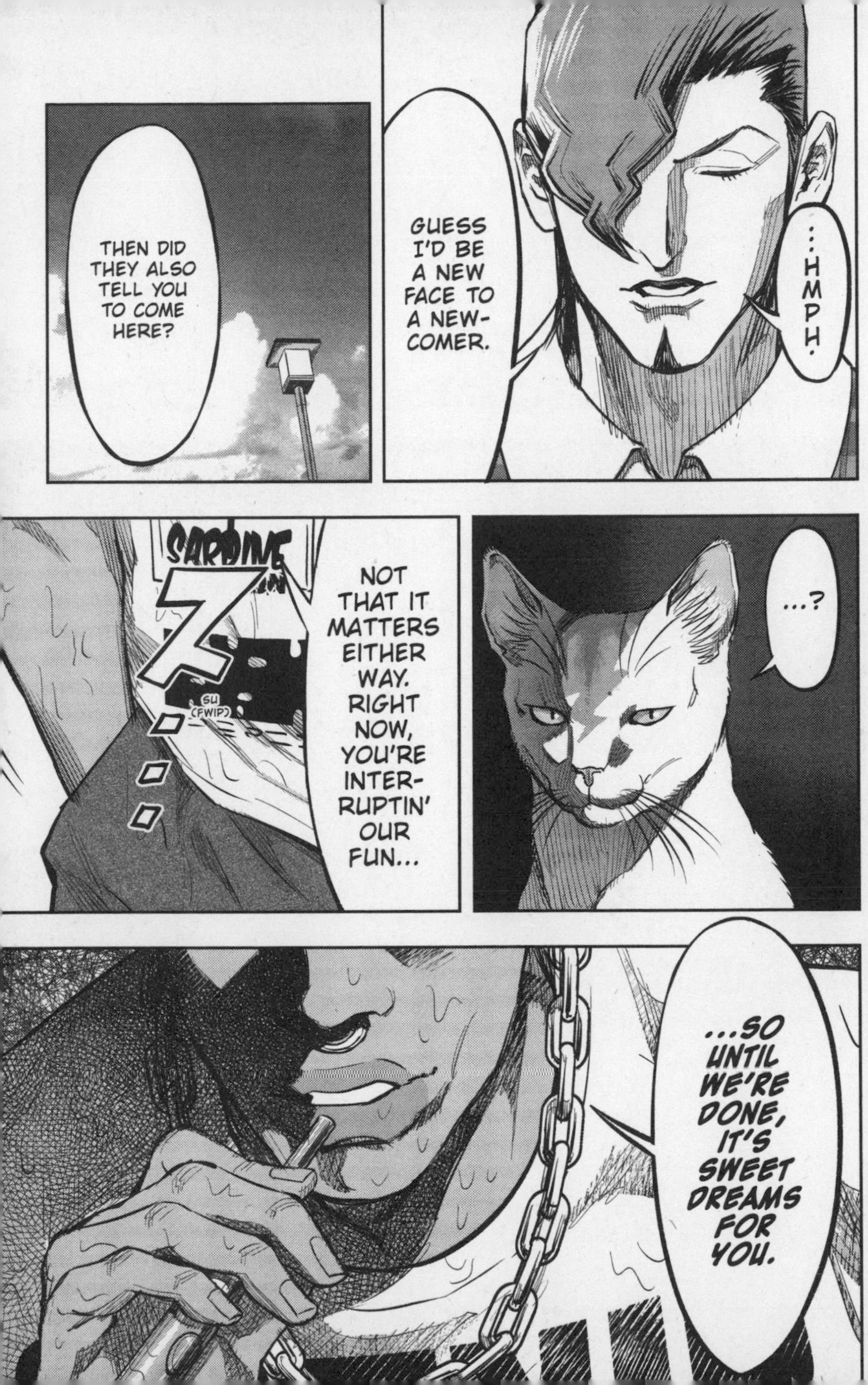
...HMPH.
GUESS I'D BE A NEW FACE TO A NEW-COMER.
THEN DID THEY ALSO TELL YOU TO COME HERE?
...?
NOT THAT IT MATTERS EITHER WAY. RIGHT NOW, YOU'RE INTER-RUPTIN' OUR FUN...
SARDINE
SU (FWIP)
...SO UNTIL WE'RE DONE, IT'S SWEET DREAMS FOR YOU.

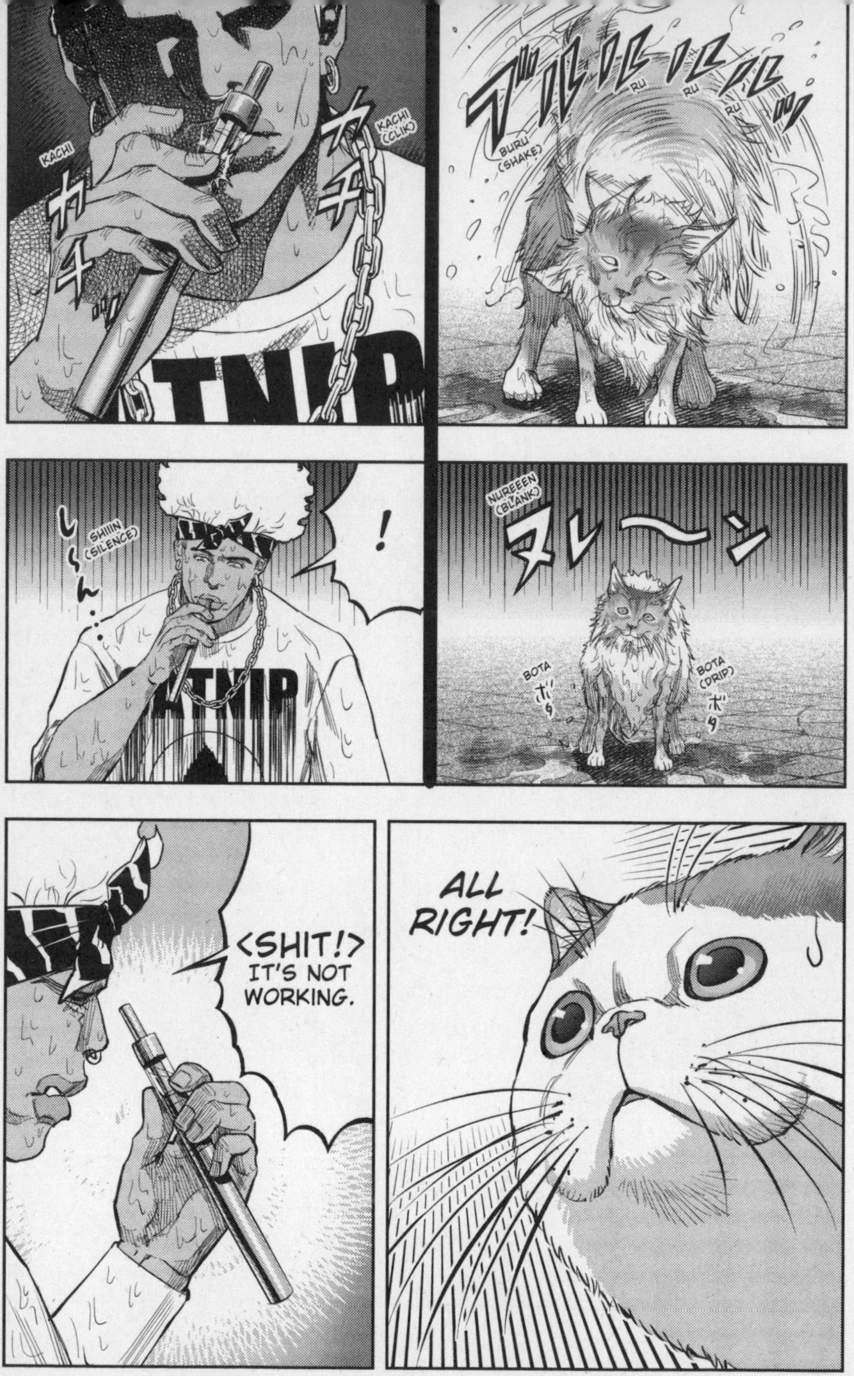
BURU (SHAKE)
RU
RU
RU
KACHI (CLIK)
KACHI
NUREEEN (BLANK)
BOTA (DRIP)
BOTA
!
SHIIIN (SILENCE)
ALL RIGHT!
<SHIT!> IT'S NOT WORKING.

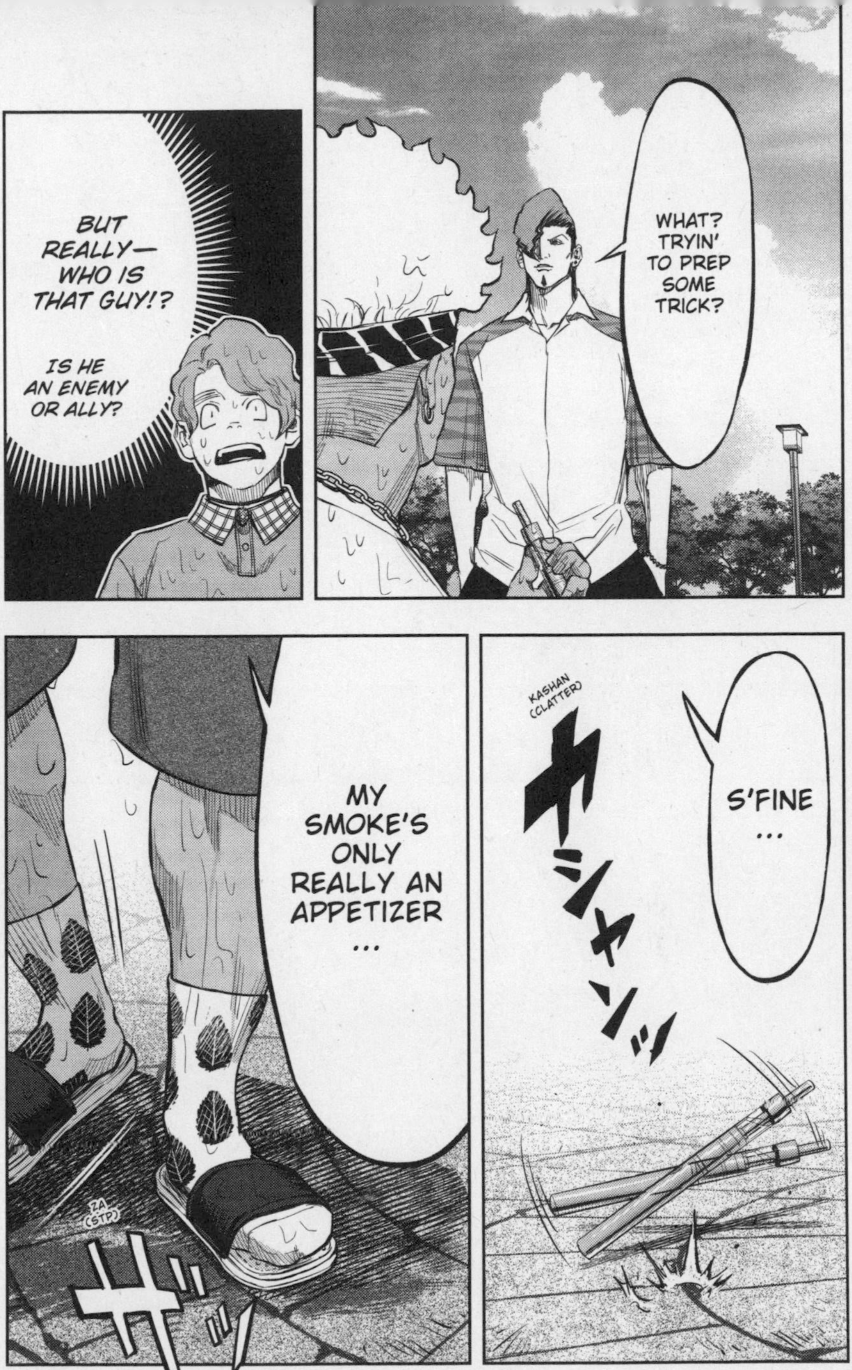
WHAT? TRYIN' TO PREP SOME TRICK?
BUT REALLY— WHO IS THAT GUY!?
IS HE AN ENEMY OR ALLY?
S'FINE ...
KASHAN (CLATTER)
カシャンッ
MY SMOKE'S ONLY REALLY AN APPETIZER ...
ZA (STP)
ザッ

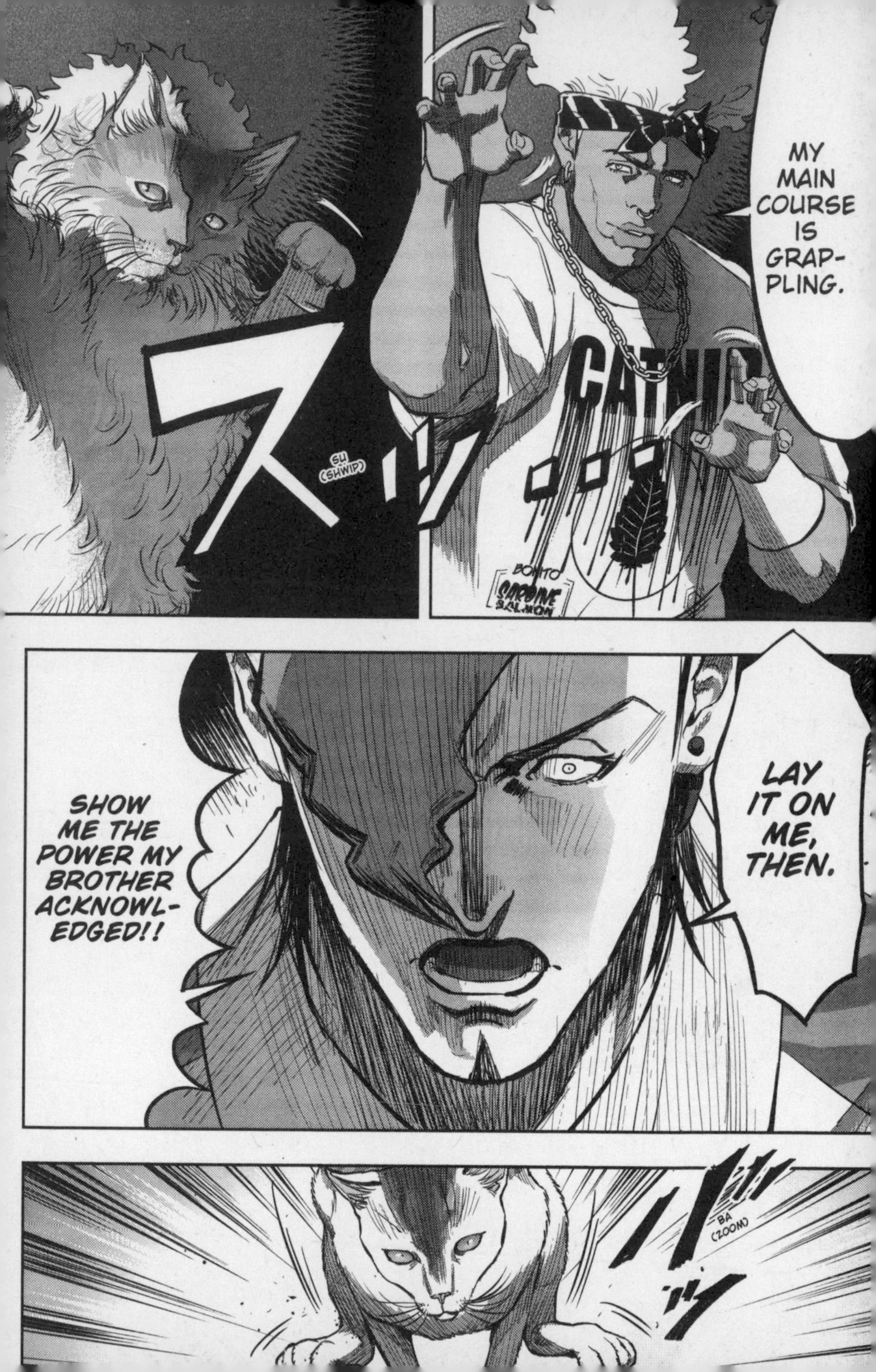
MY MAIN COURSE IS GRAP-PLING.
BONITO
SARDINE
SALMON
SU (SHWIP)
LAY IT ON ME, THEN.
SHOW ME THE POWER MY BROTHER ACKNOWL-EDGED!!
BA (ZOOM)

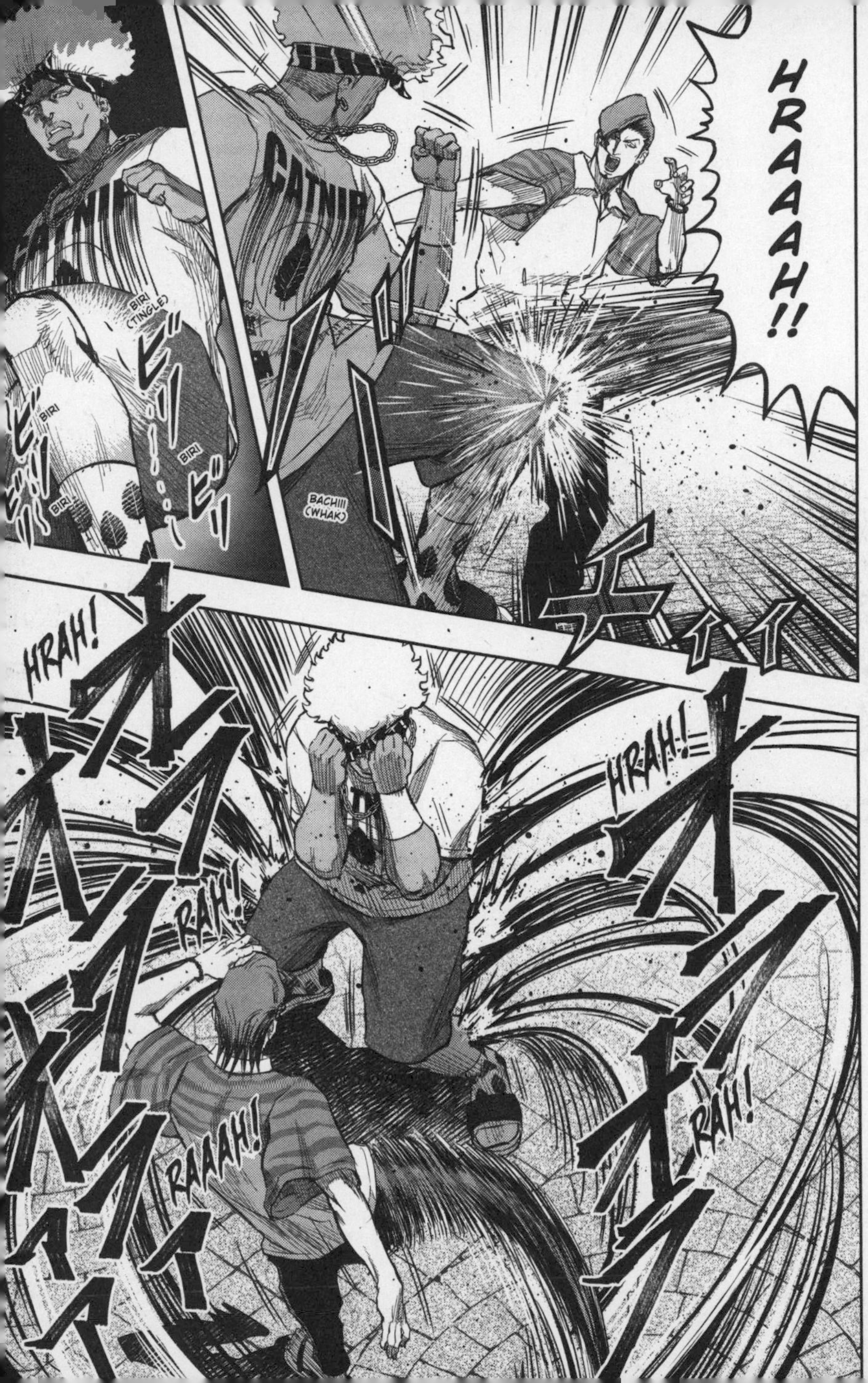
HRAAAAH!!
BACHIII
(WHAK)
BIRI
(TINGLE)
BIRI
BIRI
BIRI
HRAH!
HRAH!
RAH!
RAH!
RAAAH!

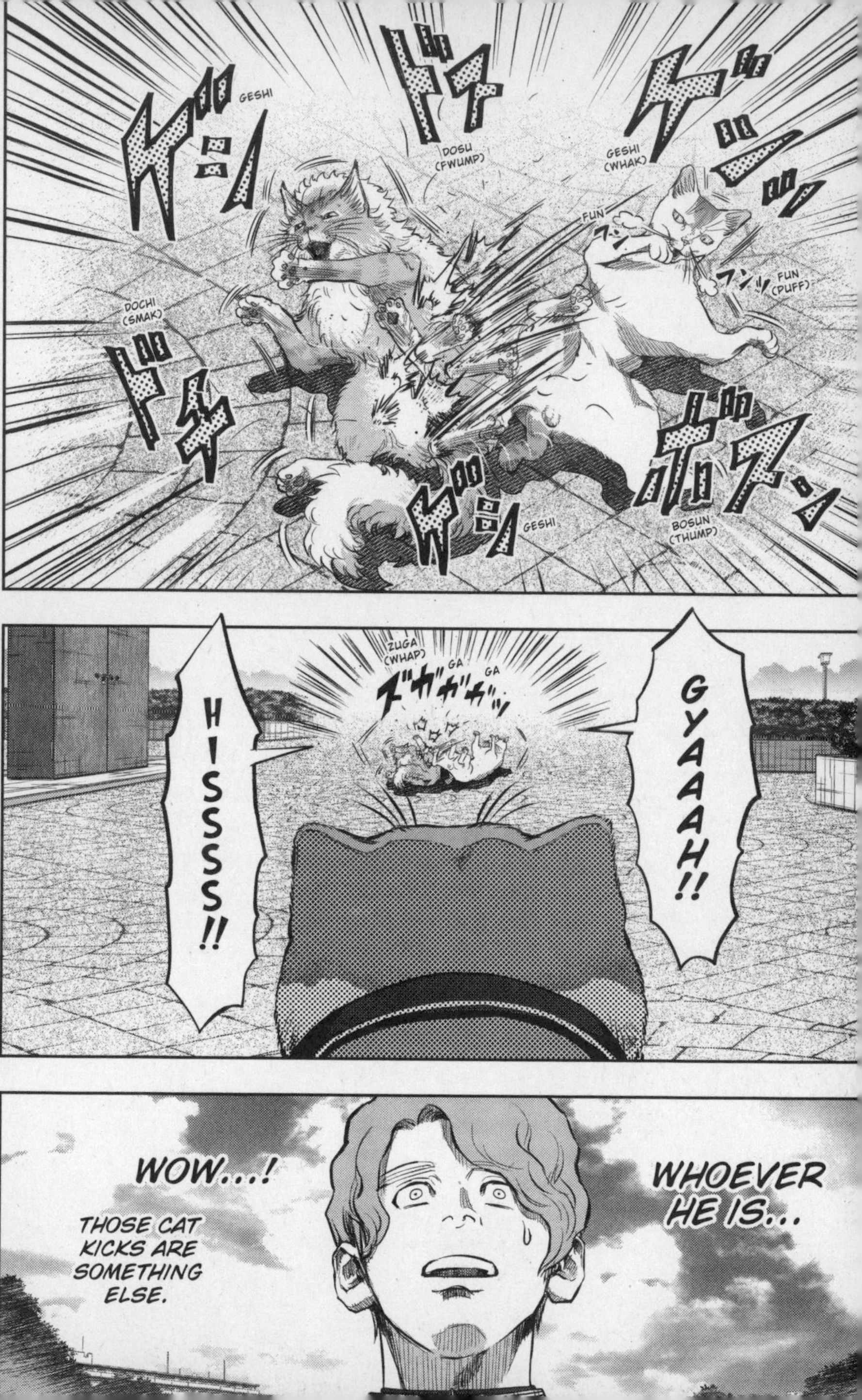
GESHI (WHAK)
FUN
FUN (PUFF)
DOSU (FWUMP)
GESHI
BOSUN (THUMP)
DOCHI (SMAK)
GESHI
GYAAAAH!!
ZUGA (WHAP)
GA
GA
HISSSS!!
WHOEVER HE IS...
WOW...!
THOSE CAT KICKS ARE SOMETHING ELSE.

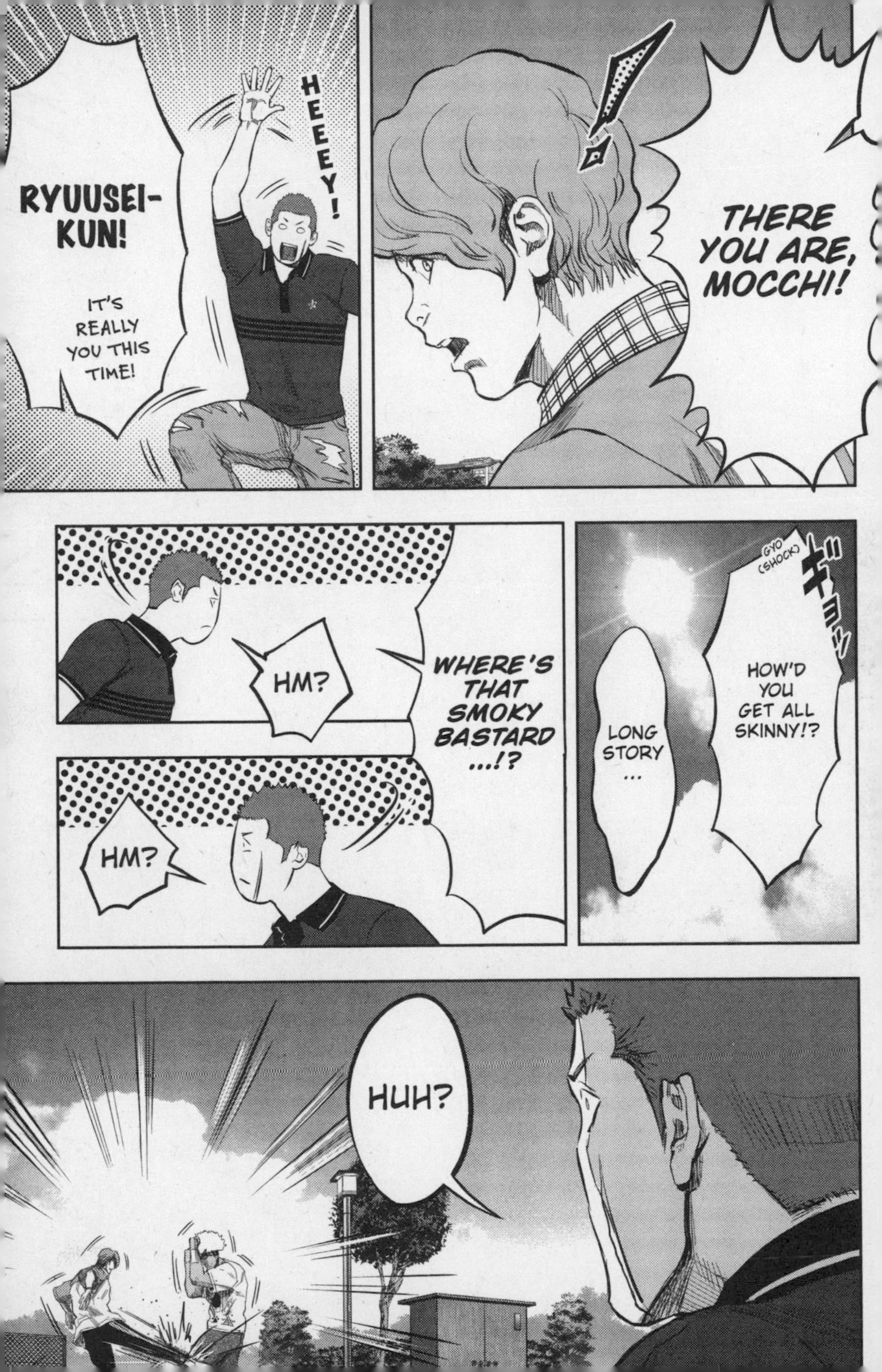
THERE YOU ARE, MOCCHI!
HEEEEY!
RYUUSEI-KUN!
IT'S REALLY YOU THIS TIME!
ギョッ
GYO (SHOCK)
HOW'D YOU GET ALL SKINNY!?
LONG STORY ...
WHERE'S THAT SMOKY BASTARD ...!?
HM?
HM?
HUH?

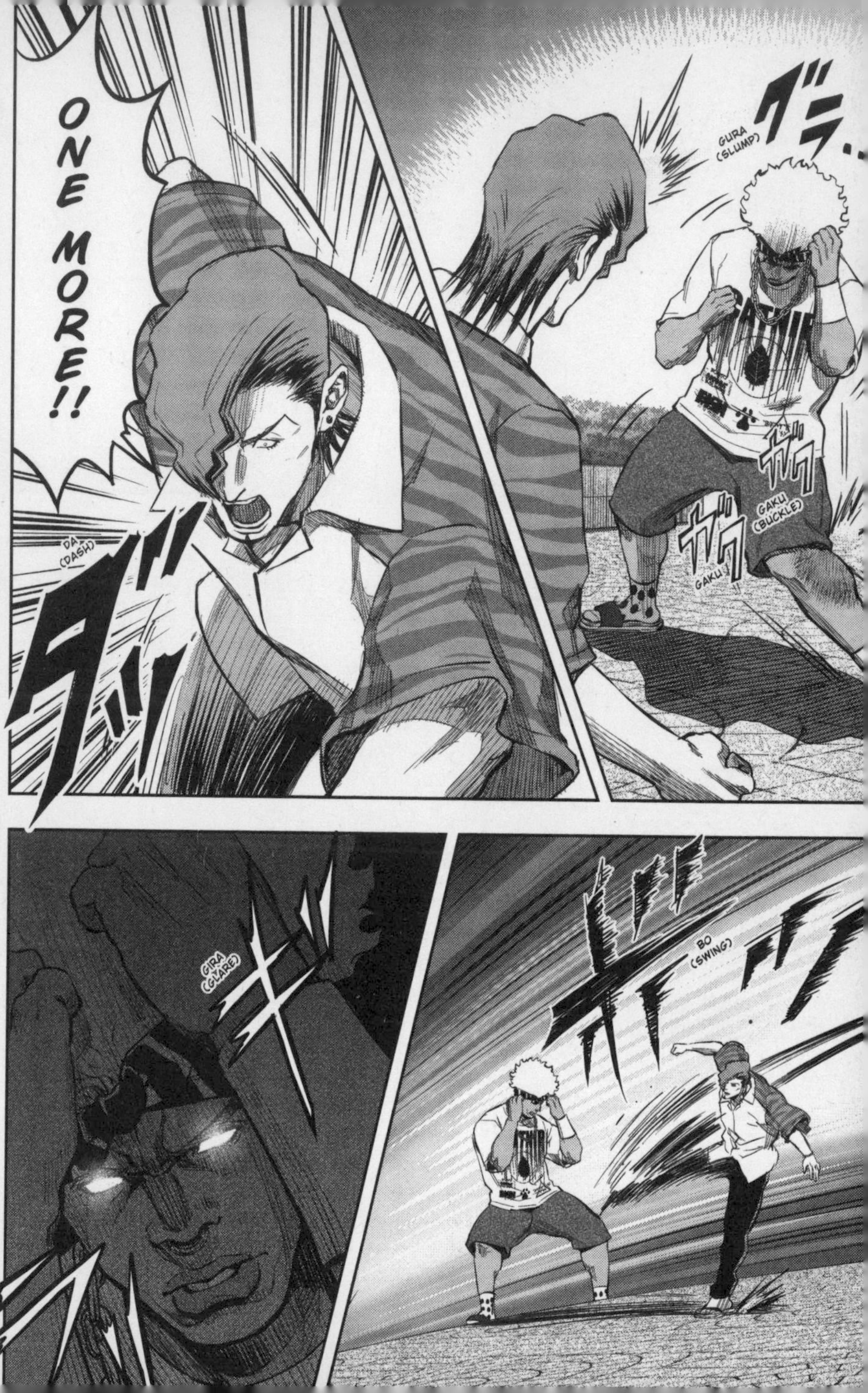

GURA (SLUMP)
GAKU (BUCKLE)
GAKU
ONE MORE!!
DA (DASH)
BO (SWING)
GIRA (GLARE)

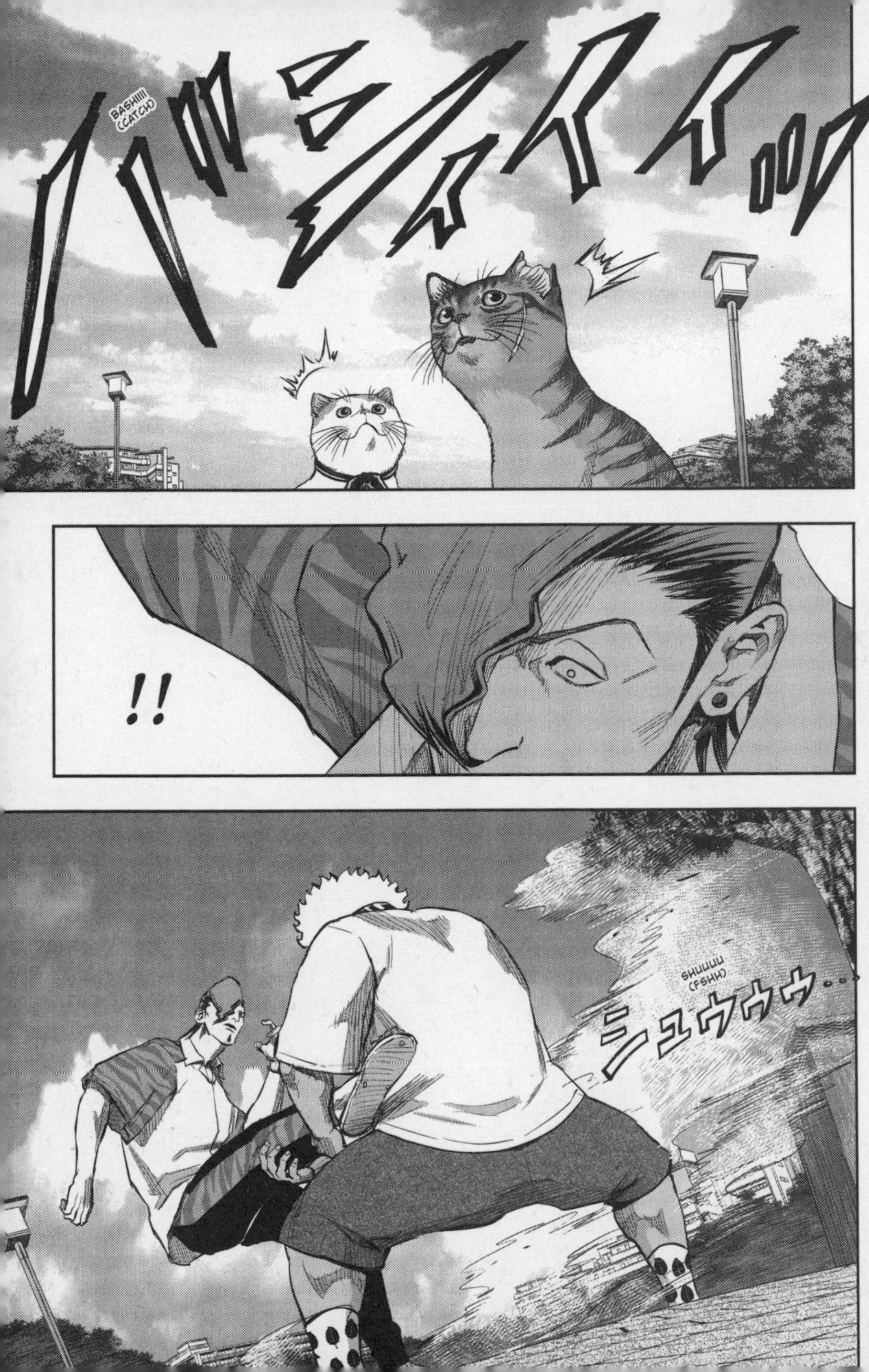
BASHIIII (CATCH)
!!
SHUUUU (FSHH)
シュウウウ…

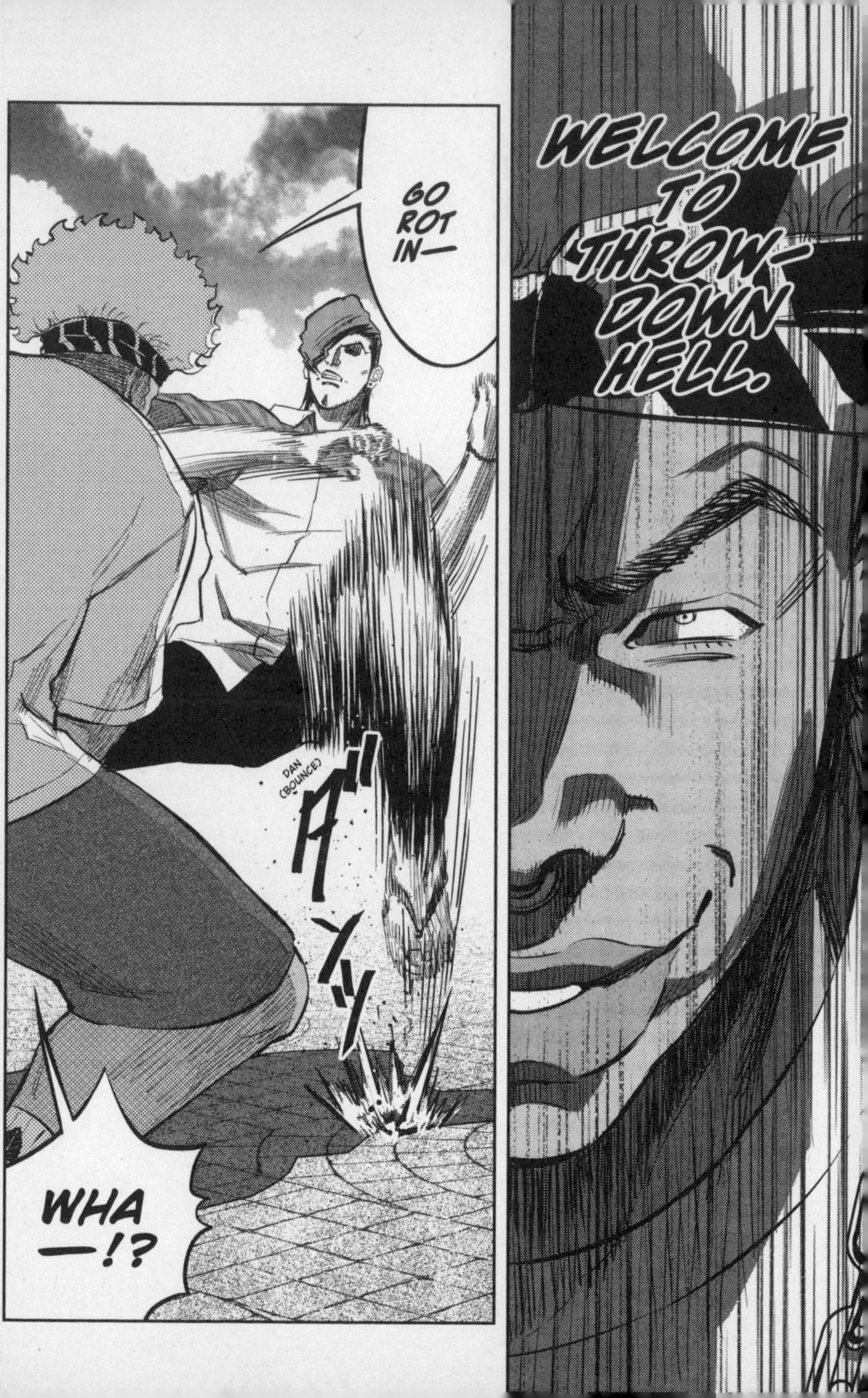
WELCOME TO THROW-DOWN HELL.
GO ROT IN—
DAN (BOUNCE)
WHA—!?

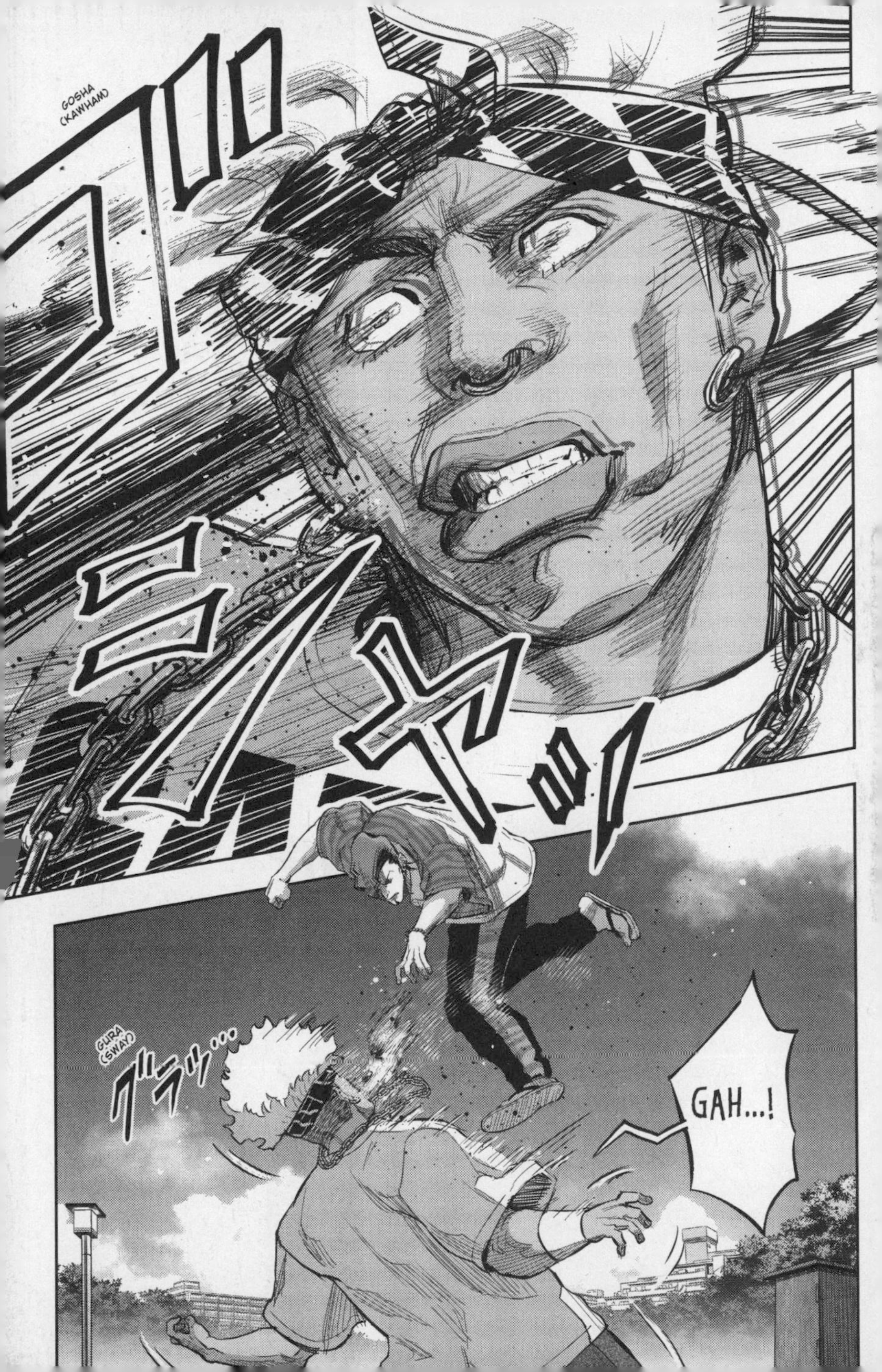
GOSHA
(KAWHAM)
GAH...!
GURA
(SWAY)

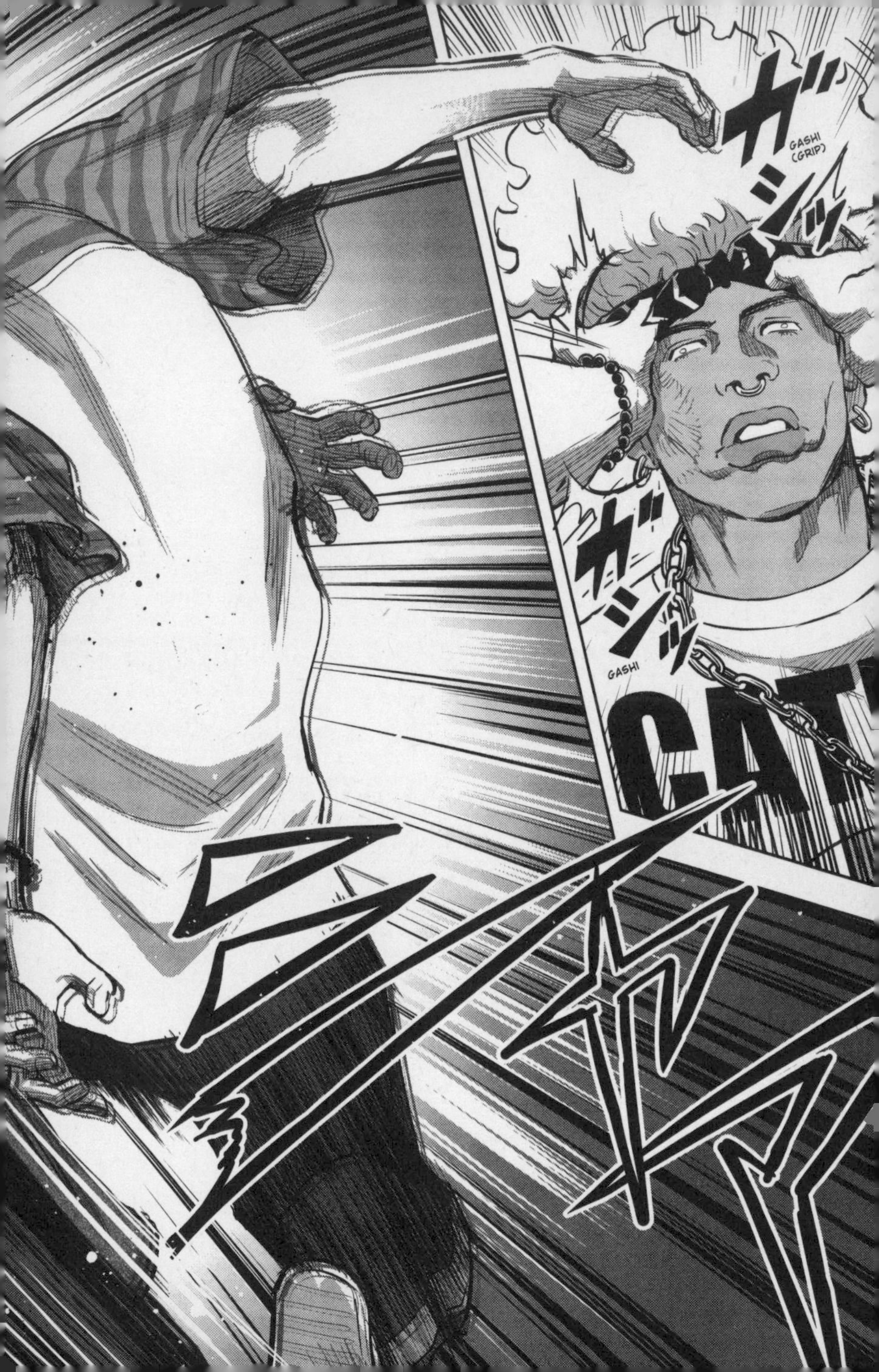
GASHI (GRIP)
GASHI

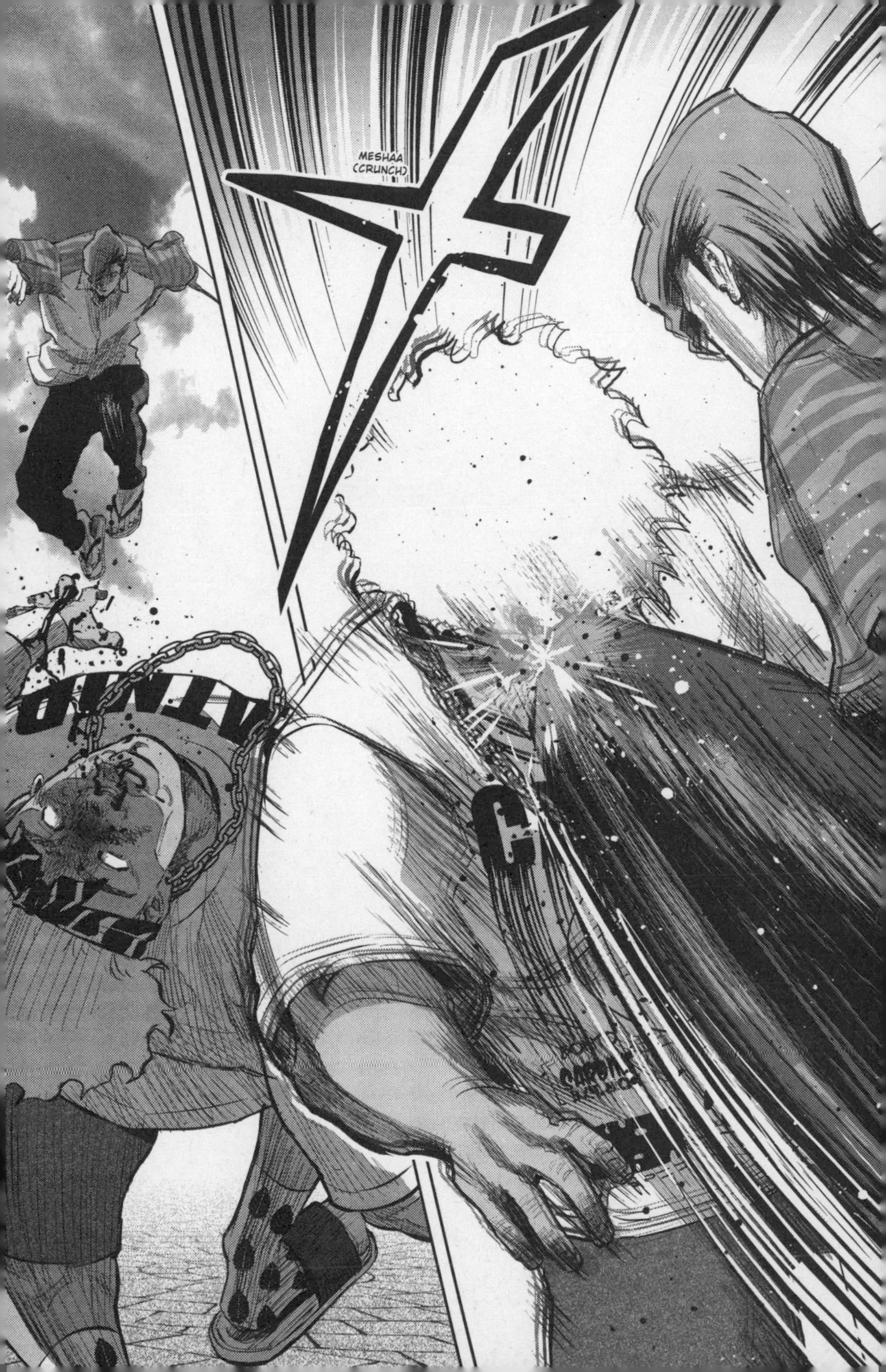
MESHAA
(CRUNCH)

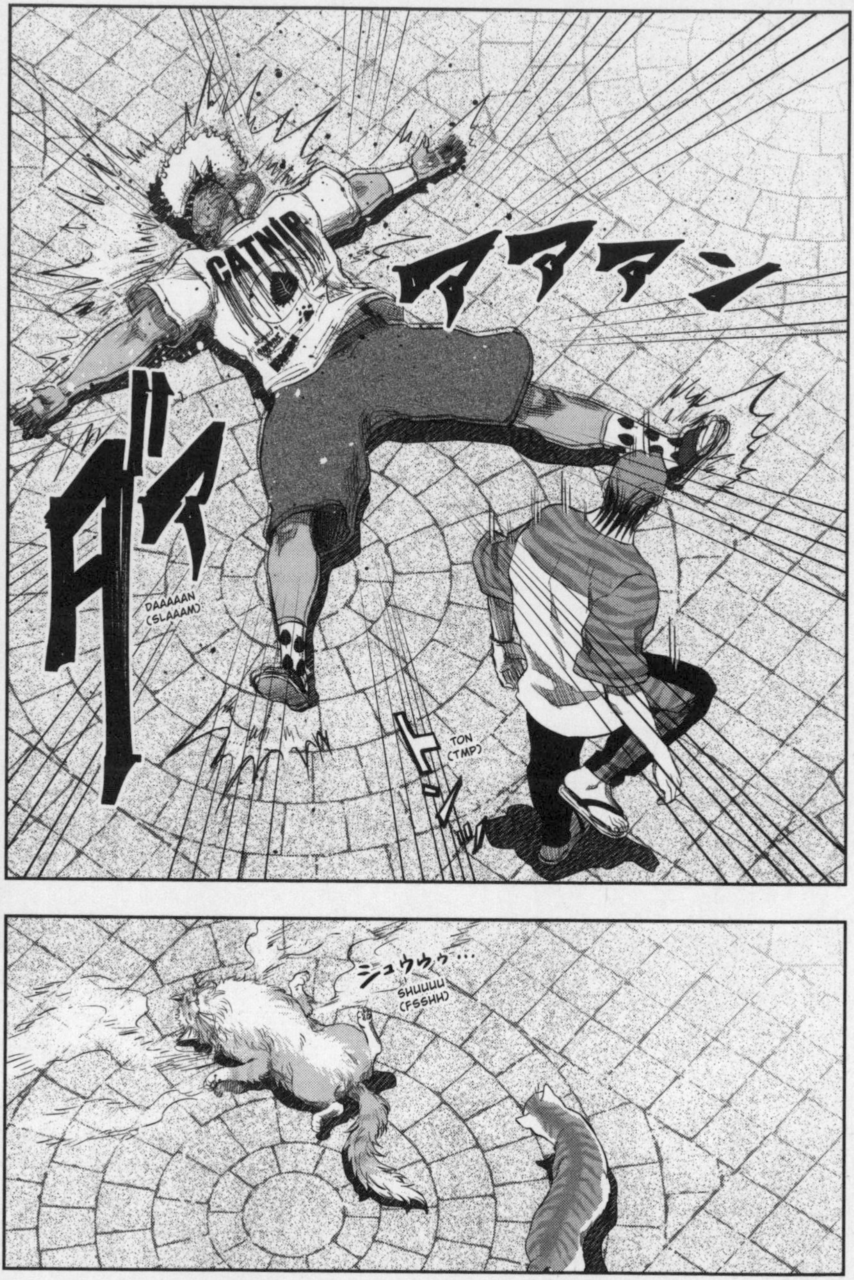
CATNIP
ダァァァン
DAAAAAN (SLAAAM)
トン
TON (TMP)
シュウウウ…
SHUUUU (FSSHH)

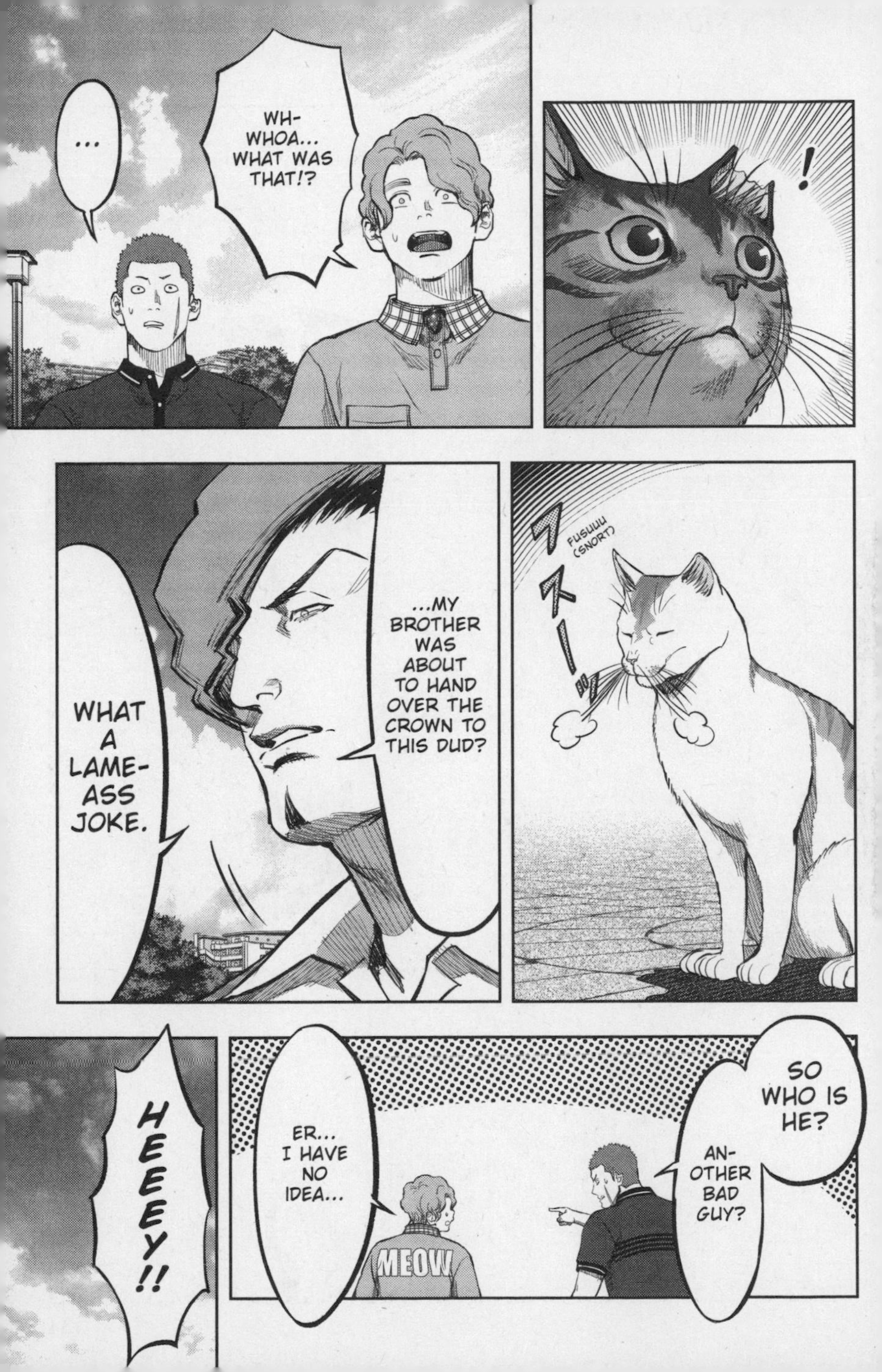
!
WH- WHOA... WHAT WAS THAT!?
...
FUSUUU (SNORT)
...MY BROTHER WAS ABOUT TO HAND OVER THE CROWN TO THIS DUD?
WHAT A LAME-ASS JOKE.
SO WHO IS HE?
AN-OTHER BAD GUY?
ER... I HAVE NO IDEA...
MEOW
HEEEY!!

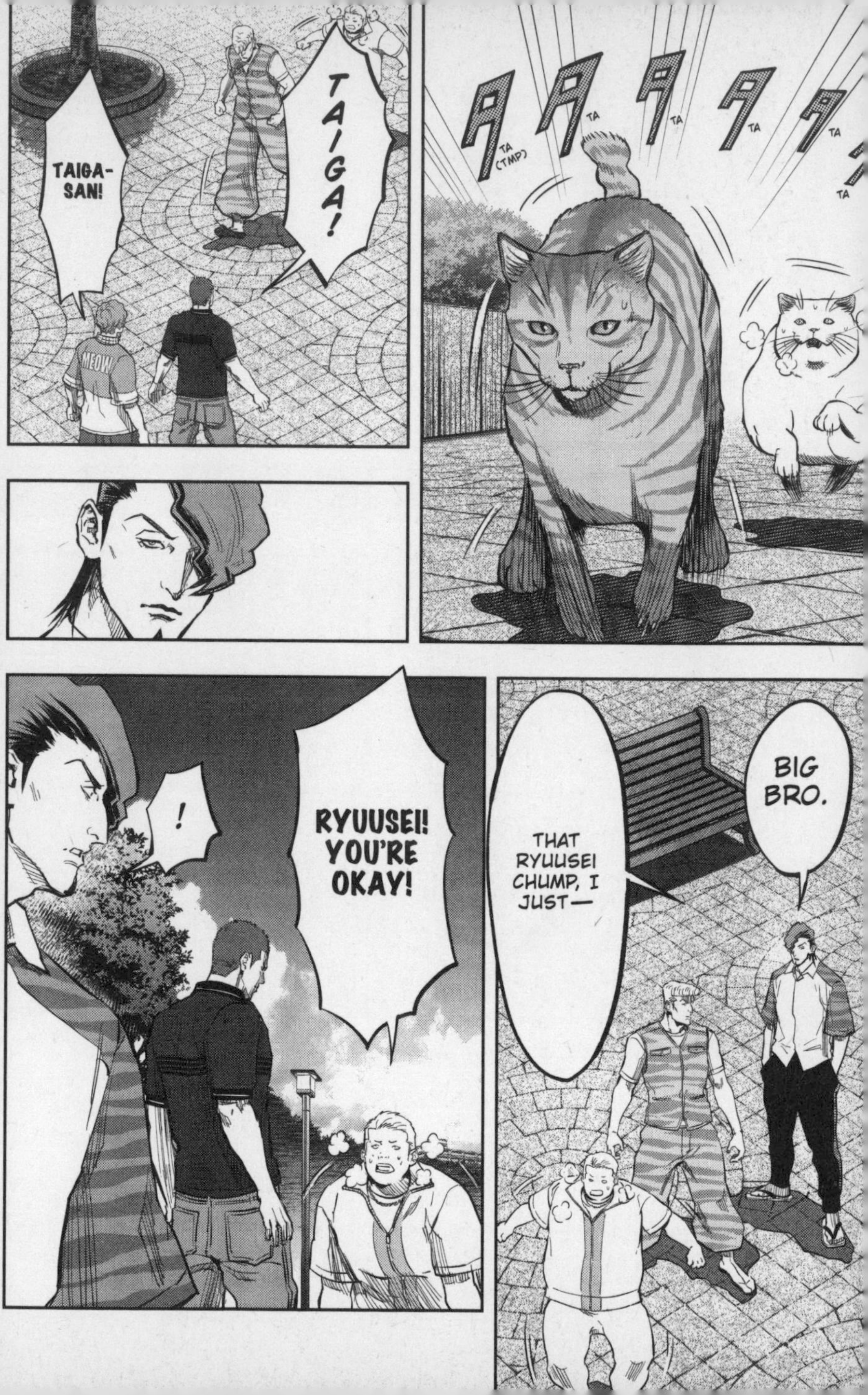
TA (TMP)
TA
TA
TA
TA
TA
TAIGA!
TAIGA-SAN!
BIG BRO.
THAT RYUUSEI CHUMP, I JUST—
RYUUSEI! YOU'RE OKAY!
!

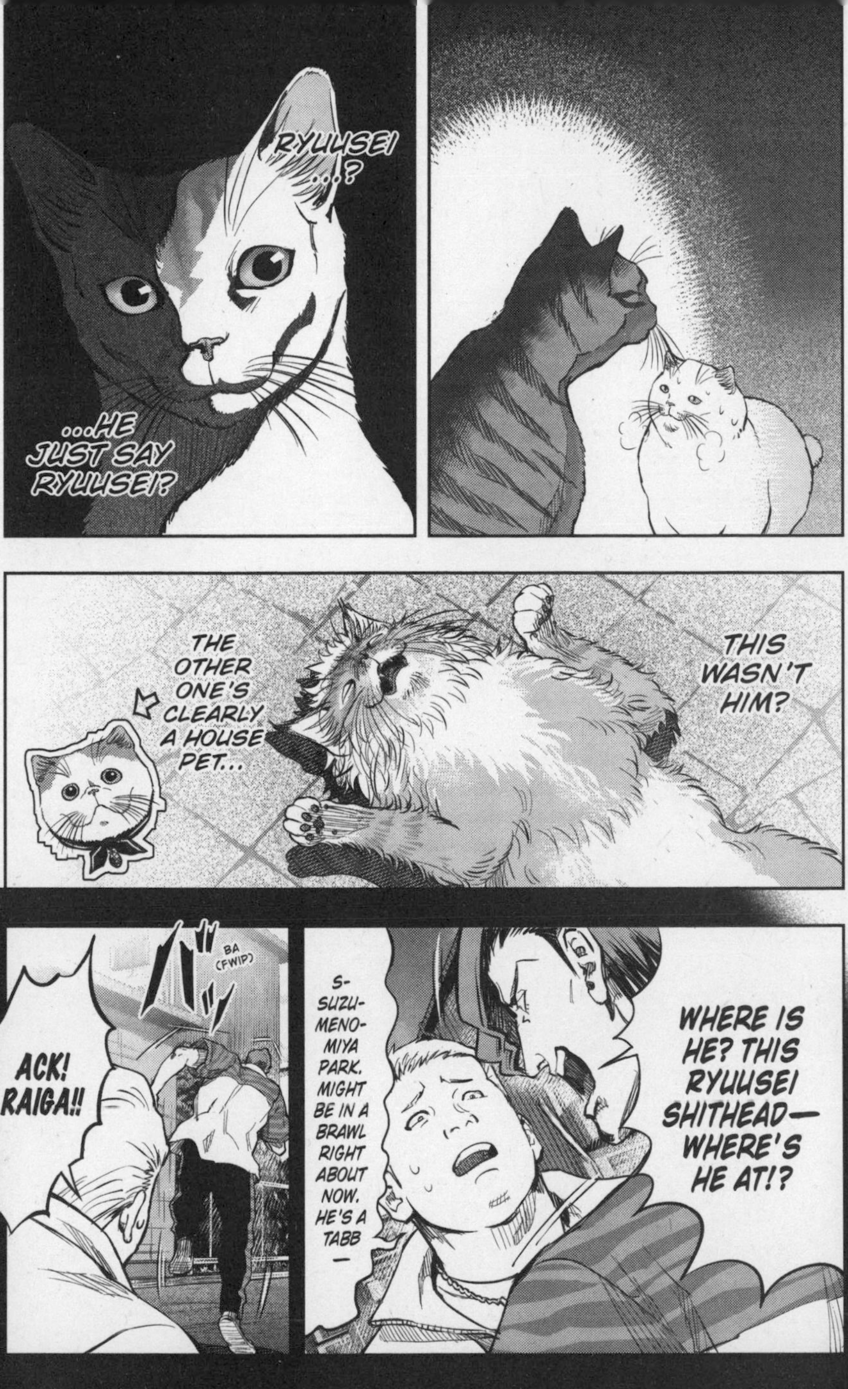
RYUUSEI ...?
...HE JUST SAY RYUUSEI?
THIS WASN'T HIM?
THE OTHER ONE'S CLEARLY A HOUSE PET...
WHERE IS HE? THIS RYUUSEI SHITHEAD—WHERE'S HE AT!?
S-SUZU-MENO-MIYA PARK. MIGHT BE IN A BRAWL RIGHT ABOUT NOW. HE'S A TABB—
BA (FWIP)
ACK! RAIGA!!

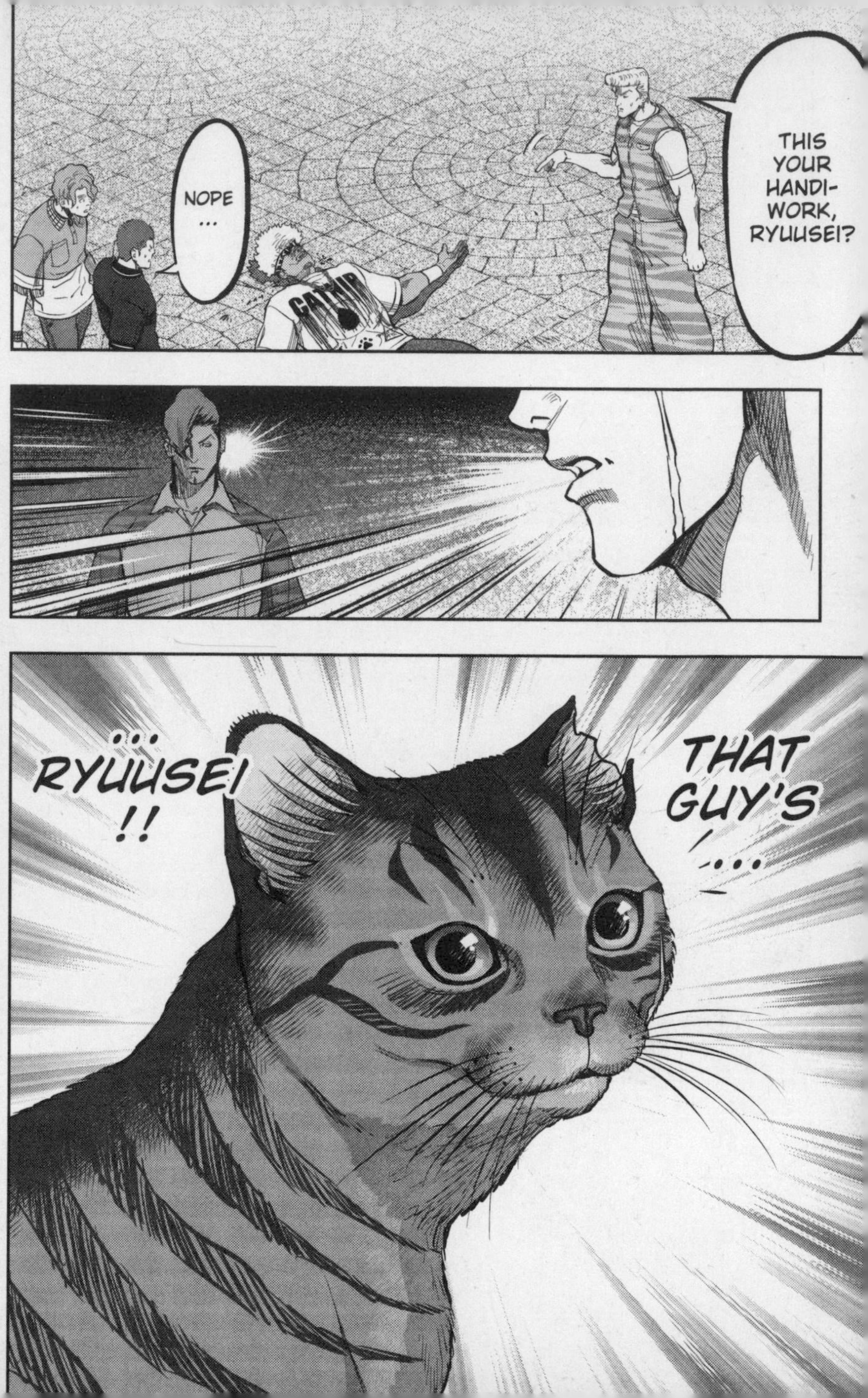
THIS YOUR HANDI-WORK, RYUUSEI?
NOPE ...
THAT GUY'S -...
... RYUUSEI !!

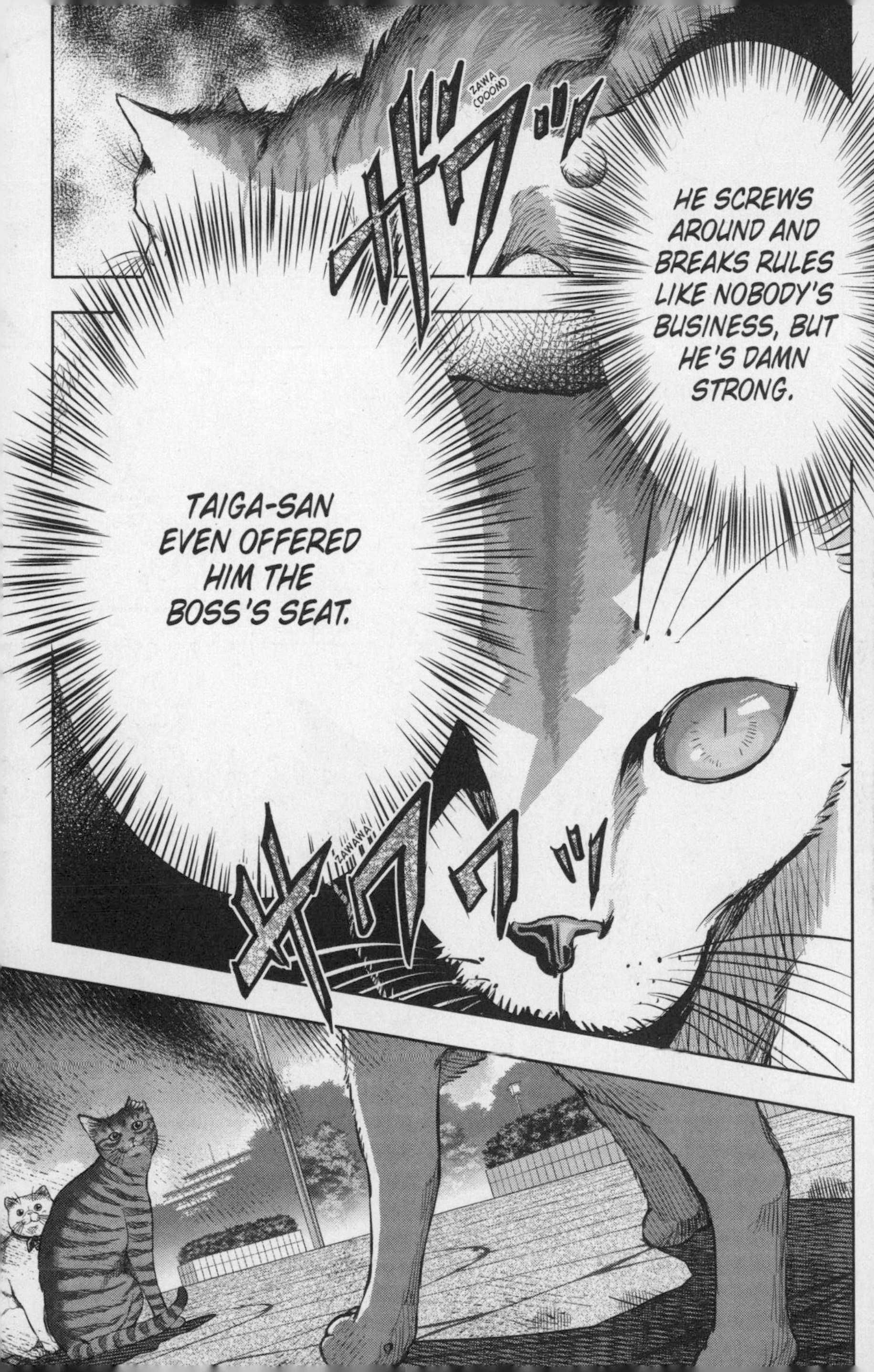
ZAWA (DOOM)
HE SCREWS AROUND AND BREAKS RULES LIKE NOBODY'S BUSINESS, BUT HE'S DAMN STRONG.
TAIGA-SAN EVEN OFFERED HIM THE BOSS'S SEAT.
ZAWAWA

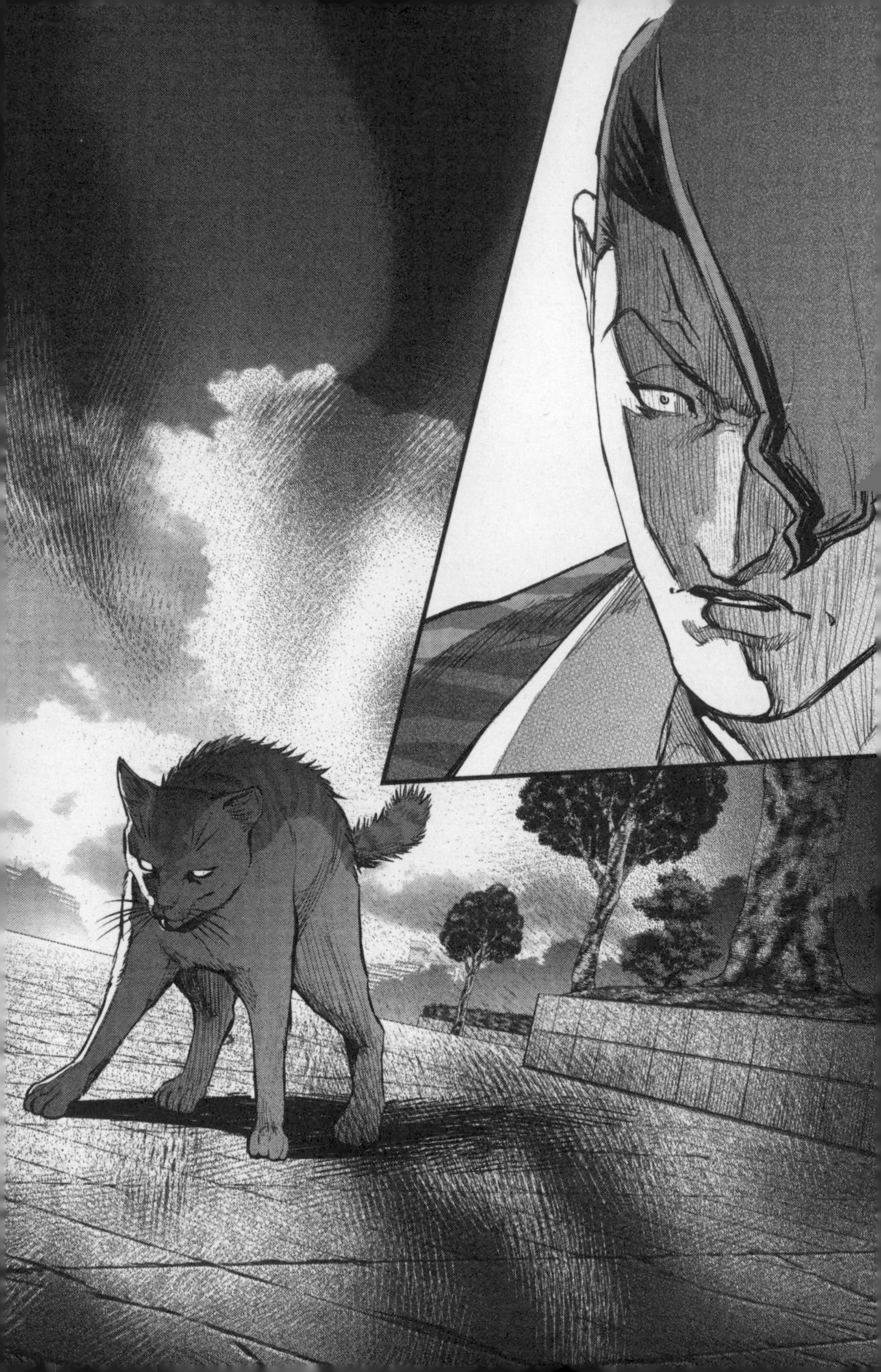

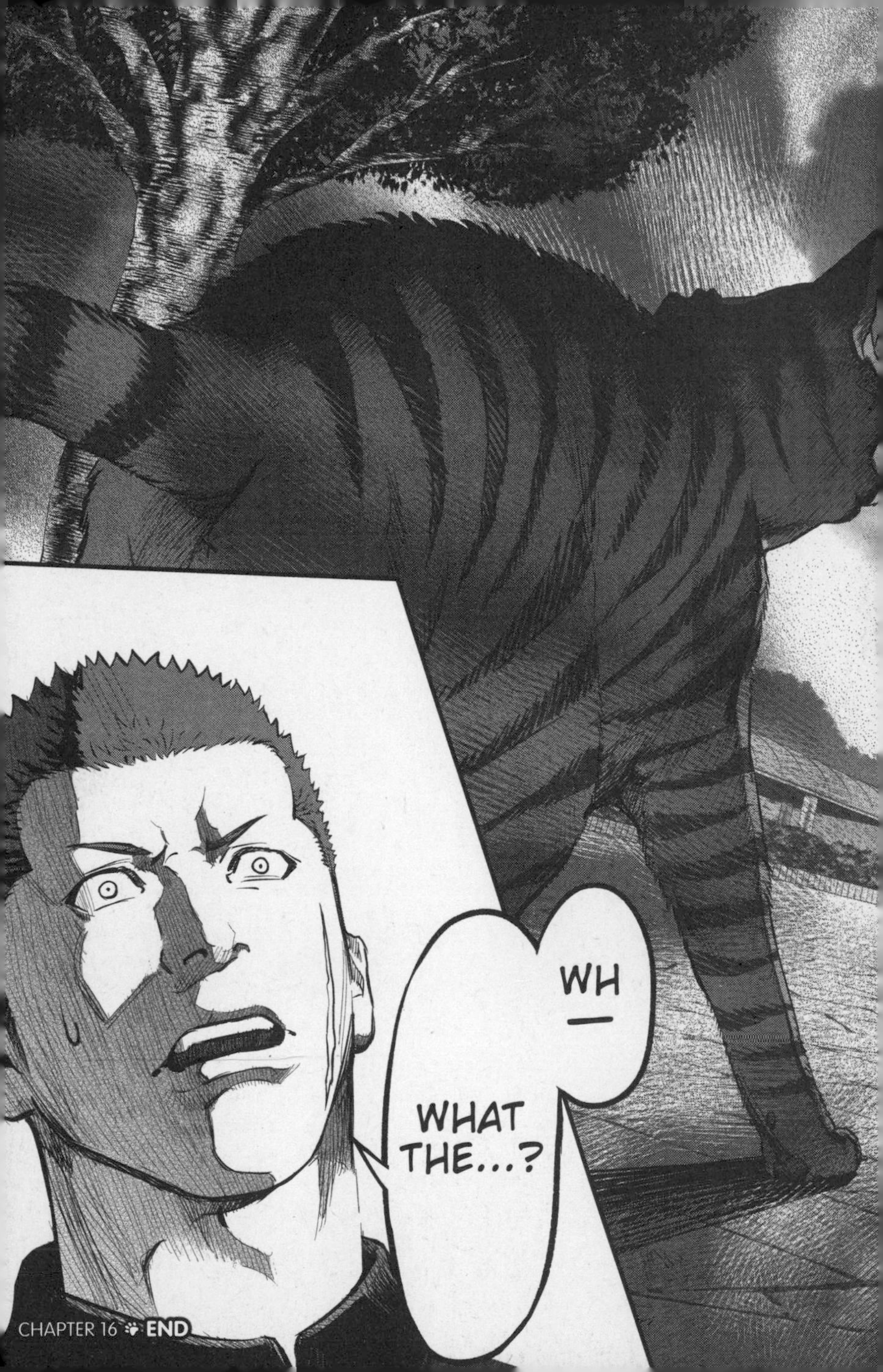
WH—
WHAT THE...?
CHAPTER 16 END

TRANSLATION NOTES

COMMON HONORIFICS

no honorific: Indicates familiarity or closeness; if used without permission or reason, addressing someone in this manner would constitute an insult.

-san: The Japanese equivalent of Mr./Mrs./Miss. If a situation calls for politeness, this is the fail-safe honorific.

-sama: Conveys great respect; may also indicate that the social status of the speaker is lower than that of the addressee.

-kun: Used most often when referring to boys, this indicates affection or familiarity. Occasionally used by older men among their peers, but it may also be used by anyone referring to a person of lower standing.

-chan: An affectionate honorific indicating familiarity used mostly in reference to girls; also used in reference to cute persons or animals of either gender.

PAGE 21
The *matatabi* in Matatabi Town means "catnip."

PAGE 125
Dave's name may feel out of place among Ryuusei, Taiga, and Madara, but it's actually a play on *debu*, meaning "chubby" or "plump" in Japanese.

Goblin Cat Tails' Boss (Female) "Sango"

Orange-brown

Black

Platinum

mole to the side of the nose

Calico pattern that looks like a bob cut

Black

Black (25%) stockings

Dr. Martens

Eight holes

Reddish Brown

NYANKEES

3

Atsushi Okada

Translation: **Caleb D. Cook**

Lettering: **Rochelle Gancio**

NYANKEES Vol.3
©Atsushi OKADA 2018
First published in Japan in 2018 by KADOKAWA CORPORATION, Tokyo. English translation rights arranged with KADOKAWA CORPORATION, Tokyo through TUTTLE-MORI AGENCY, INC., Tokyo.

English translation © 2019 by Yen Press, LLC

Yen Press
150 West 30th Street, 19th Floor
New York, NY 10001

Visit us at yenpress.com
facebook.com/yenpress
twitter.com/yenpress
yenpress.tumblr.com
instagram.com/yenpress

First Yen Press Edition: July 2019

Yen Press is an imprint of Yen Press, LLC.
The Yen Press name and logo are trademarks of Yen Press, LLC.

Library of Congress Control Number: 2018958637

ISBNs: 978-1-9753-8343-5 (paperback)
978-1-9753-8344-2 (ebook)

10 9 8 7 6 5 4 3 2 1

WOR

Printed in the United States of America